SPORTS, ADEVNTURE
AND
RECREATION TOURISM

SPORTS, ADVENTURE AND RECREATION TOURISM

By
Rajesh Kumar

2009

SBS Publishers & Distributors Pvt. Ltd.

ISBN 13 : 9788189741914

First Published in India in 2009

© Reserved

Published by:

SBS PUBLISHERS & DISTRIBUTORS PVT. LTD.
2/9, Ground Floor, Ansari Road, Darya Ganj,
New Delhi - 110002,
INDIA
Tel: 0091.11.23289119 / 41563911 / 32945311
Email: mail@sbspublishers.com
www.sbspublishers.com

Printed in India by New Z A Printers, New Delhi.

Preface

Sports, Adventure and Recreation Tourism is defined as any activity in which people are attracted to a particular centre as an event participant, an event spectator, or to attend sports attractions and business meetings. Sports Tourism is one the fastest growing industries in the world. It is also, however, one of the least talked about. Tourism has been and will continue to be one of the biggest and most profitable industries in the world. Obviously sports are a very important aspect to society in many different ways. Culturally, economically, and socially, the role sports play in today's society is immeasurable. In other words, tourism and sport are key cultural elements of today's world and have significant impact on modern society and international tourism. With this in mind, the WTO has also carried out a new study aimed at providing a more complete analysis of the role that sports tourism and sports in general among the products offered in Latin America by European tour operators and tourism websites. It embraces aspects of the relationship between sport and tourism, with clear links to work on consumption of experiences within behavioural research. This book provides readers with an introduction to tourism, sport, adventure, recreation and sports tourism. Select analysis of some adventure sports has been done in order to elaborate upon trends in international sport, adventure, recreation and travel. Focus lies on jungle tourism, adventure recreation, adventure travel, whale watching, river trekking, rafting, whitewater canoeing, tubing, watercraft paddling, mountaineering, mountain biking, multi-sport competitions, and multi-sport events. Olympic sports and related tourism activities are covered with emphasis on Olympic movement, International Olympic Committee, Organizing Committees of the Olympic games, and National Olympic Committees. Reflections are also made regarding discovering the sports and disciplines on the Programmes of the next

Olympic games and Para-Olympic shooting. The book presents details of FIFA Confederations and World Cup as a major tourist attraction with special focus on FIFA Confederations Cup, FIFA U-20 World Cup, and FIFA U-17 World Cup. Regional sports and related tourism activities are analyzed in detail with select case Studies of European football tours and tournaments, ASEAN Para Games, ASEAN football championships, ASEAN Football Federation, football at All-Africa Games, football at Pan American Games, and football at Island Games. The book also talks about Commonwealth Games and related tourism activities including the Commonwealth Games Federation, and Delhi's pact for Commonwealth Games as case studies. Similarly, the Asian Games and related tourism activities are discussed in detail with brief analysis of Asian Football Confederation, Asian Winter Games, Asian Indoor Games, and Asian Beach Games. Attempts are also made towards evolving a new tourism strategy for adventure sports training and education. Evaluation of related events and case study of Jamaica's unveiling of "New Tourism Strategy" is done. Focus also lies on outdoor education practices and frontier areas of adventure sports training. A detailed glossary and bibliography makes the book more user friendly.

Contents

List of Acronyms

AQIS	:	Australian Quarantine and Inspection Service
ASCOT	:	Australian Standing Committee on Tourism
ATC	:	Australian Tourist Commission
BTR	:	Bureau of Tourism Research
CRC	:	Cooperative Research Centres
CTC	:	Canadian Tourism Commission
CTEC	:	Canberra Tourism and Events Corporation
DIMA	:	Department of Immigration and Multicultural Affairs
DNH	:	Department of National Heritage (UK)
ETA	:	Electronic Travel Authority
GDP	:	Gross Domestic Product
IECN	:	International Event Coordinator Network
IOC	:	International Olympic Committee
ISR	:	Industry Science and Resources (Department of)
IVS	:	International Visitor Survey
NAPT	:	National Action Plan for Tourism
NSO	:	National Sporting Organisation
NVS	:	National Visitor Survey
SAST	:	South Africa Sports Tourism
SCORS	:	Standing Committee on Recreation and Sport
SIA	:	Sports Industry Australia
SRMC	:	Sport and Recreation Ministers Council
TCA	:	Tourism Council Australia
WTO	:	World Tourism Organization
WTTC	:	World Travel and Tourism Council

List of Acronyms

1

Introduction to Tourism, Sport, Adventure, Recreation and Sports Tourisms

1.1 Tourism: An Introduction

Tourism is travel for recreational or leisure purposes. The World Tourism Organization defines tourists as people who "travel to and stay in places outside their usual environment for not more than one consecutive year for leisure, business and other purposes not related to the exercise of an activity remunerated from within the place visited". Tourism has become a popular global leisure activity. In 2007, there were over 903 million international tourist arrivals, with a growth of 6.6 per cent as compared to 2006. International tourist receipts were USD 856 billion in 2007. Despite the uncertainties in the global economy, arrivals grew at around 5 per cent during the first four months of 2008, almost a similar growth than the same period in 2007.

Tourism is vital for many countries such as Egypt, Iran, Thailand and many island nations such as Fiji, due to the large intake of money for businesses with their goods and services and the opportunity for employment in the service industries associated with tourism. These service industries include transportation services such as cruise ships and taxis, accommodation such as hotels and entertainment venues, and other hospitality industry services such as resorts.

As the heritors of Ancient Persian culture, Iranians are among the world nations that are known globally for their warm and appreciatable manner of hospitality as well as French and Chinese people. It is said that the people of these three countries, receive their guests in the best possibile situations.

Definitions of Tourism

Hunziker and Krapf, in 1941, defined tourism as "the sum of the phenomena and relationships arising from the travel and stay of non-residents, insofar as they do not lead to permanent residence and are not connected with any earning activity." In 1976, the Tourism Society of England defined it as "Tourism is the temporary, short-term movement of people to destination outside the places where they normally live and work and their activities during the stay at each destination. It includes movements for all purposes." In 1981, International Association of Scientific Experts in Tourism defined Tourism in terms of particular activities selected by choice and undertaken outside the home environment.

The United Nations classified three forms of tourism in 1994 in its Recommendations on Tourism Statistics: Domestic tourism, which involves residents of the given country traveling only within this country; Inbound tourism, involving non-residents traveling in the given country; and Outbound tourism, involving residents traveling in another country.

The UN also derived different categories of tourism by combining the 3 basic forms of tourism: Internal tourism, which comprises domestic tourism and inbound tourism; National tourism, which comprises domestic tourism and outbound tourism; and International tourism, which consists of inbound tourism and outbound tourism. *Intrabound tourism* is a term coined by the Korea Tourism Organization and widely accepted in Korea. Intrabound tourism differs from domestic tourism in that the former encompasses policymaking and implementation of national tourism policies.

Recently, the tourism industry has shifted from the promotion of inbound tourism to the promotion of intrabound tourism because many countries are experiencing tough competition for inbound tourists. Some national policymakers have shifted their priority to the promotion of intrabound tourism to contribute to the local economy. Examples of such campaigns include "See America" in the United States, "Malaysia Truly Asia" in Malaysia, "Get Going Canada" in Canada, "Wow Philippines" in the Philippines, "Uniquely Singapore" in Singapore, "100 per cent Pure New Zealand" in New Zealand "Amazing Thailand" in Thailand and "Incredible India" in India.

Towards Presenting World Tourism Statistics and Rankings

Most Visited Countries

The World Tourism Organization reports the following ten countries as the most visited in 2007 by number of international travelers. When compared to 2006, Ukraine and Turkey entered the top ten list, surpassing Russia, Austria and Mexico. Most of the top visited countries continue to be on the European continent.

Rank	Country	UNWTO Regional Market	International tourist arrivals (2007)	International tourist arrivals (2006)
1.	France	Europe	81.9 million	79.1 million
2.	Spain	Europe	59.2 million	58.5 million
3.	United States	North America	56.0 million	51.1 million
4.	China	Asia	54.7 million	49.6 million
5.	Italy	Europe	43.7 million	41.1 million
6.	United Kingdom	Europe	30.7 million	30.7 million
7.	Germany	Europe	24.4 million	23.6 million
8.	Ukraine	Europe	23.1 million	18.9 million
9.	Turkey	Europe	22.2 million	18.9 million
10.	Mexico	North America	21.4 million	21.4 million

Towards Analyzing the International Tourism Receipts

International tourist receipts were USD 856 billion in 2007 (Euro 625 billion), up from USD 742 billion (Euro 879 billion), in 2006. When the export value of international passenger travel receipts is accounted for, total receipts in 2007 reached a record of USD 1.02 trillion. The World Tourism Organization reports the 10 countries (shown in table 1.1) S1 as the top ten tourism earners for the year 2007. It is noticeable that most of them are on the European continent, but the United States continues to be the top earner.

International Tourism Top Spenders

The World Tourism Organization reports the following 10 countries as the top ten biggest spenders on international tourism for the year 2007. For the fifth year in a row, German tourists continue as the top spenders. A study by Dresdner Bank study forecasts that for 2008 Germans and Europeans in general will continue to be the top spenders because of the strength of the Euro against the US dollar, with strong demand for the US in favor of other destinations:

Rank	Country	UNWTO Regional Market	International Tourism Expenditures (2007)	International Tourism Expenditures (2006)
1.	Germany	Europe	$82.9 billion	$73.9 billion
2.	United States	North America	$76.2 billion	$72.1 billion
3.	United Kingdom	Europe	$72.3 billion	$63.1 billion
4.	France	Europe	$36.7 billion	$31.2 billion
5.	China	Asia	$29.8 billion	$24.3 billion
6.	Italy	Europe	$27.3 billion	$23.1 billion
7.	Japan	Asia	$26.5 billion	$26.9 billion
8	Canada	North America	$24.8 billion	$20.5 billion
9.	Russia	Europa	$22.3 billion	$18.2 billion
10.	South Korea	Asia	$20.9 billion	$18.9 billion

Table 1.1: Analysis of the International Tourism Receipts.

Rank	Country	UNWTO Regional Market	International Tourism Receipts (2007)	International Tourism Receipts (2006)
1.	United States	North America	$96.7 billion	$85.7 billion
2.	Spain	Europe	$57.8 billion	$51.1 billion
3.	France	Europe	$54.2 billion	$46.3 billion
4.	Italy	Europe	$42.7 billion	$38.1 billion
5.	China	Asia	$41.9 billion	$33,9 billion
6.	United Kingdom	Europe	$37.6 billion	$33.7 billion
7.	Germany	Europe	$36.0 billion	$32.8 billion
8.	Australia	Oceania	$22.2 billion	$17.8 billion
9.	Austria	Europe	$18.9 billion	$16.6 billion
10.	Turkey	Europe	$18.5 billion	$16.9 billion

Most Visited Attractions

Fig. 1.1: National Mall & Memorial Parks, Washington, D.C.

Fig. 1.2: Great Wall of China, China.

Fig. 1.3: Colosseum, Rome, Italy.

Fig. 1.4: Taj Mahal, Agra, India.

Forbes Traveller *released a ranking of the world's 50 most visited tourist attractions in 2007, including both international and domestic tourists. The following are the Top 10 attractions, followed by some other famous sites included within the list of the 50 most visited: It is noticeable that 4 out of the top 5 are in the North America continent.*

Most visited attractions by domestic and international tourists in 2007 Top 10 ranking tourist attractions

World's ranking	Tourist attraction	City	Country	Number of visitors (millions)
1.	Times Square	New York City	US	35
2.	National Mall & Memorial Parks	Washington, D.C.	US	25
3.	Walt Disney World's Magic Kingdom	Lake Buena Vista, Orlando	USA	16.6
4.	Trafalgar Square	London	UK	15
5.	Disneyland	Anaheim, CA	US	14.7
6.	Niagara Falls	Ontario & N.Y.	Canada & USA	14
7.	Fisherman's Wharf & Golden Gate	San Francisco, CA	US	13
8.	Tokyo Disneyland	Tokyo	Japan	12.9
9.	Notre-Dame de Paris	Paris	France	12
10.	Disneyland Paris	Paris	France	10.6
Other selected famous destinations				
11.	The Great Wall of China	Badaling	China	10
18.	Eiffel Tower	Paris	France	6.7
31.	Grand Canyon	Arizona	US	4.4
36.	Statue of Liberty	New York	US	4.24
37.	The Vatican and its museums	Rome	Italy	4.2
39.	The Colosseum	Rome	Italy	4
47.	Giza Pyramids	Cairo	Egypt	3
50.	Taj Mahal	Agra	India	2.4

Most Visited Cities

Euromonitor released a ranking of the world's 150 most visited cities by international tourists in 2006. The following are the leading 15 cities according to Euromonitor's ranking:

Table 1.2: Most visited cities by international tourists in 2006 Top 15 ranking cities.

Ranking	City	Country	Number of intl. visitors (millions)
1.	London	United Kingdom	15.64
2.	Bangkok	Thailand	10.35
3.	Paris	France	9.70
4.	Singapore	Singapore	9.50
5.	Hong Kong	China	8.14
6.	New York City	United States	6.22
7.	Dubai	United Arab Emirates	6.12
8.	Rome	Italy	6.03
9.	Seoul	South Korea	4.92
10.	Barcelona	Spain	4.69
11.	Dublin	Ireland	4.47
12.	Bahrain	Bahrain	4.42
13.	Shangai	China	4.31
14.	Toronto	Canada	4.16
15.	Kuala Lumpur	Malaysia	4.12

Other sources report Paris as the most visited city in the world with 30 million visitors History.

Wealthy people have always traveled to distant parts of the world to see great buildings and works of art, to learn new languages, to experience new cultures, and to taste different cuisines. As long ago as the time of the Roman Republic, places such as Baiae were popular coastal resorts for the rich.

Fig. 1.5: The Persepolis in Fars, Iran.

The word *tourism* was used by 1811 and *tourist* by 1840. In 1936 the League of Nations defined *foreign tourist* as someone travelling abroad for at least twenty-four hours. It successor, the United Nations amended this definition in 1945 by including a maximum stay of six months.

Pre Twentieth Century

European tourism can be said to originate with the medieval pilgrimage. Although undertaken primarily for religious reasons, the pilgrims in the Canterbury Tales saw the experience as a holiday (the term itself being derived from the 'holy day' and its associated leisure activities). Pilgrimages created a variety of tourist aspects that still exist—bringing back souvenirs, obtaining credit with foreign banks (in medieval times utilizing international networks established by the Lombards), and making use of space available on existing forms of transport (such as the use of medieval English wine ships bound for Vigo by pilgrims to Santiago de Compostela). Religious and secular pilgrimages are still prevalent in modern tourism—such as to Lourdes or Knock in Ireland, Graceland and the grave of Jim Morrison in Père Lachaise Cemetery.

During the 17th century, it became fashionable in England to undertake a Grand Tour. The sons of the nobility and gentry were sent upon an extended tour of Europe as an educational experience. The 18th century was the golden age of the Grand Tour, and many of the fashionable visitors were painted at Rome by Pompeo Batoni.

Fig. 1.6: The Hagia Sophia, Ýstanbul, Turkey.　**Fig. 1.7:** The Great Bath at the Roman Baths, in Bath, one of the world's first health tourism sites.

Health tourism has long existed, but it was not until the eighteenth century that it became important. In England, it was associated with spas, places with supposedly health-giving mineral waters, treating diseases from gout to liver disorders and bronchitis. The most popular resorts were Bath, Cheltenham, Buxton, Harrogate, and Tunbridge Wells. Visits to take 'the waters' also allowed the visitors to attend balls and other entertainments. Continental Spas such as Carlsbad (Karlovy Vary) attracted many fashionable travellers by the nineteenth century.

Creative Tourism

Creative tourism has existed as a form of cultural tourism since the early beginnings of tourism itself. Its European roots date back to the time of the Grand Tour, which saw the sons of aristocratic families traveling for the purpose of (mostly interactive) educational experiences. More recently, creative tourism has been given its own name by Crispin Raymond and Greg Richards, who as a member of the Association for Tourism and Leisure Education (ATLAS) has directed a number of projects for the European Commission, including cultural tourism, crafts tourism or sustainable tourism. They have defined "creative tourism" as tourism related to the active participation of travelers in the culture of the host community, through interactive workshops and informal learning experiences.

Meanwhile, the concept of creative tourism has been picked up by high-profile organizations such as UNESCO, who through the Creative Cities Network have endorsed creative tourism as an engaged, authentic experience that promotes an active understanding of the specific cultural features of a place.

Leisure Travel

Leisure travel was associated with the industrialisation of United Kingdom—the first European country to promote leisure time to the increasing industrial population. Initially, this applied to the owners of the machinery of production, the economic oligarchy, the factory owners, and the traders. These comprised the new middle class. Cox & Kings were the first official travel company to be formed in 1758. Later, the working class could take advantage of leisure time.

The British origin of this new industry is reflected in many place names. At Nice, France, one of the first and best-established holiday resorts on the French Riviera, the long esplanade along the seafront is known to this day as the *Promenade des Anglais*; in many other historic resorts in continental Europe, old well-established palace hotels have names like the *Hotel Bristol*, the *Hotel Carlton* or the *Hotel Majestic*— reflecting the dominance of English customers.

Many tourists do leisure tourism in the tropics both in the summer and winter. It is often done in places such as Cuba, The Dominican Republic, Thailand, North Queensland in Australia and Florida in the United States.

Winter Tourism

Winter sports were largely invented by the British leisured classes, initially at the Swiss village of Zermatt (Valais), and St Moritz in 1864. The first packaged winter sports holidays took place in 1902 at Adelboden, Switzerland. Winter sports were a natural answer for a leisured class looking for amusement during the coldest season.

Major ski resorts are located in various mainland European countries, Canada, the United States, Australia, New Zealand, Japan, Korea, Chile and Argentina.

Mass Tourism

Mass travel could only develop with improvements in technology allowed the transport of large numbers of people in a short space of time to places of leisure interest, and greater numbers of people began to enjoy the benefits of leisure time.

In the United States, the first great seaside resort, in the European style, was Atlantic City, New Jersey, and Long Island.

In Continental Europe, early resorts included Ostend (for the people of Brussels), and Boulogne-sur-Mer (Pas-de-Calais) and Deauville (Calvados) (for Parisians), and Heiligendamm (founded 1797 as the first seaside resort at the Baltic Sea).

Recent Developments

Fig. 1.8: Machu Picchu in Cuzco, Peru, one of the most visited destinations in South America.

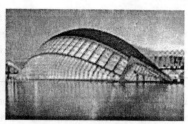

Fig. 1.9: Ciutat de les Arts i les Ciències, Valencia, Spain.

Fig. 1.10: Red Square, Moscow, Russia.

Fig. 1.11: Iguazu Falls, Argentina-Brazil border, one of the most visited ecotourism destinations in South America.

Fig. 1.12: Galapagos Islands, Ecuador. One of the most famous natural attractions in the world.

There has been an upmarket trend in the tourism over the last few decades, especially in Europe where international travel for short breaks is common. Tourists have higher levels of disposable income and greater leisure time and they are also better-educated and have more sophisticated tastes. There is now a demand for a better quality products, which has resulted in a fragmenting of the mass market for beach vacations; people want more specialised versions, such as Club 18-30, quieter resorts, family-oriented holidays, or niche market-targeted destination hotels.

The developments in technology and transport infrastructure, such as jumbo jets and low-cost airlines, and more accessible airports have made many types of tourism more affordable. There have also been changes in lifestyle, such as retiree-age people who sustain year round tourism. This is facilitated by internet sales of tourism products. Some sites have now started to offer dynamic packaging, in which an inclusive price is quoted for a tailor-made package requested by the customer upon impulse.

There have been a few setbacks in tourism, such as the September 11, 2001 attacks and terrorist threats to tourist destinations such as Bali and European cities. Some of the tourist destinations, including the beach resorts of Cancún have lost popularity due to shifting tastes. In this context, the excessive building and environmental destruction often associated with traditional "sun and beach" tourism may contribute to a destination's saturation and subsequent decline. Spain's Costa Brava, a popular 1960s and 1970s beach location is now facing a crisis in its tourism industry.

On December 26, 2004 a tsunami, caused by the 2004 Indian Ocean earthquake hit Asian countries bordering the Indian Ocean, and also the Maldives. Thousands of lives were lost, and many tourists died. This, together with the vast clean-up operation in place, has stopped or severely hampered tourism to the area.

The terms *tourism* and *travel* are sometimes used interchangeably. In this context travel has a similar definition to tourism, but implies a more purposeful journey. The terms *tourism* and *tourist* are sometimes used pejoratively, to imply a shallow interest in the cultures or locations visited by tourists.

Medical Tourism

When there is a significant price difference between countries for a given medical procedure particularly in South East Asia, India and Eastern Europe or where there are different regulatory regimes between countries in relation to particular medical procedures (eg dentistry) travelling to take advantage of the price or regulatory differences is often referred to as "medical tourism".

Educational Tourism

Educational tourism developed because of the growing popularity of teaching and learning of knowledge, and enhancing technical competency outside the classroom environment. In the educational tourism, the main focus of the tour or leisure activity includes visitation of another country to learn about the culture of the visited country (Student Exchange Program and Study Tour) or to work and apply their learning inside the classroom in different environment (International Practicum Training Program).

Other Developments

Creative tourism: More recently, creative tourism has gained popularity as a form of cultural tourism, drawing on active participation by travelers in the culture of the host communities they visit. Several countries offer examples of this type of tourism development, including the United Kingdom, Spain, Italy and New Zealand.

Adventure tourism: Tourists are looking for an adventure when they travel, see the destination more like a local would experience it. [Private tour guides] are an excellent way to get fast insight into a country and also help locals earn an income.

In recent years, second holidays or vacations have become more popular as people's discretionary income increases. Typical combinations are a package to the typical mass tourist resort, with a winter skiing holiday or weekend break to a city or national park.

Dark tourism: One emerging area of special interest tourism has been identified by Lennon and Foley (2000) as "dark" tourism. This type of tourism involves visits to "dark" sites such as battlegrounds, scenes of horrific crimes or acts of genocide, for example concentration camps. Dark tourism poses severe ethical and moral dilemmas: should these sites be available for visitation and, if so, what should the nature of the publicity involved be. Dark tourism remains a small niche market driven by varied motivations, such as mourning, remembrance, macabre curiosity or even entertainment. Its early origins are rooted in fairgrounds and medieval fairs.

Growth

The World Tourism Organization (UNWTO) forecasts that international tourism will continue growing at the average annual rate of 4 per cent. By 2020 Europe will remain the most popular destination, but its share will drop from 60 per cent in 1995 to 46 per cent. Long-haul will grow slightly faster than intraregional travel and by 2020 its share will increase from 18 per cent in 1995 to 24 per cent.

With the advent of e-commerce, tourism products have become one of the most traded items on the internet. Tourism products and services have been made available through intermediaries, although tourism providers (hotels, airlines, etc.) can sell their services directly.

This has put pressure on intermediaries from both on-line and traditional shops.

It has been suggested there is a strong correlation between Tourism expenditure per capita and the degree to which countries play in the global context. Not only as a result of the important economic contribution of the tourism industry, but also as an indicator of the degree of confidence with which global citizens leverage the resources of the globe for the benefit of their local economies. This is why any projections of growth in tourism may serve as an indication of the relative influence that each country will exercise in the future.

Space tourism is expected to "take off" in the first quarter of the 21st century, although compared with traditional destinations the number of tourists in orbit will remain low until technologies such as a space elevator make space travel cheap.

Technological improvement is likely to make possible air-ship hotels, based either on solar-powered airplanes or large dirigibles. Underwater hotels, such as Hydropolis, expected to open in Dubai in 2009, will be built. On the ocean tourists will be welcomed by ever larger cruise ships and perhaps floating cities.

Negative Impacts

Attracting a high volume of tourists can have negative impacts, such as the impact of 33 million tourists a year on the city of New York, or the potential to impact fragile environments, or the impact of the December 26, 2004 tsunami on the tourists themselves. The environment can be affected negatively by cruise ship pollution in many ways, including ballast water discharge, and by pollution from aircraft.

1.2 Sport: An Introduction

Sports is an activity that is governed by a set of rules or customs and often engaged in competitively. *Sports* commonly refer to activities where the physical capabilities of the competitor are the sole or primary determiner of the outcome (winning or losing), but the term is also used to include activities such as mind sports (a common name for some card games and board games with little to no element of chance) and motor sports where mental acuity or equipment quality are major factors. *Etymology*—"Sports" comes from the old French *desport* meaning "leisure"

Professionalism

The entertainment aspect of sports, together with the spread of mass media and increased leisure time, has led to professionalism in sports. This has resulted in some conflict, where the paycheck can be seen as more important than recreational aspects, or where the sports are changed simply to make them more profitable and popular, thereby losing certain valued traditions.

The entertainment aspect also means that sportsmen and women are often elevated to celebrity status.

Politics

At times, sports and politics can have a large amount of influence on each other.

When apartheid was the official policy in South Africa, many sports people, particularly in rugby union, adopted the conscientious approach that they should not appear in competitive sports there. Some feel this was an effective contribution to the eventual demolition of the policy of apartheid, others feel that it may have prolonged and reinforced its worst effects.

The 1936 Summer Olympics held in Berlin was an illustration, perhaps best recognised in retrospect, where an ideology was developing which used the event to strengthen its spread through propaganda.

In the history of Ireland, Gaelic sports were connected with cultural nationalism. Until the mid 20th century a person could have been banned from playing Gaelic football, hurling, or other sports administered by the Gaelic Athletic Association (GAA) if she/he played or supported association football, or other games seen to be of British origin. Until recently the GAA continued to ban the playing of soccer and rugby union at Gaelic venues. This ban is still enforced, but has been modified to allow football and rugby be played in Croke Park while Lansdowne Road (both in Dublin) is being redeveloped. Until recently, under Rule 21, the GAA also banned members of the British security forces and members of the RUC from playing Gaelic games, but the advent of the Good Friday Agreement in 1998 led to the eventual removal of the ban.

Nationalism is often evident in the pursuit of sports, or in its reporting: people compete in national teams, or commentators and audiences can adopt a partisan view. On occasion, such tensions can lead to violent confrontation among players or spectators within and beyond the sporting venue. These trends are seen by many as contrary to the fundamental ethos of sports being carried on for its own sake and for the enjoyment of its participants.

Physical Art

Gymnastics

Sports have many affinities with art. Ice skating and Tai chi, and Dancesport for example, are sports that come close to artistic spectacles in themselves. Similarly, there are other activities that have elements of sport and art in their execution, such as artistic gymnastics, Bodybuilding, Free running, performance art, professional wrestling, Yoga, bossaball, dressage, culinary arts, marching band, drum corps, etc. Perhaps the best example is Bull-fighting, which in Spain is reported in the arts pages of newspapers. The fact that art is so close to sports in some situations is probably related to the nature of sports. The definition of "sports" above put forward the idea of an activity pursued not just for the usual purposes, for example, running not simply to get places, but running for its own sake, running as well as we can.

This is similar to a common view of aesthetic value, which is seen as something over and above the strictly functional value coming from an object's normal use. So an aesthetically pleasing car is one which doesn't just get from A to B, but which impresses us with its grace, poise, and charisma.

In the same way, a sporting performance such as jumping doesn't just impress us as being an effective way to avoid obstacles or to get across streams. It impresses us because of the ability, skill, and style which is shown.

Art and sports were probably more clearly linked at the time of Ancient Greece, when gymnastics and calisthenics invoked admiration and aesthetic appreciation for the physical build, prowess and 'arete' displayed by participants. The modern term 'art' as skill, is related to this ancient Greek term 'arete'. The closeness of art and sport in these times was revealed by the nature of the Olympic Games which, as we have seen, were celebrations of both sporting and artistic achievements, poetry, sculpture and architecture.

Technology

Technology has an important role in sports, whether applied to an athlete's health, the athlete's technique, or equipment's characteristics.

Fig. 1.13: Golf, which is debatably a sport, where moving has a much lesser part than dexterity.

Equipment as sports have grown more competitive, the need for better equipment has arisen. Golf clubs, football helmets, baseball bats, soccer balls, hockey skates, and other equipment have all seen considerable changes when new technologies have been applied.

Health, ranging from nutrition to the treatment of injuries, as the knowledge of the human body has deepened over time, an athlete's potential has been increased. Athletes are now able to play to an older age, recover more quickly from injuries, and train more effectively than previous generations of athletes.

Instruction, advancing technology created new opportunities for research into sports. It is now possible to analyse aspects of sports that were previously out of the reach of comprehension. Being able to use motion capture to capture an athlete's movement, or advanced computer simulations to model physical scenarios has greatly increased an athlete's ability to understand what they are doing and how they can improve themselves.

Terminology

In British English, sporting activities are commonly denoted by the collective noun "sport". In American English, "sports" is more used. In all English dialects, "sports" is the term used for more than one specific sport. For example, "football and swimming are my favourite sports", would sound natural to all English speakers, whereas "I enjoy sport" would sound less natural than "I enjoy sports" to North Americans.

The term "sport" is sometimes extended to encompass all competitive activities, regardless of the level of physical activity. Both games of skill and motor sport exhibit many of the characteristics of physical sports, such as skill, sportsmanship, and at the highest levels, even professional sponsorship associated with physical sports. Air sports, billiards, bridge, chess, motorcycle racing, and powerboating are all recognized as sports by the International Olympic Committee with their world governing bodies represented in the Association of the IOC Recognised International Sports Federations.

Spectator Sport

As well as being a form of recreation for the participants, much sport is played in front of an audience. Most professional sport is played in a 'theatre' of some kind; be it a stadium, arena, golf course, race track, or the open road, with provision for the (often paying) public.

Large television or radio audiences are also commonly attracted, with rival broadcasters bidding large amounts of money for the 'rights' to show certain fixtures. Association football's FIFA World Cup attracts a global television audience of hundreds of millions; the 2006 Final alone attracted an estimated worldwide audience of well over 700 million. In the United States, the championship game of the NFL, the

Super Bowl, has become one of the most watched television broadcasts of the year. **Super Bowl Sunday** is a *de facto* national holiday in America; the viewership being so great that in 2007 advertising space was reported as being sold at US$2.6m for a 30 second slot.

Fig. 1.14: Rugby league match in Townsville, Queensland, Australia.

Related Topics

- ❖ Combat Sport
- ❖ Disabled sports
- ❖ Fandom
- ❖ Female sports
- ❖ History of sport
- ❖ Multi-sport events
- ❖ National sport
- ❖ Nationalism and sports
- ❖ Olympic Games
- ❖ Spectator sports
- ❖ Sponsorship
- ❖ Sport in film
- ❖ Sport governing bodies
- ❖ Sports broadcasting
- ❖ Sports club
- ❖ Sports coaching

- ❖ Sports equipment
- ❖ Sports injuries
- ❖ Sports league attendances
- ❖ Sports marketing
- ❖ Sports terms named after people

1.3 Winter Sports

A winter sport is a sport commonly played during winter. As a formal term, it refers to a sport played on snow or ice, but informally can refer to sports played in winter that are also played year-round like basketball. The main winter sports are ice hockey and figure skating, sledding events such as luge, skeleton, and bobsleigh, skiing (Alpine and Nordic) and snowboarding. Other common winter sports include snow-blading, monoskiing, skwal and tobogganing.

List of Winter Sports

Ice Skating

- ❖ Sports with asterisks denotes that it is included in the Olympics, as accurate as the 2006 Turin Olympics.
- ❖ Figure skating
- ❖ Short-track speed skating
- ❖ Speed skating
- ❖ Synchronized skating
- ❖ Xtreme Ice Skating—A sport more closely related to Extreme Inline Skating.

Snowboarding

- ❖ Freestyle snowboarding
- ❖ Alpine snowboarding
- ❖ Boardercross
- ❖ Slalom

Skiing

- ❖ Sports in which skis are used on snow.
- ❖ Alpine skiing
- ❖ Biathlon

- ❖ Cross country skiing
- ❖ Firngleiten
- ❖ Freestyle skiing
- ❖ Newschool skiing
- ❖ Nordic combined
- ❖ Ski archery
- ❖ Skiboarding
- ❖ Skibob
- ❖ Skijoring
- ❖ Ski jumping
- ❖ Snowshoe
- ❖ Speed skiing
- ❖ Telemark skiing

Sledding

Sports that use sleds going down ice tracks or pulled by something.

- ❖ Ice Blocking
- ❖ Bobsleigh
- ❖ Luge
- ❖ Skeleton
- ❖ Wok racing
- ❖ Dogsled racing

Team Sports

Sports that involve teams, played on ice.

- ❖ Bandy
- ❖ Broomball
- ❖ Curling
- ❖ Ice hockey
- ❖ Ice stock sport
- ❖ Ringette
- ❖ Sledge hockey—(Winter Para-Olympic Sport)
- ❖ Snowball Association—(Last one standing)

Recreational Sports

Some 'sports' are competed (or simply enjoyed) on a more casual basis, often by children.

- ❖ Ice boating or Ice sailing
- ❖ Tobogganing
- ❖ Snowball fight
- ❖ Building snowmen
- ❖ Shinny
- ❖ Ice swimming
- ❖ Ice fishing

Famous Winter Sport Resort Regions

- ❖ Andes
- ❖ Rocky Mountains
- ❖ Alps
- ❖ Snowy Mountains
- ❖ Karkonosze Mountains/Sudeten mountains
- ❖ Lapland
- ❖ Appalachian Mountains
- ❖ Carpathian Mountains
- ❖ Balkan Mountains
- ❖ Swiss Alps

1.4 Towards Listing of Sports

The following is a list of sports, divided by category. There are many more sports to be added. This system has a disadvantage because some sports may fit in more than one category. Soccer is currently the most watched and played sport in the world.

Physical Sports By Family

Aquatics

Ball Sports

- ❖ Underwater football
- ❖ Underwater rugby
- ❖ Water polo

Competitive Swimming

- ❖ Backstroke

- ❖ Breaststroke
- ❖ Butterfly stroke
- ❖ Freestyle swimming
- ❖ Individual Medley
- ❖ Synchronized swimming

Diving

- ❖ Diving

Underwater Hockey

- ❖ Underwater hockey

Underwater Diving

- ❖ Free-diving
- ❖ Scuba Diving
- ❖ Snorkeling

Archery

- ❖ Clout archery
- ❖ Field archery
- ❖ Flight archery
- ❖ Kyudo
- ❖ Popinjay (sport)
- ❖ Target archery

Auto Racing

- ❖ Autocross
- ❖ Autograss
- ❖ Banger racing
- ❖ Board track racing
- ❖ Demolition derby
- ❖ Dirt speedway racing
- ❖ Dirt track racing
- ❖ Drag racing
- ❖ Drifting
- ❖ Folkrace
- ❖ Hillclimbing
- ❖ Ice racing

- ❖ Kart racing
- ❖ Legends car racing
- ❖ Midget car racing
- ❖ Off-road racing
- ❖ Open wheel racing
- ❖ Production car racing
- ❖ Rallycross
- ❖ Rallying
- ❖ Road racing
- ❖ Short track motor racing
- ❖ Sports car racing
- ❖ Sprint car racing
- ❖ Sprinting
- ❖ Street racing
- ❖ Time Attack
- ❖ Touring car racing
- ❖ Truck racing

Bat-and-Ball

- ❖ Baseball
- ❖ Brännboll
- ❖ Cricket
- ❖ Test cricket
- ❖ First-class cricket
- ❖ Blind cricket
- ❖ Catchy Shubby
- ❖ Club cricket
- ❖ French cricket
- ❖ Gilli-danda
- ❖ Kilikiti
- ❖ One Day International
- ❖ Kwik cricket
- ❖ List A cricket
- ❖ Pro 40
- ❖ Limited overs cricket
- ❖ Short form cricket
- ❖ Single Wicket
- ❖ Twenty20

- ❖ Lapta
- ❖ Oina
- ❖ Old Cat
- ❖ Pesäpallo
- ❖ Podex
- ❖ Rounders
- ❖ Softball
- ❖ T-Ball

Boardsports

Sports that are played with some sort of board as the primary equipment.

- ❖ Bodyboarding
- ❖ Riverboarding
- ❖ Mountainboarding
- ❖ Kite landboarding
- ❖ Skateboarding
- ❖ Freeboarding
- ❖ Longboarding
- ❖ Streetboarding
- ❖ Skysurfing
- ❖ Streetluge
- ❖ Snowboarding
- ❖ Sandboarding
- ❖ Snowkiting
- ❖ Surfing
- ❖ Kitesurfing
- ❖ Skimboarding
- ❖ Wakeboarding
- ❖ Kneeboarding
- ❖ Windsurfing

Bowling

- ❖ Bocce
- ❖ Boccia
- ❖ Boule lyonnaise
- ❖ Bowls
- ❖ Curling

❖ Duckpin bowling
❖ Five-pin bowling
❖ Klootschieten
❖ Lawn bowls
❖ Pétanque
❖ Skittles (sport)
❖ Ten-pin bowling
❖ Varpa

Catch Games

❖ Curby
❖ Dodgeball
❖ Ga-ga
❖ Prisoner Ball
❖ Snowball fight
❖ Yukigassen

Climbing

❖ Bouldering
❖ Canyoning
❖ Mountaineering
❖ Rope climbing

Cycling

❖ Cycling sports using bicycles or unicycles.

Bicycle

❖ Artistic cycling
❖ BMX racing
❖ Bobrun cycling
❖ Cyclo-cross
❖ Mountain bicycling
❖ Road bicycle racing
❖ Track cycling
❖ FMX or foot motocross

Skibob

❖ Skibobbing

Unicycle

- ❖ Mountain unicycling
- ❖ Unicycle trials

Combat Sports

Combat sport is a competitive contact sport where two combatants fight against each other using certain rules of engagement.

Grappling

- ❖ Aikido
- ❖ Aiki-jujutsu
- ❖ Brazilian Jiu-Jitsu
- ❖ Catch wrestling
- ❖ Glima
- ❖ Judo
- ❖ Jujutsu
- ❖ Kinomichi
- ❖ Kurash
- ❖ Malla-yuddha
- ❖ Mongolian wrestling
- ❖ Pehlwani
- ❖ Sambo
- ❖ Shuai Jiao
- ❖ Ssireum
- ❖ Sumo
- ❖ Varzesh-e Pahlavani
- ❖ Wrestling
- ❖ Yaðlý Güreþ

Skirmish

- ❖ Airsoft
- ❖ Laser tag
- ❖ Paintball

Weapons

- ❖ Battojutsu
- ❖ Eskrima

- ❖ Egyptian stick fencing
- ❖ Fencing
- ❖ Gatka
- ❖ Haidong Gumdo
- ❖ Hojojutsu
- ❖ Iaido
- ❖ Iaijutsu
- ❖ Jodo
- ❖ Jogo do Pau
- ❖ Jukendo
- ❖ Juttejutsu
- ❖ Kendo
- ❖ Kenjutsu
- ❖ Kyudo
- ❖ Kyujutsu
- ❖ Modern Arnis
- ❖ Naginatajutsu
- ❖ Okinawan kobudo
- ❖ Shurikenjutsu
- ❖ Silambam
- ❖ Sojutsu

Striking

- ❖ Bajíquán
- ❖ Boxing
- ❖ Bokator
- ❖ Capoeira
- ❖ Fujian White Crane
- ❖ Karate
- ❖ Kenpo
- ❖ Kickboxing
- ❖ Lethwei
- ❖ Muay Thai
- ❖ Pradal Serey
- ❖ San shou
- ❖ Savate
- ❖ Shaolin kung fu
- ❖ Sikaran

- ❖ Silat
- ❖ Spanish Punching Derby
- ❖ Subak
- ❖ Taekkyeon
- ❖ Taekwondo
- ❖ Taido
- ❖ Wing Chun
- ❖ Wing Tsun
- ❖ Zui Quan

Mixed or hybrid

- ❖ Baguazhang
- ❖ Bando
- ❖ Bartitsu
- ❖ Bujinkan
- ❖ Hapkido
- ❖ Hwa Rang Do
- ❖ Jeet Kune Do
- ❖ Kajukenbo
- ❖ Kalarippayattu
- ❖ Krav Maga
- ❖ Kuk Sool Won
- ❖ MCMAP
- ❖ Northern Praying Mantis
- ❖ Ninjutsu
- ❖ Pankration
- ❖ Pencak Silat
- ❖ Sanshou
- ❖ Shidokan
- ❖ Shoot boxing
- ❖ Shootfighting
- ❖ Shorinji Kempo
- ❖ Systema
- ❖ Tai chi chuan
- ❖ Vajra Mushti
- ❖ Vovinam
- ❖ Xingyiquan

Cue Sports

- ❖ Carom billiards
  - ● Three-cushion
  - ● Five-pins
  - ● Balkline and straight rail
  - ● Cushion caroms
  - ● Four-ball (yotsudama)
  - ● Artistic billiards
- ❖ Novuss
- ❖ Pocket billiards (pool)
  - ● Eight-ball (and Blackball)
  - ● Nine-ball
  - ● Straight pool (14.1 continuous)
  - ● One-pocket
  - ● Three-ball
  - ● Seven-ball
  - ● Ten-ball
  - ● Rotation
  - ● Baseball pocket billiards
  - ● Cribbage (pool)
  - ● Bank pool
  - ● Artistic pool
  - ● Trick shot competition
  - ● Speed pool
  - ● Bowlliards
  - ● Kelly pool
  - ● Cutthroat
  - ● Killer
  - ● Russian pyramid
- ❖ Snooker
  - ● Snooker plus
- ❖ Hybrid carom—pocket games:
  - ● English billiards
  - ● Bottle pool
  - ● Cowboy
- ❖ Obstacle variations
  - ● Bagatelle

- Bar billiards
- Bumper pool

Dance

- ❖ Ballet
- ❖ Ballroom dance
- ❖ Breakdance
- ❖ Irish Dance
- ❖ Latin dance
- ❖ Salsa
- ❖ Tap dance
- ❖ Hip-hop
- ❖ Cheerleading
- ❖ Majorette

Equine Sports

Sports using a horse

- ❖ Barrel Racing
- ❖ Cross Country
- ❖ Dressage
- ❖ English Pleasure
- ❖ Equitation
- ❖ Equestrian vaulting
- ❖ Harness racing
- ❖ Horse racing
- ❖ Hunter
- ❖ Reining
- ❖ Rodeo
- ❖ Show Jumping
- ❖ Steeplechase
- ❖ Western Pleasure

Fishing

- ❖ Angling
- ❖ Big-game fishing
- ❖ Casting
- ❖ Noodling

- ❖ Sport fishing
- ❖ Surf fishing
  - ● Rock fishing

Flying Disc Sports

- ❖ Disc dog
- ❖ Disc golf
- ❖ Dodge disc
- ❖ Durango boot
- ❖ Double disc court
- ❖ Flutterguts
- ❖ Freestyle
- ❖ Fricket, (AKA disc cricket, cups, suzy sticks or crispy wickets)
- ❖ Friskee
- ❖ Goaltimate
- ❖ Guts
- ❖ Hot box
- ❖ Ringo
- ❖ Ultimate (sport)

Flying sports

Airplane

- ❖ Aerobatics
- ❖ Air racing

Ballooning

- ❖ Cluster ballooning
- ❖ Hopper ballooning

Football family

- ❖ Association Football
  - ● Five-a-side football
- ❖ Australian Football
- ❖ Gaelic football
- ❖ Gridiron football
  - ● American Football
  - ● Canadian Football

- Arena Football
- ❖ Rugby Football
  - Rugby League
  - Rugby Union
- ❖ Wheelchair rugby
- ❖ Footvolley

Gymnastics

- ❖ Artistic gymnastics:
  - Balance Beam
  - Floor
  - High Bar
  - Parallel Bars
  - Pommel Horse
  - Still Rings
  - Uneven Bars
  - Vault
- ❖ Cheerleading
- ❖ Majorette
- ❖ Competitive rope jumping
- ❖ Juggling
- ❖ Rhythmic gymnastics
- ❖ Sports acrobatics
- ❖ Tricking
- ❖ Trampolining
- ❖ Trapeze
  - Flying trapeze
  - Static trapeze

Handball Family

Handball games often have similarities to racquet or catch games.

- ❖ American handball
- ❖ Basketball
- ❖ European Handball
- ❖ Field handball
- ❖ Fistball
- ❖ Fives

- ● Eton Fives
- ● Rugby Fives
- ❖ Frisian handball
- ❖ Four square
- ❖ Gaelic handball
- ❖ Goalball
- ❖ Jeu de paume
- ❖ Korfball
- ❖ Netball
- ❖ Palla
- ❖ Tchoukball
- ❖ Valencian pilota
- ❖ Volleyball
- ❖ Volutobol
- ❖ Water polo

Hockey Family

- ❖ Bandy
- ❖ Broomball
- ❖ Field Hockey
  - ● Indoor field hockey
- ❖ Floorball
- ❖ Hurling (The ball can be handled so Hurling is on the periphery of the 'hockey family').
- ❖ Ice Hockey: (1) Ringette
- ❖ Knotty
- ❖ Roller hockey
  - ● Inline hockey
  - ● Road hockey
  - ● Roller hockey (Quad)
- ❖ Shinty
- ❖ Underwater hockey

Hunting

Sometimes considered blood sports.

- ❖ Beagling
- ❖ Big game hunting

- ❖ Deer hunting
- ❖ Fox hunting
- ❖ Hare coursing
- ❖ Wolf hunting

Kite Sports

- ❖ Kite buggy
- ❖ Kite fighting
- ❖ Kite landboarding
- ❖ Kitesurfing
- ❖ Snow kiting
- ❖ Sport kite (Stunt kite)

Mixed Discipline

- ❖ Biathlon
- ❖ Decathlon
- ❖ Modern pentathlon
- ❖ Pentathlon
- ❖ Triathlon

Motorboat Racing

- ❖ Drag boat racing
- ❖ F1 Powerboat Racing
- ❖ Hydroplane racing
- ❖ Jet sprint boat racing
- ❖ Offshore powerboat racing

Motorcycle Racing

- ❖ Auto Race
- ❖ Board track racing
- ❖ Cross-country rally
- ❖ Endurance racing
- ❖ Enduro
- ❖ Grand Prix motorcycle racing
- ❖ Grass Track

- ❖ Hill Climb
- ❖ Ice Racing
- ❖ Indoor short track
- ❖ Motocross
- ❖ Motorcycle drag racing
- ❖ Motorcycle speedway
- ❖ Road racing
- ❖ Superbike racing
- ❖ Supercross
- ❖ Supermoto
- ❖ Supersport racing
- ❖ Superside
- ❖ Track racing
- ❖ TT racing

Orienteering Family

- ❖ Amateur Radio Direction Finding
- ❖ Geo caching
- ❖ Orienteering

Paddle Sports

Canoeing

- ❖ Canoeing
- ❖ Outrigger canoeing

Kayaking

- ❖ Creeking
- ❖ Flyak
- ❖ Freeboating
- ❖ Royaking
- ❖ Sea kayaking
- ❖ Squirt Boating
- ❖ Surf Kayaking
- ❖ Whitewater kayaking

Rafting

- ❖ Rafting
- ❖ White water rafting

Rowing

- ❖ Coastal and ocean rowing
  - ● Surfboat
- ❖ Dragon boat racing
- ❖ Double scull
- ❖ Quad four
- ❖ Single scull
- ❖ Straight four

Parachuting

- ❖ BASE jumping
- ❖ Paragliding
- ❖ Parasailing
- ❖ Sky diving
- ❖ Skysurfing
- ❖ Wingsuit flying
- ❖ Hang Gliding

Polo

- ❖ Bicycle polo
- ❖ Canoe polo
- ❖ Elephant polo
- ❖ Equine polo
- ❖ Segway polo
- ❖ Yak polo

Racquet (or racket) Sports

Sports where a player use a racquet (or racket) to hit a ball or other objects.

- ❖ Badminton
- ❖ Ball badminton

- ❖ Bilbocatch
- ❖ Frontenis
- ❖ Jai-Alai
- ❖ Matkot
- ❖ Paddleball
- ❖ Pelota mixteca
- ❖ Pickleball
- ❖ Platform tennis
- ❖ Pington
- ❖ Racquetball
- ❖ Racquets
- ❖ Racketlon
- ❖ Rapid Ball
- ❖ Real tennis
- ❖ Soft tennis
- ❖ Speedball
- ❖ Speedminton
- ❖ Squash
- ❖ Squash tennis
- ❖ Stické
- ❖ Table tennis, Recognized by IOC in 1981
- ❖ Tennis
- ❖ Xare

Radiosports

Sports using a radio:

- ❖ Amateur Radio Direction Finding
- ❖ Radiosport/Contesting
- ❖ High Speed Telegraphy

Remote Control

- ❖ Model Aerobatics
- ❖ RC Racing
- ❖ Robot combat

Running

- ❖ Endurance
  - ● Cross-country running
  - ● Half marathon
  - ● Marathon
  - ● Ultramarathon
- ❖ Sprint
- ❖ Hurdles

Sled Sports

- ❖ Sledding
- ❖ Bobsleigh
- ❖ Luge
- ❖ Skeleton
- ❖ Toboggan

Shooting sports

Ports using a firearm:

- ❖ Clay pigeon shooting
- ❖ Field target
- ❖ Fullbore target rifle

Sport Stacking

- ❖ Sport stacking

Street Stunts

- ❖ Free running
- ❖ Tricking
- ❖ Freestyle Football

Tag Games

- ❖ British bulldogs (American Eagle)
- ❖ Hana Ichi Monme
- ❖ Hide and seek

- ❖ Kabaddi
- ❖ Kho kho
- ❖ Red rover
- ❖ Tag

Walking

- ❖ Hiking
- ❖ Race Walking

Weightlifting

- ❖ Clean and jerk
- ❖ Snatch

Mind Sports by Family

Requiring little or no physical exertion or agility mind sports are often not considered true sports. Some mind sports are recognised by sporting federations. The following list is intended to represent anything that is likely to be referred to as a mind sport, not to argue their validity as sports.

Card Games

Speedcubing

- ❖ Speedcubing

Strategy Board Games

- ❖ Chess
- ❖ Checkers
- ❖ Chinese Checkers
- ❖ Draughts
- ❖ Go
- ❖ Go-Moku
- ❖ Jacquet
- ❖ Mancala
- ❖ Mahjong (Taipei)
- ❖ Sogo (Score four)
- ❖ Stratego

- ❖ Inline speed skating
- ❖ Rowing
- ❖ Wheelchair racing
- ❖ Wood chopping
- ❖ Razza Racing
- ❖ Cross-Country Skiing

Miscellaneous

- ❖ Baton Twirling
- ❖ Boomerang Throw
- ❖ Bungee jumping
- ❖ Competitive eating
- ❖ Egg and spoon race
- ❖ Footbag (hacky sack)
- ❖ Haggis hurling
- ❖ Lumberjack
- ❖ Mattress Jumping
- ❖ Tetherball
- ❖ Three-legged race
- ❖ sack race
- ❖ Soap shoes
- ❖ Speed Typing
- ❖ Patball
- ❖ Wallball

Motorsport

Skating Sports

- ❖ Aggressive skating
- ❖ Artistic roller skating
- ❖ Bandy
- ❖ Bobrun Skating
- ❖ Ice hockey
- ❖ Ice Skating
- ❖ Inline speed skating
- ❖ Inline hockey
- ❖ Figure skating

- Ringette
- Rinkball
- Rink hockey
- Skateboarding
- Freestyle slalom skating
- Roller derby
- Roller hockey
- Roller skating
- Roller speed skating
- Short track speed skating
- Skater hockey
- Speed skating
- Synchronized skating

Snow Sports

- Skiing
- Snowball Association
- Snowboarding:
  - Boardercross
  - Freestyle snowboarding
- Snowkiting
- Snowshoeing

Strength Sports

Sports mainly based on sheer power.

- Arm Wrestling
- Thumb wrestling
- Bodybuilding
- Powerlifting
- Toe wrestling
- Tug-o-war
- Zourkhaneh
- Weightlifting
- Wife Carrying

Tables Sports

- Air hockey

- ❖ Backgammon
- ❖ Card games
- ❖ Chess
- ❖ Chinese Checkers
- ❖ Connect Four
- ❖ Cue sports:
  - ● Carom billiards
    - ■ Three-cushion:
    - ■ Five-pins
    - ■ Balkline and straight rail
    - ■ Cushion caroms
    - ■ Four-ball (yotsudama)
    - ■ Artistic billiards
    - ■ several other variants
  - ● Pocket billiards (pool)
    - ■ Eight-ball (and Blackball)
    - ■ Nine-ball
    - ■ Straight pool (14.1 continuous)
    - ■ One-pocket
    - ■ Three-ball
    - ■ Seven-ball
    - ■ Ten-ball
    - ■ Rotation
    - ■ Baseball pocket billiards
    - ■ Cribbage (pool)
    - ■ Bank pool
    - ■ Artistic pool
    - ■ Trick shot competition
    - ■ Speed pool
    - ■ Bowlliards
    - ■ Chicago
    - ■ Kelly pool
    - ■ Cutthroat
    - ■ Killer
    - ■ Russian pyramid
    - ■ many other variants
  - ● Snooker
    - ■ Snooker plus

- Hybrid carom—pocket games:
  - English billiards
  - Bottle pool
  - Cowboy
- Obstacle variations:
  - Bagatelle
  - Bar billiards
  - Bumper pool
  - many other (generally obsolete) variants
- ❖ Draughts (checker)
- ❖ Dominoes
- ❖ Go
- ❖ Go-Moku
- ❖ Jacquet
- ❖ Mancala
- ❖ Mahjong (Taipei)
- ❖ Reversi (Othello)
- ❖ Shogi
- ❖ Scrabble (and variants)
- ❖ Speedcubing
- ❖ Stratego
- ❖ Table football
- ❖ Table Tennis (Ping Pong)
- ❖ Table hockey
- ❖ Xiangqi

Target Sports

Sports where the main objective is to hit a certain target.

- ❖ Archery
- ❖ Kyûdô
- ❖ Duckpin bowling
- ❖ Atlatl
- ❖ Five-pin bowling
- ❖ Billiards
- ❖ Bar billiards
- ❖ Bowls
- ❖ Bowling Pin Shooting

- Carambole billiard
- Candlepin bowling
- Pool
- Snooker
- Bocce
- Boccia
- Boules
- Calva
- Croquet
- Curling
- Darts
- Gateball
- Disc golf
- Speed golf
- Golfcross
- Horseshoes (horseshoe throwing)
- Knife throwing
- Laser Tag
- Lawn bowls
- Marbles
- Matball
- Pall mall
- Petanque
- Paintball
- Shooting
- Skittles
- Ten-pin bowling
- Trugo
- skittles
- Skee ball
- Pitch and putt

Team Sports

Sports that involve teams.

- American football
- Kilikiti
- Association Football (soccer)

- ❖ Australian rules football
- ❖ Ball Hockey
- ❖ Bandy
- ❖ Baseball
- ❖ Basketball
- ❖ Beach handball
- ❖ Beach soccer
- ❖ Beach rugby
- ❖ Beach volleyball
- ❖ Bossaball
- ❖ Box/indoor lacrosse
- ❖ Bowling
- ❖ Basque pelota
- ❖ Broomball
- ❖ Camogie
- ❖ Canadian football
- ❖ Cricket
- ❖ Curling
- ❖ Dodgeball
- ❖ Eton Wall Game
- ❖ Field Hockey
- ❖ Fistball
- ❖ Floorball
- ❖ Cubbies
- ❖ Footballtennis
- ❖ Footvolley
- ❖ Frisian handball
- ❖ Futsal
- ❖ Gaelic football
- ❖ Gaelic handball
- ❖ Gateball
- ❖ Goalball
- ❖ Handball
- ❖ Harrow Football
- ❖ Hoover Ball
- ❖ Hornussen
- ❖ Horseshoe

- ❖ Hurling
- ❖ Indoor soccer
- ❖ Ice Hockey
- ❖ Inline hockey
- ❖ Kabaddi
- ❖ Kickball
- ❖ Korfball
- ❖ Lacrosse
- ❖ Mesoamerican ballgame
- ❖ Marching Band
- ❖ Netball
- ❖ Oina
- ❖ Paintball
- ❖ Pesäpallo
- ❖ Petanque
- ❖ Polo
- ❖ Polocrosse
- ❖ Ringette
- ❖ Rinkball
- ❖ Road hockey
- ❖ Roller Hockey (Rink Hockey)
- ❖ Rounders
- ❖ Rowing
- ❖ Royal Shrovetide Football
- ❖ Rugby football
- ❖ Rugby league
- ❖ Rugby union
- ❖ Sepak Takraw
- ❖ Shinty
- ❖ Skater hockey
- ❖ Skittles
- ❖ Slamball
- ❖ Softball
- ❖ Surfboat
- ❖ Motorcycle speedway
- ❖ Speedball
- ❖ Spongee polo

- ❖ Tennis Polo
- ❖ Tennis
- ❖ Tchoukball
- ❖ Test cricket
- ❖ Throwball
- ❖ Ultimate football
- ❖ Ultimate (Ultimate frisbee)
- ❖ Underwater football
- ❖ Underwater hockey
- ❖ Underwater rugby
- ❖ Volleyball
- ❖ Viperball
- ❖ Wallyball
- ❖ Water polo
- ❖ Wheelchair basketball
- ❖ Wheelchair tennis
- ❖ Wheelchair rugby
- ❖ Wiffle ball
- ❖ Rugby sevens
- ❖ Six-man football
- ❖ Flag football
- ❖ Touch football
- ❖ Twenty 20
- ❖ Prisoner Ball

Wind Sports

Sport which uses wind:

- ❖ Iceboating
- ❖ Land sailing
- ❖ Windsurfing
- ❖ Kitesurfing
- ❖ Kite buggy
- ❖ Kite fighting
- ❖ Kite flying
- ❖ Sailing
- ❖ Flysailing

1.5 Sports Tourism: An Introduction

There are many different definitions of sports tourism, from those involving travel for the purpose of participating in competitive sports, to those involving more leisure or adventure sporting activities.[1] Thus, the extent of sports tourism vary quite a bit.

Sports tourism involves people traveling to participate or to observe sports. These activities may include people competing in an international event, such as the Olympics, or simply sitting amongst the audience watching the World Cup match.

Inevitably, following sports tourism, there will be consequential impacts. These may be classified under economic impacts, socio-cultural impacts, health impacts and environmental impacts.

Economic Impacts

The increasing and important impact sport has in economic terms requires a more multi-disciplinary approach. The economic sector of sport has transformed itself in the last decade from a traditional Spectators-Subsidies-Sponsors-Local (SSSL)-model to a more global Media-Corporations-Merchandising-Markets or MCCM-model. The new sport model has executed forms of vertical integration in the industry and has created synergisms as an outcome of the relations between business and sport. Some of the economic developments are—Broadcasting rights, merchandising, sponsoring, organizing of mega sporting events, multiplication effect of organizing a sport event, the mobile leisure society, sport tourism, sport and the impact on health, the public-private cooperation in building of sporting infrastructures, the betting industry, raising market share of sporting goods, shoes and clothing.

The British Tourism Authority claims that 20 per cent of the tourist trips are for the prime purpose of sport participation, and 50 per cent of the tourist trips include among other purposes sport participation. The data was also validated by 1998 Canadian Travel Survey which set an evaluation of 37 per cent of the domestic trips for sport oriented activities.

In the year 2007 the first search engine for sports tourism activities was set.

Socio-Cultural Impacts

Land Use: The use of land is necessary to sports tourism. Sports take up space. Some of these sports may even require facilities to be specially built. For instance, golf will definitely require land to be allocated to build its course. Singaporeans, who want to experience golf in a bigger and more fulfilling golf course, may seek to travel to nearby Malaysia instead, and this is a form of land use for Malaysia resulting from sports tourism.

Cultural Exchanges: It is certain that cultural exchanges will take place whenever people of different cultural backgrounds meet. Sports tourists will nevertheless learn about the culture of the country they visit when they arrive at their destination, although their main purpose of travel is to participant in sports, or to observe sports (but not for cultural purposes).

Preservation of Traditions: Once-dying traditions can also be 'revived' through sports tourism. The need to display these traditions to tourists will bring these traditions 'back to life'. Showcasing traditional food, traditional costumes, culture and ethnics will not only enrich these sports tourists' experience to the country, but also help preserve the traditions, instead of letting them gradually disappear from this world.

National Identity: The national pride and prestige one feels when a mega event is held in his country is perpetual. It is a proud feeling to know that your country is able to hold an international event, because it will be broadcast worldwide, and therefore known to the rest of the world.

"In Germany "national pride" ("Nationalstolz") is often associated with the former Nazi regime. Strong displays of national pride are therefore considered poor taste by many Germans. There is an ongoing public debate about the issue of German patriotism. The World Cup in 2006, held in Germany, saw a wave of patriotism sweep the country in a manner not seen for many years. Although many were hesitant to show such blatant support as the hanging of the national flag from windows, as the team progressed through the tournament, so too did the level of support across the nation. By the time the semi-final against Italy came around, the level of national pride and unity was at its highest throughout the tournament, and the hosting of the World Cup is seen to have been a great success for Germany as a nation."

Violence: This usually occurs among the spectators who are unsatisfied with the announced results. The spectators/audiences usually from the losing side will create fights with the other side. Violence is one of the negative impacts that cam arise from sports tourism. It is an unhealthy scene as this can sour the relationship between two counterparts. Violence in sports tourism does not only happen among countries, but also within one country itself.

Health Impacts

There are various health impacts involved when looking at Sports Tourism, they are:

— Physiological impacts,
— Psychological impacts, and
— Social health impacts.

Physiological Impacts

People are generally interested and motivated to play sports when participating in Sports Tourism. Many people all over the world travel to Hawaii to surf as it is a popular destination for big waves. The physiological impact of Sports Tourism can be seen in athletes who are actively involved, going overseas to compete with other people.

These athletes typically have a good physique as it is naturally normal for them to want to improve and train to be better. They lead a lifestyle which centres on their health and physical well-being.

Psychological Impacts

Sports allows for the mind to relax when done for recreation. People who engage in Sports Tourism in a non-competitive environment typically use it as an opportunity to get away and re-charge.

Sports also cause the brain to secrete endorphins, which prevents stress and strengthens the body against pain. At the same time, it makes people increase their self-confidence and boosts their self-esteem.

Social Health Impacts

The health risks involved in Sports Tourism applies to both the athletes and fans. They might train too hard to compete, risking injuries. Also, one needs time to adapt to another country and this may sometimes be difficult, sometimes even causing sickness. For example, jet lag.

Similarly, because of the internal time difference, fans all over the world purposely stay up to watch games, and this leads to an irregular sleeping pattern. Cases of fans falling ill during these periods are common, with increased consumption of junk food combined with late nights.

Environmental Impacts

The environmental impacts of sports tourism is classified as negative impacts. It consists of pollution and depletion.

- ❖ *Pollution*: Pollution can occur in terms of air, land, water and sound. Air pollution happens basically due to the emission of harmful gases from vehicles. For example during major world games such as the Olympics and World Cup, there will be more vehicles than usual thus increasing the amount of air pollution. Sound pollution occurs due to the noise made by the spectators. As for land pollution, it usually occurs in natural habitats. For instance, sports like mountain climbing pollute the land as the equipments use can destroy the natural surroundings. Apart from that, littering caused by the masses also contribute to land pollution.
- ❖ *Depletion*: In this case, it refers to depletion of resources. For a sports events to be held (which is the main reason for sports tourism), many resources are required.

1.6 Adventure Sports: Towards Listing

Catetory and Subcategories

This category has only the following subcategory.

"Adventure sports"

- ❖ Adventure racing
- ❖ Adventure running
- ❖ Amateur Radio Direction Finding
- ❖ Antarctic Ice Marathon
- ❖ Arctic Team Challenge
- ❖ Canyoning

Caving

- ❖ Enduro
- ❖ Expedition 360
- ❖ Fox Oring
- ❖ Frontier Adventure Sports & Training
- ❖ Gerald Fusil
- ❖ Karrimor International Mountain Marathon
- ❖ La Huasteca

Lowe Alpine Mountain Marathon

- ❖ Mine exploration
- ❖ Mountain Marathon
- ❖ Primal Quest
- ❖ Radio Orienteering in a Compact Area
- ❖ Saunders Lakeland Mountain Marathon
- ❖ X-Venture

Fell Running

- ❖ Flying fox (cablecar)
- ❖ Garden pond
- ❖ Green Laning
- ❖ H. Barber and Sons
- ❖ Hazards of outdoor activities
- ❖ Heritage Conservation and Recreation Service
- ❖ High adventure
- ❖ Jeep trail
- ❖ Kloofing

Off Highway Vehicle

- ❖ Off-roading
- ❖ Outdoor exploration
- ❖ Pack station
- ❖ Pedalo
- ❖ Snow cave
- ❖ Snugpak
- ❖ Sphereing
- ❖ Swimhiking
- ❖ Woodcraft (youth movement)

❖   Zip-line

1.7 Recreation: An Introduction

Recreation is a form of entertainment derived from physical activities, without artificial rules. **Recreation** is the use of time in a non-profitable way, in many ways also a therapeutic refreshment of one's body or mind. While leisure is more likely a form of entertainment or rest, recreation is active for the participant but in a refreshing and diverting manner, usually one which is much different from day to day worries, stresses and activities.

Related categories:

❖   Games for entertainment defined by a set of rules, and
❖   Hobbies for entertainment that is more sedentary.

Subcategories

This category has the following 19 subcategories, out of 19 total.

❖   Action (genre)
❖   Airsoft
❖   Children's games
❖   Dance
❖   Diving (acrobatics)

Drinking Culture

❖   Exercise
❖   Hobbies
❖   Massage
❖   Naturism
❖   Outdoor recreation
❖   Paintball

Parkour

Pets

❖   Physical activity and dexterity toys

- ❖ Play
- ❖ Skating
- ❖ Sports
- ❖ Visitor attractions

Hobby Farm

- ❖ Hydraulophone
- ❖ Internet scavenger hunt
- ❖ Joggling board
- ❖ McFarlane Sports Picks
- ❖ Mineral spa
- ❖ Moab Jeep Safari
- ❖ Mudflat hiking
- ❖ National Playing Fields Association
- ❖ Party service
- ❖ Playground
- ❖ R&R (military)

Recreation Ecology

- ❖ Scavenger hunt
- ❖ Sleepover
- ❖ Spray pool
- ❖ Thumb twiddling
- ❖ Trade last
- ❖ Urban beach
- ❖ Vacation property
- ❖ Vandkulturhuset
- ❖ Volksmarching
- ❖ Water fight
- ❖ Western Fair

2

International Sport, Adventure, Recreation and Travel: Select Analysis of Some Adventure Sports

2.1 International Sports Federations

The International Sports Federations (IFs) are responsible for the integrity of their sport on the international level.

Organisation of the IFs

The International Federations (IFs) are international non-governmental organisations recognised by the International Olympic Committee (IOC) as administering one or more sports at world level. The national federations administering those sports are affiliated to them. While conserving their independence and autonomy in the administration of their sports, International Sports Federations seeking IOC recognition must ensure that their statutes, practice and activities conform with the Olympic Charter.

International Federations

- ❖ ASOIF: The Association of Summer Olympic International Federations.
- ❖ AIOWF: The Association of International Olympic Winter Sports Federations.
- ❖ IOC: This Association is Recognised as International Sports Federations.

Mission of the IFs

The IFs have the responsibility and duty to manage and to monitor the everyday running of the world's various sports disciplines, including the practical organisation of events during the Games, and the supervision of the development of athletes practising these sports at every level. Each IF governs its sport at world level and ensures its promotion and development. They monitor the everyday administration of their sports and guarantee the regular organisation of competitions as well as respect for the rules of fair play.

The IFs may, of course, formulate proposals addressed to the IOC concerning the Olympic Charter and the Olympic Movement in general, including the organising and holding of the Olympic Games; give their opinions concerning the candidatures for organising the Olympic Games, particularly concerning the technical capabilities of the candidate cities; collaborate in the preparation of the Olympic Congresses; and participate in the activities of the IOC commissions.

Recognised IFs whose sports appear on the Olympic programme have the status of International Olympic Federations. As such, they participate in annual meetings of the IOC Executive Board with the International Olympic Summer Federations and with their Winter counterparts.

In order to discuss common problems and decide on their events calendars, the summer Olympic federations, the winter Olympic federations and the recognised federations have formed associations: the Association of Summer Olympic International Federations (ASOIF), the Association of International Winter Sports Federations (AIOWF), the Association of IOC Recognised International Sports Federations (ARISF) and the General Association of International Sports Federations (GAISF), which also includes other sports federations.

The Association of Summer Olympic International Federations (ASOIF)

The Association of Summer Olympic International Federations (ASOIF), created in 1983, coordinates and defends the common interests of its members to ensure close cooperation between them, the members of the Olympic Movement and those of other organisations. They do so with the aim of preserving the Olympic

Movement while maintaining the authority, independence and autonomy of the member International Federations.

The Association of International Olympic Winter Sports Federations (AIOWF)

The Association of International Olympic Winter Sports Federations (AIOWF) works in close cooperation with the International Sports Federations which govern a sport featured on the Olympic programme as well as those affiliated to the General Association of International Sports Federations (GAISF). It encourages cooperation between its members.

The AIOWF is the qualified spokesperson dealing with specific questions connected with winter sports in general, and with the Olympic Games in particular. The AIOWF is also responsible for choosing the joint delegation and/or appointments of the winter sports representatives on the commissions of the International Olympic Committee (IOC) and other international organisations. AIOWF also deals with the coordination of the competitions calendar as well as the submission to the IOC of proposals regarding the distribution of the share of television rights revenues.

The Association of the IOC Recognised International Sports Federations (ARISF)

Founded in 1983, the Association of the IOC Recognised International Sports Federations has several aims, namely:

- ❖ to act as a spokesperson, and to defend and coordinate the common interests of its members whilst maintaining their authority, independence and autonomy. However, the Rules of the Olympic Charter prevail and no ARISF rule can go against these principles,
- ❖ to determine the consensus of the member federations on questions of common interest in relation to the Olympic Movement,
- ❖ to ensure the largest possible participation in the Congresses, programmes and projects of the International Olympic Committee (IOC),

❖ to decide on nominations of ARISF representatives on commissions of the IOC and/or other international sports organisations.

The General Association of International Sports Federations (GAISF)

The General Association of International Sports Federations (GAISF), founded in 1967, groups together the International Sports Federations and various associations with the aim of defending world-wide sport, becoming better informed and making themselves known, and cooperating and coordinating their activities. Its aim is to create a forum which brings together all the sports bodies once a year for an exchange of views on subjects of common interest. Its mission is to maintain the authority and autonomy of its members, promote closer links between its members and all sports organisations, coordinate and protect common interests and collect, verify and disseminate information.

2.2 Jungle Tourism

Jungle tourism is a rising subcategory of adventure travel defined by active multifaceted physical means of travel in the jungle regions of the earth. Although similar in many respects to adventure travel, jungle tourism pertains specificalluy to the context of region, culture and activity. According to the *Glossary of Tourism Terms*, jungle tours have become a major component of green tourism in tropical destinations and are a relatively recent phenomenon of Western international tourism.

Of the regions that take part in tourism-driven sustainable development practices and eco tourism, Mexican, Central and South American practices are the most pervasive in the industry; notably Mayan jungle excursions. Other regions include jungle territories in Africa, Australia, and the South Pacific.

Jungle tourism in Central and South America

The majority of jungle tour operators are concentrated in what is known as the Mayan World or "Ruta Maya". The Mayan World encompasses five different countries that hosted the entirety of the Mayan Civilization: Mexico, Guatemala, Belize, Honduras and El Salvador.

Most tours consist of visits to popular Mayan archaeological sites such as Tikal, Guatemala, Chichen Itza, and Copan. These day visits will usually consist of a guided tour of a heavily tourist-concentrated Mayan and archaeological site. Tikal and Chichen Itza are prime examples of popular day-visit sites. Such sites involve a tour guide, designated either by the state government or by a private company, for the tourists. These tour guides are predominantly trained professionals, certified to take large parties of fifty through heavily populated archaeological sites.

Although most of the visits to these more prominent sites involve day trips, there are also many jungle tour operators that showcase less-known, remote Mayan jungle ruins such as Nakum, Yaxha, and El Mirador. These tours involve much more preparation, time and funding to explore as they are usually in very remote and generally inaccessible regions of the Mayan jungles. These ruins and sites are reached by alternative and physically taxing means of travel such as bicycle, canoe, horseback or hiking. This is what essentially differentiates jungle tourism from any other sort of adventure travel tours. There are several tour operators that will even employ the use of machetes during tours.

Another significant and noteworthy difference is the fact that the majority of tour operators that travel deep into the Central and South American Jungle will cap the number of persons traveling in the group at ten to fifteen. This is done to minimize the impact on the jungle flora and fauna. Federal laws in some countries prohibit any given group large than fifteen people traveling through the Mayan jungle, a generally protected region, but very limited resources have kept such practices from occurring under the radar.

2.3 Adventure Recreation

Adventure recreation refers to active and outdoor activities such as backpacking (wilderness), rafting, climbing, and outdoor survival. A few universities give degrees in adventure recreation, which aim to teach graduates how to run a business in the field of adventure recreation. Along with hands-on training on activities included in adventure recreation, basic courses needed for any business, such as accounting, are required to obtain a degree. Some adventure recreation businesses cater to tourists, while others, such as indoor rock climbing, appeal to people wanting to be active on a regular basis.

In contemporary society, the term outdoor adventure generally implies an educational or recreational activity that is exciting and physically challenging. Adventure recreation can be any number of leisure pursuits which provide exposure to physical danger.

University Outdoor Recreation programs are becoming more popular in the United States. Universities often offer indoor rock climbing walls, equipment rental, ropes courses and trip programming.

2.4 Adventure Travel

Adventure travel is a type of tourism involving exploration or travel to remote, exotic and possibly hostile areas, where the traveler should "expect the unexpected". Adventure tourism is rapidly growing in popularity as tourists seek different kinds of vacations. According to the U.S.-based Adventure Travel Trade Association, "adventure travel" may be any tourist activity including two of the following three components: a physical activity, a cultural exchange or interaction, and engagement with nature.

Adventure tourism gains much of its excitement by allowing its participants to step outside of their comfort zone. This may be from experiencing culture shock, or through the performance of acts that require significant effort and involve some degree of risk (real or perceived) and/or physical danger. This may include activities such as mountaineering, trekking, bungee jumping, mountain biking, rafting, zip-lining and rock climbing. Some obscure forms of adventure travel include disaster and ghetto tourism. Other rising forms of adventure travel include social and jungle tourism.

Access to inexpensive consumer technology with respect to navigation systems, flashpacking, social networking and photography have increased the worldwide interest in adventure travel.

Tour Operators, Travel Agencies & Retailers

Many organizations and companies worldwide cater to adventure clientèle. Some of these include Intrepid Travel, GAP Adventures, Far Frontiers, Mountain Equipment Co-op, BadAss Travel, BikeHike Adventures Rainforest Expeditions and Scott Walking Adventures. Some geographic regions are promoted by both private and public agencies as adventure travel destinations. One of the premier and pioneer adventure companies is Mountain Travel, of California, founded in 1968 by mountaineers/adventurers Leo LeBon, Allen Steck and Barry Bishop.

Disabled

With the trend of increasing accessible tourism available to disabled persons around the world, some tourism areas are developing adventure tourism specifically for the disabled. Whistler, British Columbia and Vancouver, British Columbia, Canada have been taking the lead with the 2010 Para-Olympics. Adventure travel for the disabled has become a $13 billion USD a year industry in North America.

Notable disabled adventurers include Erik Weihenmeyer, the first blind person to climb Mt. Everest; Casey Pieretti, an amputee skater; and Caroline Walsh, founder of the Access to Marine Conservation for All International.

Some adventure travel destinations offer diverse programs and job opportunities developed specifically for the differently abled. Esprit Rafting, located in Pontiac Regional County Municipality in Quebec, Canada designs rafting trips for people with spinal cord damage. Accessible Canadian Adventures in Ontario, Canada offers hunting, fishing and wildlife photography adventures for those requiring assistance.

Media

Some prominent adventure travel personalities, media sources and organizations include:

❖ Adventure Travel Magazine, a UK based adventure travel magazine published since 1995.

❖ *Anthony Bourdain*: No Reservations, a program on the Travel Channel that focuses on the adventure of authentic food and experiences in various locales.

❖ Nat Geo Adventure, a subscription TV channel part of National Geographic Channels International.

National Geographic Adventure, a magazine affiliated with the National Geographic Society.

Outpost, a Canadian adventure travel magazine.

"Whatever You Do, Don't Run" is a collection of true stories from Peter Allison, who worked as a safari guide in South Africa, Botswana and Namibia.

There are many blogs and websites dedicated to this form of tourism including ComeBackAlive.com, the official website of Robert Young Pelton, author of The World's Most Dangerous Places, the official website of Adventure Travel Magazine.

2.5 Whale Watching

Whale watching is the practice of observing whales and other cetaceans in their natural habitat. Whales are watched most commonly for recreation (cf. bird watching) but the activity can also be for scientific or educational reasons. While individuals do organize private trips, whale watching is primarily a commercial activity, estimated to be worth up to $1 billion per annum worldwide to whale watching operations and their local communities. The size and rapid growth of the whale watching industry has led to complex and unconcluded debates with the whaling industry about the best use of whales as a natural resource.

History

Whale watching as an organized activity dates back to 1950 when the Cabrillo National Monument in San Diego was declared a public spot for the observation of Gray Whales. In 1955 the first water-based whale watching commenced in the same area, charging customers $1 per trip to view the whales at closer quarters. The spectacle proved popular, attracting 10,000 visitors in its first year and many more in subsequent years. The industry spread throughout the western coast of the United States over the following decade.

In 1971 the Montreal Zoological Society commenced the first commercial whale watching activity on the eastern side of North America, offering trips in the St. Lawrence River to view Fin and Beluga Whales.

In the late 1970s the industry mushroomed in size thanks to operations in New England. By 1985 more visitors watched whales from New England than California. The rapid growth in this area has been attributed to the relatively dense population of Humpback Whales, whose acrobatic behaviour such as breaching (jumping out of the water) and tail-slapping was an obvious crowd-pleaser, and the close proximity of whale populations to the large cities on the east coast of the US.

Throughout the 1980s and 1990s whale watching spread throughout the world. In 1998 Erich Hoyt carried out the largest systematic study of whale watching yet undertaken and concluded that whale watching trips were now available in 87 countries around the world, with over 9 million participants generating an income to whale watcher operators and supporting infrastructure (such as accommodation, restaurants and souvenirs) of over one billion dollars. His estimate for 2000 was for 11.3 million participants spending $1.475 billion, representing a five-fold increase over the decade.

Whale watching is of particular importance to developing countries as coastal communities start to profit directly from the whales' presence, significantly adding to popular support for the full protection of these animals from any resumption of commercial whaling.

Regulation

Environmental campaigners, concerned by what they consider the "quick-buck" mentality of some boat owners, continue to strongly urge all whale watcher operators to contribute to local regulations governing whale watching (no international standard set of regulations exist because of the huge variety of species and populations). Common rules include:

❖   Minimize speed/"No wake" speed,

❖ Avoid sudden turns,
❖ Minimize noise,
❖ Do not pursue, encircle or come in between whales,
❖ Approach animals from angles where they will not be taken by surprise,
❖ Consider cumulative impact—minimize number of boats at any one time/per day,
❖ Do not coerce dolphins into bow-riding, and
❖ Do not allow swimming with dolphins. This last rule is more contentious and is often disregarded in, for-example, the Caribbean.

Almost all popular whale watching regions now have such regulations. Campaigners hope that a combination of peer pressure, the economic benefit of being advertised and promoted by ethical tourism operators and operators' own passion for marine wildlife forces them to adhere to such regulations.

One example of such regulations is the Be Whale Wise campaign of the Northeast Pacific.

Locations

Around the world, whale watching can be had in various locations and climates. By area, they are:

Northeast Atlantic

Much of Europe is surrounded by water. Tidal straits, inlets, lagoons, and varying water temperatures, make it ideal for various species to live here from the Arctic Circle to the warm turquoise waters off of Greece. Whales are seen in good numbers off the coast of Great Britain, Ireland, Iceland, Scandinavia, Spain, and France. Commercial car ferries crossing the Bay of Biscay from Britain and Ireland to Spain and France often pass by animals as large as blue whales and as small as pods of harbor porpoise and land based tours of these waters are not unheard of. In Northern Norway, Orcas are observed in Vestfjord, Tysfjord and Ofotfjord in Nordland as the herring gathers in the fjords to stay over the winter as well as being observed off the Lofoten islands during the summer. At Andenes on Andøya in Vesterålen, sperm whales can be observed all year round, although whale watching trips are only offered from May till September. There is also a possibility to go whale watching for sperm whales and other whales from Tromsø. The continental shelf [Eggakanten] and deep water where the sperm whales congregate, is very close to shore, beginning only 7000m from the Andenes harbour. Also, in the middle of the Northeast Atlantic, in the Azores Archipelago whale watching can be easily done. The most common whale in the region is the sperm whale, especially groups of females with calves.

Northeast Pacific

On the West Coast of the United States and Canada, excellent whale watching can be found in Alaska (summer), British Columbia, and the San Juan Islands/Puget Sound in Washington, where pods of orca are sometimes visible from shore. In California good whalewatching can be found in spring, summer, and fall at the Farallon Islands off San Francisco, Monterey Bay, the usual suspects including humpbacks, greys, and blue whales. In Mexico, the various lagoons of Baja California Sur become whale breeding habitat in February and March. Tourists come here during this time to see the whales. A number of towns in the Mexican state have festivals celebrating the whale's arrival such as Guerrero Negro, in the first half of February and the port of San Blas on the 24 and 25 of February.

Northwest Pacific

In the Philippines, over thirty species of whales and dolphins can be observed around Central Visayas, Davao Gulf, the northern coast of the province-island Palawan, and in Batanes. The Visayas is particularly known area for dolphin sightings, and is home to one of the larger populations of the Fraser's Dolphin in the world. Dolphin species in the Visayas are known to be attracted to fish lures and to commercial fishing operations. In the northermost province of Batanes, at least 12 species of whales and dolphins has been sighted, making it the single location in the country with the highest cetacean diversity. There seems to be no definitive whale watching season in the Philippines, although the calmer waters of the summer season typically provides the best conditions. Some populations, like those of the Humpback Whales in Batanes, appear migratory, but other populations have yet to be studied. Some former coastal whaling communities in the Philippines have also started to generate income through whale watching tours.

Southwest Pacific

Kaikoura in New Zealand is a world-famous site for whales (in particular Sperm Whales) and Albatrosses.

Hervey Bay in Queensland, Australia offers reliable whale watching conditions for Southern Humpback Whales from the beginning of August through to the end of November each year. Whale numbers and activity have increased markedly in recent years. Sydney, Eden, Port Stephens and Byron Bay in New South Wales are other popular hot spots for tours from May to November. Southern Right Whales are seen in winter (June-August) along the south coast of Australia. They are often readily viewed from the coast around Encounter Bay near Victor Harbor and up to a hundred at a time may be seen from the cliff tops at the head of the Great Australian Bight near Yalata.

Northwest Atlantic

In New England and off the east coast of Long Island, the whale watching season typically takes place from about mid-spring through October, depending both on weather and precise location. It is here that the Northern Humpback Whale, Fin Whale, Minke Whale, and the very endangered/heavily protected North Atlantic Right Whale are often observed. For generations, areas like the Gulf of Maine and Stellwagen Bank National Marine Sanctuary (part of the inner waters formed by Cape Cod's hooked shape) have been important feeding grounds for these species and in the past this area was a whaling capital for the U.S. whaling industry, particularly Nantucket, an island just off the coast of Massachusetts.) Though strict laws prohibit the molestation of these large wild mammals, it is not unknown for the whales to approach the boats entirely on their own, particularly calves and juveniles. In recent years it is also not uncommon from time to time to see these huge animals playing and feeding in harbors of large cities, including New York. Due to the frequent visits of these mammals, a very large amount of research on large cetaceans takes place, in particular Woods Hole Oceanographic Institute.

In Canada, a popular whale-watching area is at Tadoussac, Quebec, where Beluga Whales favour the extreme depth and admixture of cold fresh water from the Saguenay River into the inland end of the Gulf of Saint Lawrence. In addition, the Maritimes shares a population of humpbacks living in the Bay of Fundy during the summer and moving south and out to the ocean during the winter.

Southwest Atlantic

In Brazil, humpback whales are observed off Salvador in Bahia State and at the National Marine Park of Abrolhos during their breeding season in austral winter and spring. Likewise, Southern Right Whales are observed from shore in Santa Catarina State during the same season, as mother/calf pairs can come as close to shore as 30 meters (about 100 feet). Income from whale watching has bolstered many a coastal community in Brazil and has made the township if Imbituba, Santa Catarina, recognized as a Brazilian "whale capital".

Africa

In South Africa, the town of Hermanus is one of the world centers for whale watching. During the winter months (MAY—DEC) Southern Right Whales come so close to the Cape shoreline that visitors can watch whales from their hotels. The town employs a "whale crier" (cf town crier) to walk through the town announcing where whales have been seen.

Southeast Indian

In Western Australia, whales are watched not far from Cape Leeuwin and Cape Naturaliste.

In Australia, whale watching occurs in many spots up and down the East Coast. From headlands you will often seen them making their migration south. At times, whales even make it into Sydney Harbour.

Whaling and Whale Watching

All three of the current major whaling nations (Norway, Japan and Iceland) have large and growing whale watching industries. Indeed Iceland had the fastest-growing whale watching industry in the world between 1994 and 1998.

Many conservationists now espouse the economic argument that a whale is worth more alive and watched than dead in order to try to persuade the governments of whaling nations to curtail whaling activities. The correctness of this argument is the subject of much debate at the International Whaling Commission, particularly since whaling countries complain about the 'scarcity' of whale meat which supposedly has caused it to become a luxury item, increasing its value. However, whale meat markets have collapsed and in Japan the government keeps its flow artificially through subsidies and whale meat distribution in schools and other forms of whale meat promotion. In 1997 2,000 tonnes of whale meat were sold for $30m—a single 10 tonne Minke Whale would thus have been worth $150,000. There is no agreement as to how to value a single animal to the whale watching industry, though it is probably much higher. It is possible to construct arguments that 'prove' a single whale is worth either much more or much less than this figure. However, it is clear from most coastal communities that are involved in whale watching that profits can be made and are more horizontally distributed throughout the community than if the animals were killed by a whaling industry.

Upon the resumption of whaling in Iceland in August 2003, pro-whaling groups, such as fishermen who argue that increased stocks of whales are depleting fish populations, suggested that sustainable whaling and whale watching could live side-by-side. Whale watching lobbyists, such as Húsavík Whale Museum curator Asbjorn Bjorgvinsson, counter that the most inquisitive whales, which approach boats very closely and provide much of the entertainment on whale-watching trips, will be the first to be killed by whalers. Pro-whaling organisations such as the High North Alliance on the other hand, have claimed that whale watching is not profitable and that some whale-watching companies in Iceland are surviving only because they receive funding from anti-whaling organizations.

Conservation Aspects

The rapid growth of the number of whale watching trips and the size of vessel used to watch whales has led to concerns that whale behaviour, migatory patterns and breeding cycles may be affected. There is now strong evidence that whalewatching can significantly affect the biology and ecology of whales and dolphins. Unfortunately management responses are lagging far behind the rapid growth of the sector and much is needed to improve the sustainability of whalewatching in most locations in the world.

2.6 River Trekking

River trekking or river tracing is a form of hiking or outdoor adventure activity, particularly popular in Hong Kong and Taiwan, and, in some ways, similar to canyoning or canyoneering. River trekking is a combination of trekking and climbing and sometimes swimming along the river. It involves particular techniques like rock climbing, climbing on wet surfaces, understanding the geographical features of river and valleys, knotting, dealing with sudden bad weather and find out possible exits from the river.

River Trekking in Different Countries

Hong Kong

River trekking has developed in Hong Kong since mid-20th century. Currently, there are numerous hiking groups organize regular trekking activities in Hong Kong. However, river trekking is a bit underground. There are no formal schools, formal coaches, formal sites, official recognition or qualifications on river trekking, even though it involves particular skills and certain level of risks. In Hong Kong, any natural rivers can be found in the country side, there would be the possible sites for river trekking.

Attractions and Popularity

River trekking is especially popular in Hong Kong because it is totally a surprise that in this highly developed region are preserved a number of excellent geographical features in its rivers in the countryside. Through river trekking, it is possible to access numerous waterfalls, large ponds, pot holes, other special geographical features as well as special species of animals and plants. Also, it is a very cheap activity in comparison with other challenging outdoor activities like rock climbing, rowling and wind-surfing. No training courses are needed because there is no one in Hong Kong who would provide training for river trekking. However, river trekking has long been one of the most popular outdoor activities in Hong Kong, even though most of the river trekking routes or sites are indicated as "danger" or "no entry" by the government. There is a trend that more and more foreigners and even tourists are taking part in this activity.

The Nine Big Rivers

The Nine Big Rivers are the nine rivers that are most popular among river trekkers in Hong Kong. The Nine Big Rivers include:

1. Tai Shing River located in Tsuen Wan
2. Wan Chung River located in Tai Po
3. Ng Tung River located in Tai Po
4. Wong Lung River located on Lantau Island near Tung Chung
5. Sheng Luk River located in Sai Kung
6. Man Cheng Po located in the west of Lantau Island
7. Lotus River located in Tai Lam Country Park
8. Ngon Sam River located on Lantau Island near Great Buddha
9. Ping Nam River located close to the border between Hong Kong and mainland China

Taiwan

This sport is popular throughout Taiwan, where it is generally called **river tracing**.

Rating of Difficulties

As river trekking has a certain level of risk, experienced river trekkers or hiking groups have developed rating systems about difficuties on different rivers. The ratings usually are various from 1 to 5 stars, even though a few rivers can be more than 5 stars because of their extreme difficulties. Such ratings are largely subjective, depends largely on river trekker's own experience. Therefore, different people or hiking groups would give different number of stars on the same river. According to Hong Kong Adverntruer, an English Website about hiking and river trekking in Hong Kong, difficult scale of different rivers as:

❖   *1 star*: can be handled by normal healthy persons

- ❖ *2 stars*: not too easy
- ❖ *3 stars*: fairly difficult
- ❖ *4 stars*: difficult, absolutely not for beginners
- ❖ *5 stars*: very difficult, very demanding in term of strength and skill

Risk and Danger

River trekking has certain level of risk. There are occasional accidents in river trekking, including falls from steep cliffs or waterfalls, drownings, exhaustion, or getting lost. Risks that should be prepared for include the following:

First, sudden changes in weather, like rainstorms, can cause rapid rises in water levels and speed in the river. Also, the number of viable paths and climbing areas inside the river valley would be reduced suddenly in a very short period. Besides this, bad or misty weather would also cause low visibility. Low visibility may come in to quickly for trekkers to adapt to. Therefore, a torch (flashlight), preferably a head-mounted one, is a must for river trekking.

Second, steep cliffs inside river valleys require a certain level of rock climbing skills. However, because of the humid environment inside the river valley, some rock surfaces can be very wet and some rocks can be very loose despite appearing solid. To deal with such wet climbing conditions, a pair of professional river-trekking boots are strongly advised.

Damage to Stream Systems Caused by River Trekking

Due to the increasing popularity of river trekking, the activity has resulted in some damage to certain streams. The most noticeable kinds of damage are:

- ❖ Rubbish left by river trekking groups.
- ❖ Use of aerosol spraypaints to mark route directions on rocks and trees.
- ❖ Discarded climbing equipment and unnecessary bolting.

❖ Damage to trees and other flora when used as leverage by trekkers.
❖ Graffiti written in paint, ink and correction fluid.
❖ Such damage is, unfortunately, quite common in Hong Kong and goes against the philosophy of leave no trace, which most outdoor adventure sports adhere to.

2.7 Rafting

Rafting or whitewater rafting is a challenging recreational activity utilizing a raft to navigate a river or other bodies of water. This is usually done on whitewater or different degrees of rough water, in order to thrill and excite the raft passengers. The development of this activity as a leisure sport has become popular since the mid 1970s.

History

Rafting is one of the earliest means of transportation, used as a means for shipping people, hunting, and transferring food.

1842 : Lieutenant John Fremont of the U.S. Army first journalized his rafting expedition on the Platte River. Horace H. Day designed the equipment he used in rafting. Day's rafts were constructed from four independent rubber cloth tubes and wrap-around floor.

1960s : Rafting was then recognized and paths like Grand Canyon were routed and whitewater rafting companies were established.

1970s : Rafting marked its major development as a leisure sport when it was then included in the Munich Olympic Games.

1980s : As rafting continued to gain its popularity, many rivers were opened for rafting activities including rivers in South America and Africa.

1990s : Rafting was included in major game events like the Barcelona Games in 1992, Atlanta Games in 1996, and the whitewater events of the Summer Olympic Games hosted by Ocoee River in Tennessee Valley. In addition, the International Federation of Rafting was instituted in 1997 and in 1999 the first Official International Championship was held.

Currently, river rafting is still gaining popularity among extreme water sports in order to thrill and excite the raft passengers.

Whitewater Rafts

Rafts were originally the simplest form of man's transportation in water and were then made of several logs, planks or reeds which were fastened together. Nowadays, inflatable boat were used as rafts which were later adopted by the military for beach assaults. It consists of very durable, multi-layered rubberized or vinyl fabrics with several independent air chambers. Its length varies between 3.5 m (11 ft) and 6 m (20 ft), the width between 1.8 m (6 ft) and 2.5 m (8 ft). The exception to this size rule is usually the packraft, which is designed as a portable single-person raft and may be as small as 1.5m long and weigh as little as 4 lbs.

Rafts come in a few different forms. In Europe the most common is the symmetrical raft steered with a paddle at the stern. Other types are the asymmetrical, rudder-controlled raft and the symmetrical raft with central helm (oars). Rafts are usually propelled with ordinary paddles and typically hold 4 to 12 persons. In Russia rafts are often hand made and are often a catamaran style with two inflatable tubes attached to a frame. Pairs of paddlers navigate these rafts. Catamaran style rafts have become popular in the western United States as well, but are typically rowed instead of paddled.

Rivers with high current are used for White water rafting. Specially, White Water Rafting is popular in Nepal due to high current of water falling through hills and rocky mountains.

Classes of Whitewater

Class 1: Very small rough areas, requires no maneuvering. (Skill Level: None).

Class 2: Some rough water, maybe some rocks, might require maneuvering. (Skill Level: Basic Paddling Skill).

Class 3: Whitewater, small waves, maybe a small drop, but no considerable danger. May require significant maneuvering.(Skill Level: Experienced paddling skills)

Class 4: Whitewater, medium waves, maybe rocks, maybe a considerable drop, sharp maneuvers may be needed. (Skill Level: Whitewater Experience).

Class 5: Whitewater, large waves, possibility of large rocks and hazards, possibility of a large drop, requires precise maneuvering (Skill Level: Advanced Whitewater Experience).

Class 6: Class 6 rapids are considered to be so dangerous as to be effectively unnavigable on a reliably safe basis. Rafters can expect to encounter substantial whitewater, huge waves, huge rocks and hazards, and/or substantial drops that will impart severe impacts beyond the structural capacities and impact ratings of most all rafting equipment. Traversing a Class 6 rapid has a dramatically increased likelihood of ending in serious injury or death compared to lesser classes. (Skill Level: Successful completion of a Class 6 rapid without serious injury or death is widely considered to be a matter of luck or extreme skill).

Safety

Whitewater rafting can be a dangerous sport, especially if basic safety precautions are not observed. Both commercial and private trips have seen their share of injuries and fatalities, though private travel has typically been associated with greater risk. Depending on the area, legislated safety measures may exist for rafting operators. These range from certification of outfitters, rafts, and raft leaders, to more stringent regulations about equipment and procedures. It is generally advisable to discuss safety measures with a rafting operator before signing on for a trip. The equipment used and the qualifications of the company and raft guides are essential information to be considered.

Like most outdoor sports, rafting in general has become safer over the years. Expertise in the sport has increased, and equipment has become more specialized and increased in quality. As a result the difficulty rating of most river runs has changed. A classic example would be the Colorado River in the Grand Canyon, which has swallowed whole expeditions in the past, leaving only fragments of boats but is now run safely by commercial outfitters hundreds of times each year, with relatively untrained passengers.

Risks in whitewater rafting stem from both environmental dangers and from improper behavior. Certain features on rivers are inherently unsafe and have remained consistently so despite the passage of time. These would include "keeper hydraulics", "strainers" (*e.g.* fallen trees), dams (especially low-head dams, which tend to produce river-wide keeper hydraulics), undercut rocks, and of course dangerously high waterfalls. Rafting with experienced guides is the safest way to avoid such features. Even in safe areas, however, moving water can always present risks—such as when a swimmer attempts to stand up on a rocky riverbed in strong current, risking foot entrapment. Irresponsible behavior related to rafting while intoxicated has also contributed to many accidents.

To combat the illusion that rafting is akin to an amusement park ride, and to underscore the personal responsibility each rafter faces on a trip, rafting outfitters generally require customers to sign waiver forms indicating understanding and acceptance of potential serious risks. Rafting trips often begin with safety presentations to educate customers about problems that may arise.

Due to this the overall risk level on a rafting trip with experienced guides using proper precautions is low. Thousands of people safely enjoy raft trips every year.

Issues with Rafting

Like all wilderness sports, rafting has to balance the conflict between nature protection and nature use. Because of frequent problems in the past, some rivers now have regulations restricting or specifying the annual and daily operating times.

Conflicts have also arisen with environmentalists when rafting operators, often in co-operation with municipalities and tourism associations, alter the riverbed by dredging and/or blasting in order to eliminate safety risks or create more interesting whitewater features in the river. Incongruously these measures usually are only temporary, since a riverbed is subject to permanent changes.

On the other hand, rafting contributes to the economy of many alpine regions which in turn may contribute to the protection of rivers from hydroelectric power generation and other development. Additionally, white water rafting trips can promote environmentalism. By experiencing first hand the beauty of a given river, individuals who would otherwise be indifferent to the environmental concerns of an area may gain a strong desire to protect and preserve that area because of a positive outdoors experience.

2.8 Whitewater Canoeing

Whitewater canoeing is the sport of paddling a canoe on a moving body of water, typically a whitewater river. Whitewater canoeing can range from simple, carefree gently moving water, to demanding, dangerous whitewater. River rapids are graded like ski runs according to the difficulty, danger or severity of the rapid. Whitewater grades (or classes) range from I or 1 (the easiest) to VI or 6 (the most difficult/ dangerous). Grade/Class I can be described as slightly moving water with ripples. Grade/Class VI can be described as severe or almost unrunnable whitewater, such as Niagara Falls.

Design

The canoe (or just 'boat') used in casual whitewater canoeing is different from those used in whitewater racing. Traditionally, canoes were made of tree bark, sewn with tree roots and sealed with resin. Early whitewater boats were fiberglass or kevlar, and this is still preferred for racing due to the light weight, but most modern whitewater boats are typically rotomoulded from a tough plastic that is slightly flexible and very durable, if easily scratched. Boats can range in size from barely long enough to hold the paddler (around 6 ft (1.8 m) long), up to 12 ft (3.7 m) or longer.

History

Paddling on rivers, lakes and oceans is as old as the Stone Age. The raft, the catamaran, the canoe and the kayak evolved depending on the needs and environment of the indigenous peoples in different parts of the world. The modern day canoe most likely originated about 8,000 years ago.

The Greek, Herodotus, 484-425 BC, wrote in his travel diaries about boats with which merchandise was brought from Armenia to Babylon. The boats were made of a wooden framework that was covered with animal skins. Mules hauled the precious skins back to Armenia.

The Scot, John MacGregor published in 1866 the book *A Thousand Miles in the Roy Rob Canoe*. The timing was right and the book became a resounding success. With the Industrial Revolution leading to more leisure time in the middle of the 19th century, people in Europe started to enjoy floating down rivers in all kinds of contraptions taking in nature previously only available to a selected few.

Types

There are several 'sub-categories' in whitewater canoeing:

River Running

River running can be thought of as a tour down a river, to enjoy the scenery as well as experiencing challenging whitewater. River running includes short day trips as well as longer multi-day trips. Multi-day canoe trips often entail the use of gear-toting rafts to allow a more comfortable experience without a heavily-laden canoe. Whitewater racing is the competitive aspect of this sub-category, racing canoes down a river as fast as possible.

Creeking

Creeking is perhaps best thought of as a subcategory of river running, involving very technical and difficult rapids, typically in the Grade/Class IV to VI range. While people will differ on the definition, creeking generally involves higher gradient (approaching or in excess of 100 ft per mi (19 m per km), and is likely to include running ledges, slides, and waterfalls on relatively small and tight rivers, though some will allow for very large and big volume rivers in their definition. Canoes used for creeking usually have higher volume (more gallons or liters of displacement) and more rounded bow and stern, as these features provide an extra margin of safety' against the likelihood of pinning, and will resurface more quickly and controllably when coming off larger drops. Creek boats usually have increased "rocker," or rise, on the bow to go up and over obstacles and obstructions within the river. Extreme racing is a competitive form of this aspect of whitewater canoeing, in which canoers race down steep sections and or generally dangerous sections of whitewater.

Slalom

Slalom is a technical competitive form of canoeing, and the only whitewater event to appear in the Olympic Games. Racers attempt to make their way from the top to the bottom of a designated section of river as fast as possible, while correctly negotiating gates- (a series of double-poles suspended vertically over the river). There are usually 18-25 gates in a race which must be navigated in sequential order. Green gates must be negotiated in a downstream direction, red gates in an upstream direction. The events are typically conducted on Grade/ Class II to Grade/Class IV water, but the placement of the gates, and precision necessary to paddle them fast and "clean" (without touching a pole and adding 2 seconds to the total time), makes the moves much harder than the water's difficulty suggests. (Slalom has been described as performing class V moves with class III consequences.) Pro level slalom competitions have specific length (350 cm (140 in) for kayaks—new rules), width, and weight requirements for the boats, which will be made out of kevlar/fiberglass/carbon fiber composites to be light weight and have faster hull speed. Plastic whitewater canoes can be used in citizen-level races.

Playboating

Playboating, also known as Freestyle or Rodeo, is a more gymnastic and artistic kind of canoeing. While the other varieties of canoeing generally involve going from Point A to Point B, playboaters often stay in one spot in the river (usually in a hole, pourover or on a wave) where they work with and against the dynamic forces of the river to perform a variety of maneuvers. These can include surfing, spinning, and various vertical moves (cartwheels, loops, blunts, pistol and donkey flips, and many others), spinning the boat on all possible axis of rotation. More recently, aerial moves have become accessible, where paddlers perform tricks having gained air from using the speed and bounce of the wave. Canoes used for playboating generally have relatively low volume in the bow and stern, allowing the paddler to submerge the ends of the canoe with relative ease. Competitions for playboating or freestyle are sometimes called whitewater rodeo in the US, but more frequently just referred to as freestyle events in UK and Europe.

Techniques

Boofing

Boofing, in whitewater canoeing, refers to the raising of the canoe's bow during freefall, while descending a ledge, ducking behind a boulder, or running a waterfall. This technique is used to avoid submerging the bow of the canoe by ensuring it lands flat when it hits the base of the waterfall. The term is an onomatopoeia which mimics the sound that is usually created when the hull of the canoe makes contact with water at the base of the waterfall.

Another type of boof is the "rock boof" which is a move that uses a glancing impact with a boulder at the top of a ledge to bounce the boater over a downstream feature, often finished with a mid-air eddy turn. Rock boofs result in sounds both at the top of the drop (boat impacting rock) and the bottom (boat bellyflopping into the water).

2.9 Tubing (Recreation)

Tubing, also known as inner tubing or even toobing, is a recreational activity of riding an inner tube, either on water, snow, or through the air. The tubes themselves are also known as "donuts" or "biscuits" because of their shape.

Variations

Water

Tubing on water generally consists of two forms: towed and free-floating, also known as river tubing.

Towed tubing usually takes place on a large body of water such as a lake or river. One or more tube riders (often called "tubers") tether their tubes to a powered watercraft such as a motor boat or a personal watercraft. The riders are then towed through the water by the watercraft.

In free-floating tubing, the tube riders are untethered and often conveyed by the current of a waterway. Texas and much of the southern U.S.A. have adopted the spelling of 'toobing' and 'toobers'. People paddle with their hands to steer. Without steering, you generally float towards the bank of the river. Groups of tubers often rope their tubes together creating a large floating group. This generally slows down the float but allows the group to pass food, drink, and other party implements around the group. Because of this, free-floating tubing often takes place on rivers and streams (natural or artificial). Longer expeditions often include tubes mounted with coolers for food and beverages.

Popular riverside tube rentals normally warn against glass due to riverside dangers. Some law enforcement offices have prohibited kegs which were popularly chilled in metal tubs harnessed within larger tubes.

Major water parks often have specially designed courses for tubing. These may consist of a circular, artificial river on which riders are conveyed or a linear course such as a water slide.

Kite Tubing

A variant of towed tubing dubbed "kite tubing" has begun to emerge.

When tubes being towed on water reach high speeds, they may begin to experience a tendency to take flight. This is because the body of the tube acts as an airfoil and creates lift. In this way, the tube becomes a kite. A tube's ability to achieve and maintain flight depends on a number of factors including the speed at which the tube is traveling, the shape and size of the tube, the weight of the rider, and how the tube itself is oriented. As most tubes are not designed for flight, the rider often has little or no control over a tube after it takes to the air. This can lead to a violent crash as the rider, with or without the tube, falls back to the surface of the water.

To address the poor flight characteristics of most tubes and to target thrill seekers, tubes specially designed for kite tubing have been introduced. These tubes may feature channels to allow air to flow through the tube's body, a transparent "window" for the rider to signal the boat operator, as well as more streamlined, aerodynamic designs.

As of July 2006, 39 injuries and two deaths from kite tubing have been reported. Injuries have included a broken neck, punctured lung, cracked ribs, a concussion and injuries to the chest, back and face. Some accidents have been linked to gusts of wind that unexpectedly altered the flight characteristics and ejected the riders.

In cooperation with the U.S. Consumer Product Safety Commission (CPSC), Sportsstuff Inc. voluntarily withdrew the Wego Kite Tube from the market on July 13th of 2006.

Snow

Tubing on snow is a wintertime activity that is similar to sledding. This kind of tubing is almost always performed on a hill or slope, using gravity to propel the rider to the bottom of the grade. The rider often returns to the top of the slope with the tube to repeat the process. The low amount of friction between most tubes and snow allows tubers to reach considerable speeds while riding, especially on steep slopes. Because of the circular shape of snow tubes, controlling the course and speed of a tube while riding on snow is extremely difficult. While a sled rider can drag their arms on the snow to brake or steer to a degree, attempting this on a tube will often cause the tube to spin. This lack of control has led to injuries, some serious, when riders have struck obstacles such as trees while tubing on snow.

Some ski resorts offer courses devoted solely to tubing. Such courses often have slopes or barriers on the periphery to guide the tubes along a safe course. Motorized pulley towlines are often used to tow riders and their tube back to the top of the course after riding to the bottom.

It is also possible to tow a tube through the snow behind a snowmobile. This is similar to towed tubing on water, only the watercraft is replaced by a snowmobile and the water with snow-covered ground.

Popular River Tubing Locations

Africa

Nile River, Jinga, Uganda.

South East Asia

Vang Vieng, Laos.

Europe

Paznaun, Tirol, Austria.

Middle East

Jordan River, Israel.

North America

- ❖ Avalanche Xpress (York, PA).
- ❖ Apple River (Wisconsin).
- ❖ Bear River, Placer County, California (between Colfax and the Dog Bar Bridge).
- ❖ Boulder Creek (Colorado).
- ❖ Chattahoochee River, Helen, Georgia.
- ❖ Colorado River, Glenwood Springs, CO.
- ❖ Cowichan River, Cowichan Valley, British Columbia.
- ❖ Deerfield River, Massachusetts.
- ❖ Big Rapids, Michigan.
- ❖ Delaware Water Gap, New Jersey/Pennsylvania.
- ❖ Doe River, Elizabethon, Tennessee.
- ❖ Guadalupe River, New Braunfels, Texas.
- ❖ San Marcos River, San Marcos, Texas.
- ❖ Gunpowder Falls River, Maryland.
- ❖ Hiwassee River, Reliance, Tennessee.
- ❖ Ichetucknee River, Florida.
- ❖ Kern River, Kern County, California.
- ❖ Kettle River, Midway, British Columbia, Canada.
- ❖ Little Wolf River, Waupaca County, Wisconsin.
- ❖ Martinez Lake, Yuma, Arizona.
- ❖ Maury River in Rockbridge County, Virginia.
- ❖ New River, North Carolina.
- ❖ Niobrara River, Valentine, Nebraska.
- ❖ Penticton River Channel, between Okanagan Lake and Skaha Lake, in Penticton, B.C.
- ❖ Platte River, Royalton, Minnesota.

❖ Saluda River (South Carolina).
❖ Salt River, Mesa, Arizona.
❖ Styx River, Alabama.
❖ Polar Wave (Batavia, NY).
❖ Hood Canal (Hood Canal, WA).

South America

Equipment

Tubing can require varying pieces and kinds of equipment depending on the variety of tubing one wishes to engage in.

The one common piece of equipment across all forms of tubing is the tube itself. While tubes vary in construction, all share the general characteristics of being:

❖ Inflatable,
❖ Made of a thin, flexible, synthetic material such as rubber or PVC plastic, and
❖ Donut or disk shaped.

Water

Tubes for use as towables on water are generally not true inner tubes but rather specially designed tubes for the purpose of recreation. These tubes are often fairly durable and come in either donut or disk shapes. A sleeve of synthetic fabric often covers the tube to prevent it from becoming elongated during towing. Such sleeves commonly have handles for the rider to grasp and an anchoring point for the tow line to be attached at.

Towing a tube or tubes also requires a powered watercraft such a motorboat or personal watercraft as well as rope to tether the tubes to such craft.

Tubes used for free-floating tubing have traditionally been true inner tubes, but commercially-sold tubes for the same purpose are becoming common place. These tubes are almost always donut-shaped to allow the rider to sit comfortably on their back across the top of the tube with buttocks in the center. This kind of tube rarely has handles or a sleeve and would perform poorly as a towable.

Tubing can also be performed by paddling a lesser known third method of entertainment.

Snow

Tubes used for riding on snow are usually specially designed tubes with dimpled centers rather than a "donut" hole. This prevents the rider and the tube itself from dragging on the snow. Snow tubes commonly have handles.

2.10 Watercraft Paddling

With regard to watercraft, paddling is the act of propelling a boat using the motion of a paddle in the water. The difference between paddling and rowing is that with rowing the oars have a mechanical connection with the boat whereas with paddling the paddles are hand-held with no mechanical connection.

Canoeing

Canoeing is the activity of paddling a canoe for the purpose of recreation (also called a float trip), sport, or transportation. It usually refers exclusively to using a paddle to propel a canoe with only human muscle power.

Fig. 2.1: A family in a canoe.

Outrigging

Outrigger Canoe Racing is a team paddling sport which utilises the outrigger canoe. The sport is also known as *Wa'a racing* in some parts of the Pacific and *Waka ama* (Maori) in New Zealand.

Kayaking

Kayaking is the use of a kayak for moving across water. Kayaking is differentiated from canoeing by the fact that a kayak has a closed cockpit and a canoe has an open cockpit. Kayakers also use a two bladed paddle. Another major difference is in the way the paddler sits in the boat. Kayakers sit in a seat on the bottom of the boat with their legs extended out in front of them. Canoeists will either sit on an elevated bench seat or kneel directly on the bottom of the boat.

Dragonboating

For racing events, dragon boats are always rigged with decorative Chinese dragon heads and tails and are required to carry a large drum aboard. At other times the decorative regalia is usually removed, although the drum often remains aboard for training purposes.

Fig. 2.2: A Dragon boat (traditional Chinese) is a very long and narrow human powered boat used in the team paddling sport or Dragon boat racing which originated in China.

Rafting

Rafting or whitewater rafting is a recreational activity utilizing a raft to navigate a river or other bodies of water. This is usually done on whitewater or different degrees of rough water, in order to thrill and excite the raft passengers. The development of this activity as a leisure sport has become popular since the mid 1970s.

2.11 Mountaineering

Mountaineering is the sport, hobby or profession of walking, hiking, trekking and climbing up mountains. It is also sometimes known as alpinism, particularly in Europe. While it began as an all-out attempt to reach the highest point of unclimbed mountains, it has branched into specializations addressing different aspects of mountains and may now be said to consist of three aspects: rock-craft, snow-craft and skiing, depending on whether the route chosen is over rock, snow or ice. All require great athletic and technical ability, and experience is also very important.

Technique

Snow

While certain compacted snow conditions allow mountaineers to progress on foot, frequently crampons are required to travel efficiently over snow and ice. Crampons have 8-14 spikes and are attached to a mountaineer's boots. They are used on hard snow (neve) and ice to provide additional traction and allow very steep ascents and descents. Varieties range from lightweight aluminum models intended for walking on snow covered glaciers, to aggressive steel models intended for vertical and overhanging ice and rock. Snowshoes can be used to walk through deep snow. Skis can be used everywhere snowshoes can and also in steeper, more alpine landscapes, although it takes considerable practice to develop strong skills for difficult terrain. Combining the techniques of alpine skiing and mountaineering to ascend and descend a mountain is a form of the sport by itself, called Ski Mountaineering. Ascending and descending a snow slope safely requires the use of an ice axe and many different footwork techniques that have been developed over the past century, mainly in Europe. The progression of footwork from the lowest angle slopes to the steepest terrain is first to splay the feet to a rising traverse, to kicking steps, to front pointing the crampons. The progression of ice axe technique from the lowest angle slopes to the steepest terrain is to use the ice axe first as a walking stick, then a stake, then to use the front pick as a dagger below the shoulders or above, and finally to swing the pick into the slope over the head. These various techniques may involve questions of differring ice-axe design depending on terrain, and even whether a mountaineer uses one or two ice axes. Anchors for the rope in snow are sometimes unreliable, and include snow stakes, called pickets, deadman devices called flukes which are fashioned from aluminum, or devised from buried objects that might include an ice axe, skis, rocks or other objects. Bollards, which are simply carved out of consolidated snow or ice, also sometimes serve as anchors.

Glaciers

When traveling over glaciers, crevasses pose a grave danger. These giant cracks in the ice are not always visible as snow can be blown and freeze over the top to make a *snowbridge*. At times snowbridges can be as thin as a few inches. Climbers use a system of ropes to protect themselves from such hazards. Basic gear for glacier travel includes crampons and ice axes. Teams of two to five climbers tie into a rope equally spaced. If a climber begins to fall the other members of the team perform a self-arrest to stop the fall. The other members of the team enact a crevasse rescue to pull the fallen climber from the crevasse.

Ice

Multiple methods are used to safely travel over ice. If the terrain is steep but not vertical, then protection in the form of ice screws can be placed in the ice and attached to the rope by the lead climber. Each climber on the team must clip past the anchor, and the last climber picks up the anchor itself. Occasionally, slinged icicles or bollards are also used. This allows for safety should the entire team be taken off their feet. This technique is known as Simul-climbing and is sometimes also used on steep snow and easy rock.

If the terrain becomes steeper then standard ice climbing techniques are used in which each climber is belayed, moving one at a time.

Shelter

Climbers use a few different forms of shelter depending on the situation and conditions. Shelter is a very important aspect of safety for the climber as the weather in the mountains may be very unpredictable. Tall mountains may require many days of camping on the mountain.

Base Camp

The 'Base Camp' of a mountain is an area used for staging an attempt at the summit. Base camps are positioned to be safe from the harsher conditions above. There are base camps on many popular or dangerous mountains. Where the summit cannot be reached from base camp in a single day will have additional camps above base camp. For example, the southeast ridge route on Mount Everest has Base Camp plus (normally) camps I through IV.

Hut

The European alpine regions, in particular, have a network of mountain huts (called 'refuges' in France, 'rifugi' in Italy, 'cabanes' in Switzerland and 'hytte' in Norway). Such huts exist at many different heights, including in the high mountains themselves—in extremely remote areas, more rudimentary shelters may exist. The mountain huts are of varying size and quality, but each is typically centred on a communal dining room and have dormitories equipped with mattresses, blankets or duvets, and pillows—guests are expected to bring and to use their own sleeping bag liner. The facilities are usually rudimentary but, given their locations, huts offer vital shelter, make routes more widely accessible (by allowing journeys to be broken and reducing the weight of equipment needing to be carried), and offer good value. In Europe, all huts are staffed during the summer (mid-June to mid-September) and some are staffed in the spring (mid-March to mid-May). Elsewhere, huts may also be open in the fall. Huts also may have a part that is always open, but unmanned, a so-called winter hut. When open and manned, the huts are generally run by full-time employees, but some are staffed on a voluntary basis by members of Alpine clubs (such as Swiss Alpine Club and Club alpin français). The manager of the hut, termed a guardian or warden in Europe, will usually also sell refreshments and meals—both to those visiting only for the day and to those staying overnight. The offering is surprisingly wide—given that most supplies, often including fresh water, must be flown in by helicopter—and may include glucose-based snacks (such as Mars and Snickers bars) on which climbers and walkers wish to stock up, cakes and pastries made at the hut, a variety of hot and cold drinks (including beer and wine), and high carbohydrate dinners in the evenings. Not all huts offer a catered service, though, and visitors may need to provide for themselves. Some huts offer facilities for both, enabling visitors wishing to keep costs down to bring their own food and cooking equipment and to cater using the facilities provided. Booking for overnight stays at huts is deemed obligatory, and in many cases is essential as some popular huts—even with more than 100 bed spaces—may well be full during good weather and at weekends. Once made, the cancellation of a reservation is advised as a matter of courtesy—and, indeed, potentially of safety, as many huts keep a record of where climbers and walkers state they planned to walk to next. Most huts may be contacted by telephone and most take credit cards as a means of payment.

Bivouac (Bivy)

In the mountaineering context, a bivouac or 'bivy' is a makeshift resting or sleeping arrangement in which the climber has less than the full complement of shelter, food and equipment that would normally be present at a conventional campsite. This may involve simply getting a sleeping bag and Bivouac sack and lying down to sleep. Many times small partially sheltered areas such as a bergschrund, cracks in rocks or a trench dug in the snow are used to provide additional shelter from wind. These techniques were originally used only in emergency; however some climbers steadfastly committed to alpine style climbing specifically plan for bivouacs in order to save the weight of a tent when suitable snow conditions or time is unavailable for construction of a snow cave. The principal hazard associated with bivouacs is the greater level of exposure to cold and the elements.

Tent

Tents are the most common form of shelter used on the mountain. These may vary from simple tarps to much heavier designs intended to withstand heavy snow loads and storm winds. In exposed positions, windbreaks of snow or rock may be required to shelter the tent. One of the downsides to tenting is that high winds and snow loads can be dangerous and may ultimately lead to the tent's failure and collapse. In addition, the constant flapping of the tent fabric can hinder sleep and raise doubts about the security of the shelter.

Snow Cave

Where conditions permit snow caves are another way to shelter high on the mountain. Some climbers do not use tents at high altitudes unless the snow conditions do not allow for snow caving, since snow caves are silent and much warmer than tents. They can be built relatively easily, given sufficient time, using a snow shovel. A correctly made snow cave will hover around freezing, which relative to outside temperatures can be very warm. They can be dug anywhere there is at least four feet of snow. Another shelter that works well is a quinzee, which is excavated from a pile of snow that has been work hardened or sintered (typically by stomping). Igloos are used by some climbers, but are deceptively difficult to build and require specific snow conditions.

Hazards

Dangers in mountaineering are sometimes divided into two categories: objective hazards that exist without regard to the climber's presence, like rockfall, avalanches and inclement weather, and subjective hazards that relate only to factors introduced by the climber. Equipment failure and falls due to inattention, fatigue or inadequate technique are examples of subjective hazard. A route continually swept by avalanches and storms is said to have a high level of objective danger, whereas a technically far more difficut route that is relatively safe from these dangers may be regarded as objectively safer.

In all, mountaineers must concern themselves with eight chief dangers: falling rocks, falling ice, snow-avalanches, the climber falling, falls from ice slopes, falls down snow slopes, falls into crevasses and dangers from weather. To select and follow a route using one's skills and experience to mitigate these dangers is to exercise the climber's craft.

Falling Rocks

Every rock mountain is slowly disintegrating due to erosion, the process being especially rapid above the snow-line. Rock faces are constantly swept by falling stones, which may be possible to dodge. Falling rocks tend to form furrows in a mountain face, and these furrows (couloirs) have to be ascended with caution, their sides often being safe when the middle is stoneswept. Rocks fall more frequently on some days than on others, according to the recent weather. Ice formed during the night may temporarily bind rocks to the face but warmth of the day or lubricating water from melting snow or rain may easily dislodge these rocks. Local experience is a valuable help on determining typical rockfall on such routes.

The direction of the dip of rock strata sometimes determines the degree of danger on a particular face; the character of the rock must also be considered. Where stones fall frequently debris will be found below, whilst on snow slopes falling stones cut furrows visible from a great distance. In planning an ascent of a new peak or an unfamiliar route, mountaineers must look for such traces. When falling stones get mixed in considerable quantity with slushy snow or water a mud avalanche is formed (common in the Himalaya). It is vital to avoid camping in their possible line of fall.

Fig. 2.3: Rocky mountains tend to be hazardous.

Falling Ice

The places where ice may fall can always be determined beforehand. It falls in the broken parts of glaciers (seracs) and from overhanging cornices formed on the crests of narrow ridges. Large icicles are often formed on steep rock faces, and these fall frequently in fine weather following cold and stormy days. They have to be avoided like falling stones. Seracs are slow in formation, and slow in arriving (by glacier motion) at a condition of unstable equilibrium. They generally fall in or just after the hottest part of the day. A skillful and experienced ice-man will usually devise a safe route through a most intricate ice-fall, but such places should be avoided in the afternoon of a hot day. Hanging glaciers (*i.e.* glaciers perched on steep slopes) often discharge themselves over steep rock-faces, the snout breaking off at intervals. They can always be detected by their debris below. Their track should be avoided.

Falls from Rocks

The skill of a rock climber is shown by one's choice of handhold and foothold, and his adhesion to those once he has chosen. Much depends on a correct estimate of the firmness of the rock where weight is to be thrown upon it. Many loose rocks are quite firm enough to bear a person's weight, but experience is needed to know which can be trusted, and skill is required in transferring the weight to them without jerking. On rotten rocks the rope must be handled with special care, lest it should dislodge loose stones on to those below. Similar care must be given to handholds and footholds, for the same reason. When a horizontal traverse has to be made across very difficult rocks, a dangerous situation may arise unless at both ends of the traverse there be firm positions. Mutual assistance on hard rocks takes all manner of forms: two, or even three, people climbing on one another's shoulders, or using an ice axe propped up by others for a foothold. The great principle is that of co-operation, all the members of the party climbing with reference to the others, and not as independent units; each when moving must know what the climber in front and the one behind are doing. After bad weather steep rocks are often found covered with a veneer of ice (verglas), which may even render them inaccessible. Crampons are useful on such occasions.

Avalanches

The avalanche is the most underestimated danger in the mountains. People generally think that they will be able to recognize the hazards and survive being caught. The truth is a somewhat different story. Every year, 120—150 people die in small avalanches in the Alps alone. The vast majority are reasonably experienced male skiers aged 20-35 but also include ski instructors and guides. There is always a lot of pressure to risk a snow crossing. Turning back takes a lot of extra time and effort, supreme leadership, and most importantly there seldom is an avalanche to prove the right decision was made. Making the decision to turn around is especially hard if others are crossing the slope, but any next person could become the trigger.

There are many types of avalanche, but two types are of the most concern:

❖ *Slab avalanche*: This type of avalanche occurs when a plate of snow breaks loose and starts sliding down; these are the largest and most dangerous.

❖ *Hard slab avalanche*: This type of avalanche is formed by hard-packed snow in a cohesive slab. The slab will not break up easily as it slides down the hill, resulting in large blocks tumbling down the mountain.

❖ *Soft slab avalanche*: This type of avalanche is formed again by a cohesive layer of snow bonded together, the slab tends to break up more easily.

❖ *Loose snow avalanche*: This type of avalanche is triggered by a small amount of moving snow that accumulates into a big slide. Also known as a "wet slide or point release" avalanche. This type of avalanche is deceptively dangerous as it can still knock a climber or skier off their feet and bury them, or sweep them over a cliff into a terrain trap.

Dangerous slides are most likely to occur on the same slopes preferred by many skiers: long and wide open, few trees or large rocks, 30 to 45 degrees of angle, large load of fresh snow, soon after a big storm, on a slope 'lee to the storm'. Solar radiation can trigger slides as well. These will typically be a point release or wet slough type of avalanche. The added weight of the wet slide can trigger a slab avalanche. Ninety percent of reported victims are caught in avalanches triggered by themselves or others in their group.

When going off-piste or traveling in alpine terrain, parties are advised to always carry: (a) Avalanche beacon, (b) Probe, and (c) Shovel (retrieving victims with a shovel instead of your hands is five times faster) and to have had avalanche training! Paradoxically, expert skiers who have avalanche training make up a large percentage of avalanche fatalities; perhaps because they are the ones more likely to ski in areas prone to avalanches, and certainly because most people do not practice enough with their equipment to be truly fast and efficient rescuers.

Even with proper rescue equipment and training, there is a one-in-five chance of dying if caught in a significant avalanche, and only a 50/50 chance of being found alive if buried more than a few minutes. The best solution is to learn how to avoid risky conditions.

Ice Slopes

For travel on slopes consisting of ice or hard snow, crampons are a standard part of a mountaineer's equipment. While step-cutting can sometimes be used on snow slopes of moderate angle, this can be a slow and tiring process, which does not provide the higher security of crampons. However, in soft snow or powder, crampons are easily hampered by balling of snow, which reduces their effectiveness. In either case, an ice axe not only assists with balance but provides the climber with the possibility of self-arrest in case of a slip or fall. On a true ice slope however, an ice axe is rarely able to effect a self-arrest. As an additional safety precaution on steep ice slopes, the climbing rope is attached to ice screws buried into the ice.

True ice slopes are rare in Europe, though common in mountains located in the tropics, where newly-fallen snow quickly thaws on the surface and becomes sodden below, so that the next night's frost turns the whole mass into a sheet of semi-solid ice.

Snow Slopes

Snow slopes are very common, and usually easy to ascend. At the foot of a snow or ice slope is generally a big crevasse, called a *bergschrund*, where the final slope of the mountain rises from a snow-field or glacier. Such *bergschrunds* are generally too wide to be stepped across, and must be crossed by a snow bridge, which needs careful testing and a painstaking use of the rope. A steep snow slope in bad condition may be dangerous, as the whole body of snow may start as an avalanche. Such slopes are less dangerous if ascended directly, rather than obliquely, for an oblique or horizontal track cuts them across and facilitates movement of the mass. New snow lying on ice is especially dangerous. Experience is needed for deciding on the advisability of advancing over snow in doubtful condition. Snow on rocks is usually rotten unless it is thick; snow on snow is likely to be sound. A day or two of fine weather will usually bring new snow into sound condition. Snow cannot lie at a very steep angle, though it often deceives the eye as to its slope. Snow slopes seldom exceed 40°. Ice slopes may be much steeper. Snow slopes in early morning are usually hard and safe, but the same in the afternoon are quite soft and possibly dangerous; hence the advantage of an early start.

Crevasses

Crevasses are the slits or deep chasms formed in the substance of a glacier as it passes over an uneven bed. They may be open or hidden. In the lower part of a glacier the crevasses are open. Above the snow-line they are frequently hidden by arched-over accumulations of winter snow. The detection of hidden crevasses requires care and experience. After a fresh fall of snow they can only be detected by sounding with the pole of the ice axe, or by looking to right and left where the open extension of a partially hidden crevasse may be obvious. The safeguard against accident is the rope, and no one should ever cross a snow-covered glacier unless roped to one, or even better to two companions. Anyone venturing onto crevasses should be trained in crevasse rescue.

Weather

The primary dangers caused by bad weather centre around the changes it causes in snow and rock conditions, making movement suddenly much more arduous and hazardous than under normal circumstances.

Whiteouts make it difficult to retrace a route while rain may prevent taking the easiest line only determined as such under dry conditions. In a storm the mountaineer who uses a compass for guidance has a great advantage over a merely empirical observer. In large snow-fields it is, of course, easier to go wrong than on rocks, but intelligence and experience are the best guides in safely navigating objective hazards.

Summer thunderstorms may produce intense lightning. If a climber happens to be standing on or near the summit, they risk being struck. There are many cases where people have been struck by lightning while climbing mountains. In most mountainous regions, local storms develop by late morning and early afternoon. Many climbers will get an "alpine start"; that is before or by first light so as to be on the way down when storms are intensifying in activity and lightning and other weather hazards are a distinct threat to safety.

Altitude

Rapid ascent can lead to altitude sickness. The best treatment is to descend immediately. The climber's motto at high altitude is "climb high, sleep low", referring to the regimen of climbing higher to acclimatize but returning to lower elevation to sleep. In the South American Andes, the chewing of coca leaves has been traditionally used to treat altitude sickness symptoms.

Common symptoms of altitude sickness include severe headache, sleep problems, nausea, lack of appetite, lethargy and body ache. Mountain sickness may progress to HACE (High Altitude Cerebral Edema) and HAPE (High Altitude Pulmonary Edema), both of which can be fatal within 24 hours.

In high mountains, atmospheric pressure is lower and this means that less oxygen is available to breathe. This is the underlying cause of altitude sickness. Everyone needs to acclimatize, even exceptional mountaineers that have been to high altitude before. Generally speaking, mountaineers start using bottled oxygen when they climb above 7,000 m. Exceptional mountaineers have climbed 8000-metre peaks (including Everest) without oxygen, almost always with a carefully planned program of acclimatization.

In 2005, researcher and mountaineer John Semple established that above-average ozone concentrations on the Tibetan plateau may pose an additional risk to climbers.

Locations

Mountaineering has become a popular sport throughout the world. In Europe the sport largely originated in the Alps, and is still immensely popular there. Other notable mountain ranges frequented by climbers include the Caucasus, the Pyrenees, Rila Mountain the Tatra mountains and Carpathian Mountains. In North America climbers frequent the Rockies and Sierra Nevada of California, the Cascades of the Pacific Northwest and the high peaks of Alaska. There has been a long tradition of climbers going on expeditions to the Greater Ranges, a term generally used for the Andes and the high peaks of Asia including the Himalaya, Pamirs and Tien Shan. In the past this was often on exploratory trips or to make first ascents. With the advent of cheaper long-haul air travel mountaineering holidays in the Greater Ranges are now undertaken much more frequently and ascents of even Everest and Vinson Massif (the highest mountain in Antarctica) are offered as a "package holiday". Other mountaineering areas of interest include the Southern Alps of New Zealand, the Japanese Alps, the Coast Mountains of British Columbia, the Scottish Highlands, and the mountains of Scandinavia, especially Norway.

History

Though it is unknown whether his intention was to reach a summit, Ötzi ascended at least 3,000 m in the Alps about 5,300 years ago. His remains were found at that altitude, preserved in a glacier.

The first recorded mountain ascent in the Common Era is Roman Emperor Hadrian's ascent of Etna (3,350 m) to see the sun rise in 121. Peter III of Aragon climbed Canigou in the Pyrenees in the last quarter of the 13th century. The first ascent of the Popocatépetl (5,426 m in Mexico) was reported in 1289 by members of a local tribe (Tecanuapas) Jean Buridan climbed Mont Ventoux around 1316. The Italian poet Petrarch wrote that on April 26, 1336 he, together with his brother and two servants, climbed to the top of Mont Ventoux

(1,909 m). His account of the trip was composed later as a letter to his friend Dionigi di Borgo San Sepolcro. The Rochemelon (3,538 m) in the Italian Alps was climbed in 1358. In the late 1400s and early 1500s ascents were made of numerous high peaks in the Andes, for religious purposes by the citizens of the Inca Empire and their subjects. They constructed platforms, houses and altars on many summits and carried out sacrifices, including human sacrifices. The highest peak they are known for certain to have climbed is Llullaillaco (6,739 m). They may also have ascended the highest peak in the Andes, Aconcagua (6,962 m) as a sacrifice victim has been found at over 5,000 m on this peak.

In 1492 the ascent of Mont Aiguille was made by order of Charles VIII of France. The Humanists of the 16th century adopted a new attitude towards mountains, but the disturbed state of Europe nipped in the bud the nascent mountaineering of the Zurich school. Leonardo da Vinci climbed to a snow-field in the neighborhood of the Val Sesia and made scientific observations. In 1642 Darby Field made the first recorded ascent of Mount Washington, then known as Agiocochook, in New Hampshire. Konrad Gesner and Josias Simler of Zurich visited and described mountains, and made regular ascents. The use of ice axe and rope were locally invented at this time. No mountain expeditions of note are recorded in the 17th century. Richard Pococke and William Windham's historic visit to Chamonix was made in 1741, and set the trend for visiting glaciers. In 1744 the Titus was climbed, the first true ascent of a snow-mountain.

The first attempt to ascend Mont Blanc was made in 1775 by a party of natives. In 1786 Dr Michel Paccard and Jacques Balmat gained the summit for the first time. Horace-Bénédict de Saussure, the initiator of the first ascent followed next year.

The Norwegian mountain climber, Jens Esmark was the first person to ascend Snøhetta in 1798, part of the Dovrefjell range in Southern Norway. The same year he lead the first expedition to Bitihorn, a small mountain in the southernmost outskirts of Jotunheimen, Norway. In 1810 he was the first person to ascend Mount Gaustatoppen in Telemark, Norway. The Grossglockner was climbed in 1800, the Ortler in 1804, the Jungfrau in 1811, the Finsteraarhorn in 1812, and the Breithorn in 1813. Thereafter, tourists showed a tendency to climb, and the body of Alpine guides began to come into existence as a consequence. Citlaltépetl (5720 m in Mexico) was first climbed in 1848 by F. Maynard & G. Reynolds. Systematic mountaineering, as a sport, is usually dated from Sir Alfred Wills's ascent of the Wetterhorn in 1854. The first ascent of Monte Rosa was made in 1855.

The Alpine Club was founded in London in 1857, and was soon imitated in most European countries. Edward Whymper's ascent of the Matterhorn in 1865 marked the close of the main period of Alpine conquest—the Golden age of alpinism—during which the craft of climbing was invented and 'perfected', the body of professional guides formed and their traditions fixed.

Passing to other ranges, the exploration of the Pyrenees was concurrent with that of the Alps. The Caucasus followed, mainly owing to the initiative of D. W. Freshfield; it was first visited by exploring climbers in 1868, and most of its great peaks were climbed by 1888.

The Edelweiss Club Salzburg was founded in Salzburg in 1881, and had 3 members make the first ascent on two Eight-thousanders, Broad Peak (1957) and Dhaulagiri (1960).

Trained climbers turned their attention to the mountains of North America in 1888, when the Rev. W. S. Green made an expedition to the Selkirk Mountains. From that time exploration has gone on apace, and many English and American climbing parties have surveyed most of the highest peaks; Pikes Peak (14,115 ft) having been climbed by Mr. E. James and party in 1820, and Mt. Saint Elias (18,008 ft) by the Duke of the Abruzzi and party in 1897. The exploration of the highest Andes was begun in 1879-1880, when Whymper climbed Chimborazo and explored the mountains of Ecuador. The Cordillera between Chile and Argentina was visited by Dr. Gussfeldt in 1883, who ascended Maipo (17,270 ft) and attempted Aconcagua (22,841 ft). That peak was first climbed by the Fitzgerald expedition in 1897.

The Andes of Bolivia were first explored by Sir William Martin Conway in 1898. Chilean and Argentine expeditions revealed the structure of the southern Cordillera in the years 1885-1898. Conway visited the mountains of Tierra del Fuego.

New Zealand's Southern Alps were first visited in 1882 by the Rev. W. S. Green, and shortly afterwards a New Zealand Alpine Club was founded, and by their activities the exploration of the range was pushed forward. In 1895, Major Edward Arthur Fitzgerald, made an important journey in this range. Tom Fyfe and party climbed Aoraki/ Mount Cook on Christmas Day 1894, denying Fitzgerald the first ascent. Fitzgerald was en route from Britain with Swiss guide Matthias Zurbriggen to claim the peak. So piqued at being beaten to the top of Mount Cook, he refused to climb it and concentrated on other peaks in the area. Later in the trip Zubriggen soloed Mount Cook up a ridge that now bears his name. The first mountains of the arctic region explored were those of Spitsbergen by Sir W. M. Conway's expeditions in 1896 and 1897. Of the high African peaks, Kilimanjaro was climbed in 1889 by Dr. Hans Meyer, Mt. Kenya in 1899 by Halford John Mackinder, and a peak of Ruwenzori by H. J. Moore in 1900.

The Asiatic mountains were initially surveyed on orders of the British Empire. In 1892 Sir William Martin Conway explored the Karakoram Himalaya, and climbed a peak of 23,000 ft (7,000 m) In 1895 Albert F. Mummery died while attempting Nanga Parbat, while in 1899 D. W. Freshfield took an expedition to the snowy regions of Sikkim. In 1899, 1903, 1906 and 1908 Mrs Fannie Bullock Workman made ascents in the Himalayas, including one of the Nun Kun peaks (23,300 ft). A number of Gurkha sepoys were trained as expert mountaineers by Major the Hon. C. G. Bruce, and a good deal of exploration was accomplished by them. The Rucksack Club was founded in Manchester, England in 1902. The American Alpine Club was founded in 1902.

In 1902, the Eckenstein-Crowley Expedition, lead by mountaineer Oscar Eckenstein and occultist Aleister Crowley, was the first to attempt to scale Chogo Ri (now known as K2 in the west). They reached 22,000 feet (6,700 m) before turning back due to weather and other mishaps. In 1905, Aleister Crowley led the first expedition to Kanchenjunga, the third highest mountain in the world. Four members of that party were killed in an avalanche. Some claims say they reached around 21,300 feet (6,500 m) before turning back, however Crowley's autobiography claims they reached about 25,000 feet (7,600 m). A few Olympics in the 1920s included prizes for alpinism, but these were discontinued after World War II.

The 1950s saw the first ascents of all the eight-thousanders but two, starting with Annapurna in 1950 by Maurice Herzog and Louis Lachenal. The world's highest mountain (above mean sea level), Mount Everest (8,848 m) was first climbed on May 29, 1953 by Sir Edmund Hillary and Tenzing Norgay from the south side in Nepal. Just a few months later, Hermann Buhl made the first ascent of Nanga Parbat (8,125 m), a siege style expedition culminating in a remarkable solo push for the summit, it's the only eight-thousander to be summited solo on the first ascent. K2 (8,611 m), the second highest peak in the world was first scaled in 1954. In 1964, the final eight-thousander to be climbed was Shishapangma (8,013 m), the lowest of all the 8,000 metre peaks.

2.12 Mountain Biking

Mountain biking entails the sport of riding bicycles off-road, often over rough terrain, whether riding specially equipped mountain bikes or hybrid road bikes. Most mountain bikes share similar characteristics that underscore durability and performance in rough terrain: wide, knobby tires, large frame tubing, front fork or dual suspension shock absorbers. The durability factor means a far heavier bicycle weight to rider ratio than their road touring cousins.

Mountain biking is roughly broken down into four categories: cross country, downhill, freeride, and trials/street riding. Each has differing levels of safety-consciousness with different types of mountain bikes and riding gear.

This individual sport requires endurance, bike handling skills and self-reliance, and can be performed almost anywhere from a back yard to a gravel road, but the majority of mountain bikers ride off-road trails, whether country back roads, fire roads, or *singletrack* (narrow trails that wind through forests, mountains, deserts, or fields). There are aspects of mountain biking that are more similar to trail running than regular bicycling. Because riders are often far from civilization, there is a strong ethic of self-reliance in the sport. Riders learn to repair their broken bikes or flat tires to avoid being stranded miles from help. This reliance on survival skills accounts for the group dynamics of the sport. Club rides and other forms of group rides are common.

History of Mountain Biking

Bicycles have been ridden off-road since their invention. However, the modern sport of mountain biking primarily originated in the 1970s. There were several groups of riders in different areas of the U.S.A. who can make valid claims to playing a part in the birth of the sport. Riders in Crested Butte, Colorado and Cupertino, California tinkered with bikes and adapted them to the rigors of off-road riding. Other riders around the country were probably copying their friends with motorcycles and riding their bikes on trails and fire roads. However, a group in Marin County, California is recognized by the Mountain Bike Hall of Fame to have played a central role in the birth of the sport as we know it today. They began racing down Mount Tamalpais (Mt Tam) on old 1930s and '40s Schwinn bicycles retrofitted with better brakes and fat tires. This group included Joe Breeze, Otis Guy, Gary Fisher, and Keith Bontrager, among others. It was Joe Breeze who built the first new, purpose-made mountain bike in 1977. Tom Ritchey built the first regularly available mountain bike frame, which was accessorized by Gary Fisher and Charlie Kelly and sold by their company called MountainBikes (later changed to Fisher Mountain Bikes then bought by Trek, still under the name Gary Fisher). The first two mass produced mountain bikes were sold in 1982: the Specialized Stumpjumper and Univega Alpina Pro.

In 1988, the Mountain Bike Hall of Fame was founded to chronicle the history of mountain biking, and to recognize the individuals and groups that have contributed significantly to this sport.

Equipment

Mountain bikes differ from road touring bicycles in several ways. They have a smaller, reinforced frame, knobby, wide and high profile tires which are mounted on a rim that is stronger than a standard bicycle rim, a larger range of gears to facilitate climbing up steep hills and over obstacles, a wider flat or upwardly-rising handlebar that allows a more upright riding position, and often some form of suspension system for either the front wheel or both wheels. The inherent comfort and flexibility of the modern mountain bike has led to an estimated 80 per cent market share in the United States, United Kingdom, Canada,

Australia and New Zealand and others. Mountain bikes often come with disc brakes similar to those used in automobiles, rather than rim brakes used on road bikes.

Fig. 2.4: A hardtail mountain bike.

- ❖ *Bicycle pedals* vary from simple *platform* pedals, where the rider simply places the shoes on top of the pedals, to *clipless*, where the rider uses a specially equipped shoe with a sole that engages mechanically into the pedal. Pedals with cages are rarely used, as the rough terrain (whether rock or tree roots and branches) can easily catch a cage and cause the rider to fall.
- ❖ *Helmets* provide mandatory head protection, as falls can occur over rough, rocky, sandy, or mountainous terrain. Helmets include full-faced helmets or regular streamline.
- ❖ *Gloves* differ from road touring gloves, are made of heavier construction, and often have covered thumbs or all fingers covered for hand protection. They are sometimes made with high-impact Kevlar and carbon fiber knuckles.
- ❖ *Glasses*, lightweight cycling, help protect against debris while on the trail. Filtered lenses, whether yellow for cloudy days or shaded for sunny days, protect the eyes from strain. Glasses are available with interchangeable lenses.
- ❖ *Shoes* are chosen for their comfort and ability to withstand backcountry terrain, whether used with clipless pedals or not.
- ❖ *Clothing* is chosen for comfort during physical exertion in the

backcountry, and its ability to withstand rough terrain. Road touring clothes are often inappropriate due to their delicate fabrics and construction.

❖ *Hydration systems* are imperative for mountain bikers in the backcountry, ranging from simple water bottles to toteable water bags with drinking tubes in lightweight backpacks (*e.g.*, Camelbaks).

❖ *GPS System* is often added to the handlebars and is used to display and monitor progress on trails downloaded from the internet or pre-made mapping systems, record trails on the fly, and keep track of trip times and other data. The GPS system is often a handheld GPS device with color screen and rugged, waterproof (IPX7) design. Good GPS mapping systems have topographic or aerial maps to help keep you aware of changing elevation and avoid sudden dropoffs or other hazards.

❖ *Pump* to inflate flat tires.

❖ *Bike tools* and extra bike tubes are important, as mountain bikers frequently find themselves miles from help (where their cell phones don't work), with flat tires or other mechanical problems (*e.g.*, chainsuck) that must be handled by the rider.

❖ *Body armor* Similar to the armor worn on motorcross bikes. These can consist of knee pads, elbow pads, padded shorts or armored under jackets. Body armor provides an extra layer of protection. These are made by companies like Dainese, sixsixone, Alpinestars and many others

Types of Mountain Biking

Mountain biking is dominated by these four major categories:

Cross-Country (XC)

Cross-Country (XC) is the most popular form of mountain biking, and the standard for most riders. It generally means riding point-to-point or in a loop including climbs and descents on a variety of terrain. A typical XC bike weighs around 25-30 lbs, and has 0-4 inches of suspension travel front and sometimes rear. Some XC riders aspire to *XC racing*, which is even more physically demanding than regular XC, and like all sports at an elite level requires years of training to compete at a national level.

Dirt Jumping (DJ)

Dirt Jumping (DJ) is one of the names given to the practice of riding bikes over shaped mounds of dirt or soil and becoming airborne. The idea is that after riding over the 'take off' the rider will become momentarily airborne, and aim to land on the 'landing'. Dirt jumping can be done on almost anything with wheels, but it is usually executed on a bicycle. tricks e.g backflips are performed in the air as well.

Downhill (DH)

Downhill (DH) is, in the most general sense, riding mountain bikes downhill. The rider usually travels to the point of descent by other means than cycling, such as a ski lift or automobile, as the weight of the downhill mountain bike often precludes any serious climbing. While cross country riding inevitably has a downhill component, Downhill (or DH for short) usually refers to racing-oriented downhill riding. Downhill-specific bikes are universally equipped with front and rear suspension, large disc brakes, and use heavier frame tubing than other mountain bikes. Because of their extremely steep terrain (often located in summer at ski resorts), downhill courses are one of the most physically demanding and dangerous venues for mountain biking. They include large jumps (up to and including 40 feet), drops of 10+ feet, and are generally rough and steep top to bottom. To negotiate these obstacles at race speed, racers must possess a unique combination of total body strength, aerobic and anaerobic fitness, and mental control. Minimum body protection in a true downhill setting is knee pads and a full face helmet with goggles, although riders and racers commonly sport full body suits to protect themselves. Downhill bikes now weigh around 35-40 lbs, while professional downhill mountain bikes can weigh as little as 33 lbs, fully equipped with custom carbon fibre parts, air suspension tubeless tires and more. Downhill frames get anywhere from 7 to 10 inches of travel and are usually mounted with an 8 inch travel dual-crown fork.

Freeride/Big Hit/Hucking

Freeride, as the name suggests is a 'do anything' discipline that encompasses everything from downhill racing without the clock to jumping, riding 'North Shore' style (elevated trails made of interconnecting bridges and logs), and generally riding trails and/or stunts that require more skill and aggressive techniques than XC. Freeride bikes are generally heavier and more amply suspended than their XC counterparts, but usually retain much of their climbing ability. It is up to the rider to build his or her bike to lean more toward a preferred level of aggressiveness. "Slopestyle" type riding is an increasingly popular genre that combines big-air, stunt-ridden freeride with BMX style tricks. Slopestyle courses are usually constructed at already established mountain bike parks and include jumps, large drops, quarter-pipes, and other wooden obstacles. There are always multiple lines through a course and riders compete for judges' points by choosing lines that highlight their particular skills. A "typical" freeride bike is hard to define, but 30-40 lbs with 4-7 inches of suspension front and rear is a good generalization.

Trials

Trials riding consists of hopping and jumping bikes over obstacles. It can be performed either off-road or in an urban environment. It requires an excellent sense of balance. As with Dirt Jumping and BMX-style riding, emphasis is placed on style, originality and technique. Trials bikes look almost nothing like mountain bikes. They use either 20", 24" or 26" wheels and have very small, low frames, some types without a saddle.

Short Cross or Speed Cross (SC)

Short Cross or Speed Cross (SC) is the newest form of mountain biking. The idea is to ride short, narrow forest paths with rocks, roots and dints, but not necessarily any ramps on them. The optimal length of the paths are from a few tens to hundreds of meters. The shortness is to provide extreme speed and thrilling to get trough the hindrances as fast as possible without crashing. The altitude of the paths does not have to vary much. The ultimate direction of the paths from vertical aspect can be the both ways, either up or down. The transitions between these essential parts are to be taken lightly and stopping at the beginning of every path is to provide maximum amount of thrilling action gained through the speed. The bikes for this purpose can vary from XC to FR.

Advocacy

Mountain bikers have faced land access issues from the beginnings of the sport. Areas where the first mountain bikers have ridden have faced serious restrictions or elimination of riding.

Many trails were originally fireroads, animal paths, hiking trails, or multi-use paths that were simply used for these new trail users. Single-track mountain biking creates more conflict with hikers, particularly in forested areas. There is also some concern single-track biking leads to erosion. Because of these conflicts, the interpretation of the Wilderness Act was revised by the National Park Service to be able to exclude bicycles in certain areas.

Opposition to the sport has led to the development of local, regional, and international mountain bike groups. The different groups that formed generally work to create new trails, maintain existing trails, and help existing trails that may have issues. Groups work with private and public entities from the individual landowner to city parks departments, on up through the state level at the DNR, and into the federal level. Different groups will work individually or together to achieve results.

Advocacy organizations work through a variety of means including education, trail work days, and trail patrols. Examples of the education an advocacy group can provide include: Educate local bicycle riders, property managers, and other user groups on the proper development of trails, and on the International Mountain Bicycling Association's rules of the Trail. Examples of trail work days can include: Flagging, cutting, and signing a new trail, or removing downed trees after a storm. A trail patrol is a bike rider who has had some training to help assist other (including non cyclists) trail users.

The International Mountain Bicycling Association, or IMBA, is a non-profit advocacy group whose mission is to create, enhance and preserve trail opportunities for mountain bikers worldwide. IMBA serves as an umbrella organization for mountain biking advocacy worldwide, and represents more than 700 affiliated mountain biking groups. In 1988, five California mountain bike clubs linked to form IMBA. The founding clubs were: Concerned Off Road Bicyclists Association, Bicycle Trails Council East Bay, Bicycle Trails Council

Marin, Sacramento Rough Riders, and Responsible Organized Mountain Pedalers. IMBA developed "Rules of the Trail" to promote responsible and courteous conduct on shared-use trails.

IMBA Rules of the Trail

1. Ride On Open Trails Only > 2. Leave No Trace > 3. Control Your Bicycle > 4. Yield to Others > 5. Never Scare Animals > 6. Plan Ahead

Environmental Impacts of Mountain Biking

Studies reported in the IMBA (International Mountain Bike Association) Trail Solutions manual found that a mountain bike's impact is comparable to that of a hiker and substantially less than that of an equestrian.

Studies that find mountain biking has little environmental impact have been criticized as underestimating the real impact of mountain biking on the environment. In 2003, Jason Lathrop wrote a critical literature review on the ecological impacts of mountain biking, raising some questions found nowhere else. He quotes the BLM: "An estimated 13.5 million mountain bicyclists visit public lands each year to enjoy the variety of trails. What was once a low use activity that was easy to manage has become more complex". He also notes that few studies take mountain biking into account.

The environmental impacts of mountain biking can be greatly reduced by not riding on muddy or sensitive trails, not skidding or locking the rear wheel when braking and by staying on the trail.

2.13 Multi-Sport Competitions

Subcategories

This category has the following 6 subcategories, out of 6 total.

1. Adventure race
2. Biathlon
3. Modern pentathlon
4. Nordic combined

5.   Strongmen competitions
6.   Triathlon

"Multi-Sport Competitions"

❖   Adventure racing
❖   Alpine Ironman
❖   Aquathlon
❖   Biathle
❖   Biathlon
❖   Chess boxing
❖   Coast to Coast (race)
❖   Decathlon
❖   Decathlon scoring tables

Duathlon

❖   Frontier Adventure Sports & Training
❖   Heptathlon
❖   International King of Sports
❖   Karrimor International Mountain Marathon
❖   Korean National Sports Festival
❖   Military patrol
❖   Modern Biathlon
❖   Multisport
❖   Octathlon
❖   Off-road duathlon

Off-Road Triathlon

❖   Pentathlon
❖   Women's pentathlon
❖   Quadrathlon
❖   SOS triathlon
❖   Triathlon
❖   Triathlon equipment
❖   Triathlon one 0 one
❖   Ultraman (endurance challenge)
❖   World's Strongest Man
❖   World's Strongest Woman
❖   XTERRA Triathlon

2.14 Multi-Sport Events

This category contains articles about sports events which feature separate competitions in two or more sports.

For sports in which individual competitors utilise more than one sporting skill (*e.g.*, triathlon) see: Category: Multi-sport competitions.

Subcategories

This category has the following 67 subcategories, out of 67 total.

Multi-sport competitions:

- ❖ 1987 in multi-sport events
- ❖ 1989　　"　　　"　　　"
- ❖ 1990　　"　　　"　　　"
- ❖ 1991　　"　　　"　　　"
- ❖ 1992　　"　　　"　　　"
- ❖ 1993　　"　　　"　　　"
- ❖ 1994　　"　　　"　　　"
- ❖ 1995　　"　　　"　　　"
- ❖ 1996　　"　　　"　　　"
- ❖ 1997　　"　　　"　　　"
- ❖ 1998　　"　　　"　　　"
- ❖ 1999　　"　　　"　　　"
- ❖ 2000　　"　　　"　　　"
- ❖ 2001　　"　　　"　　　"
- ❖ 2002　　"　　　"　　　"
- ❖ 2004　　"　　　"　　　"
- ❖ 2005　　"　　　"　　　"
- ❖ 2006　　"　　　"　　　"
- ❖ 2007　　"　　　"　　　"
- ❖ 2008　　"　　　"　　　"

2009 In Multi-Sport Events

- ❖ 2011 in multi-sport events
- ❖ ASEAN Para Games
- ❖ AST Dew Tour
- ❖ All-Africa Games
- ❖ Arctic Winter Games

❖ Asian Games
❖ Black Sea Games
❖ Bolivarian Games
❖ Canada Games
❖ Central American and Caribbean Games
❖ Central Asian Games
❖ Commonwealth Games
❖ Commonwealth Youth Games
❖ Deaflympics
❖ East Asian Games
❖ European Youth Olympic Festivals
❖ Extremity Games
❖ FINA World Aquatics Championships
❖ Gay Games
❖ Goodwill Games
❖ Highland games
❖ Island Games

Jeux de la Francophonie

❖ Kingdom Games
❖ Lusophony Games
❖ Mediterranean Games
❖ Micronesian Games
❖ Military World Games
❖ Olympics
❖ Pan American Games
❖ Pan Arab Games
❖ Panhellenic Games
❖ Para-Olympics
❖ Red Bull sports events
❖ Games of the Small States of Europe
❖ South American Games
❖ South Asian Games
❖ South Pacific Games
❖ Southeast Asian Games
❖ Special Olympics
❖ Universiade
❖ World Games

- ❖ World Outgames
- ❖ World Wheelchair and Amputee Games
- ❖ X Games

"Multi-sport Events"

The following 83 are in this category:

Multi-sport event:

1. 2011 Military World Games
2. 2011 Pacific Games
3. 3rd World Festival of Youth and Students
4. AAU Junior Olympic Games
5. Afro-A(3)sian Games
6. Alabama Sports Festival
7. All Comers Track Meets
8. All-time Para-Olympic Games medal table
9. Ancient Olympic Games
10. Arafura Games
11. Arctic Winter Games
12. Aryan Games
13. Australasian Masters Games
14. Big Sky State Games
15. Black Sea Games
16. 2007 Black Sea Games
17. Bolivarian Games
18. CARIFTA Games
19. CPLP Games
20. California State Games
21. Canada Games
22. Central African Games
23. Central Asian Games
24. Children of Asia International Sports Games
25. Commonwealth Games

Commonwealth Youth Games

1. Cotswold Games
2. Deaflympics

3. Défi sportif
4. East Asian Games
5. Eurogames (LGBT sporting event)
6. European Youth Olympic Festival
7. Extremity Games
8. GANEFO
9. Games of the Small States of Europe
10. Goodwill Games
11. Gravity Games
12. Indian Ocean Island Games
13. Inter-Allied Games
14. International Island Games Association
15. Jeux de la Francophonie
16. LG action sports world tour
17. Lusophony Games
18. Maccabiah Games
19. 2010 Micronesian Games
20. Micronesian Games
21. Military World Games
22. Military pentathlon
23. Naadam
24. National Congress of State Games
25. National Sports Festival of Japan
26. Nordic Games
27. North American Indigenous Games

Olympic Games

1. Pacific Games
2. Pan American Games
3. Pan-Armenian Games
4. Panathenaic Games
5. Para-Olympic Games
6. Prairie Rose State Games
7. Respect Gaymes
8. Rhieia
9. SELL Student Games
10. Senior Olympics
11. South American Games

12. South Asian Games
13. Southeast Asian Games
14. Spartakiad
15. Special Olympics World Games
16. Sports carnival
17. State Games of North Carolina
18. Thailand National Games
19. Thailand National Youth Games
20. Universiade
21. West Asian Games
22. Western Canada Summer Games
23. Women's Islamic Games
24. World Masters Games
25. World Mind Sports Games
26. World Police and Fire Games
27. Youth Friendship Games
28. Youth Olympic Games

3

Olympic Sports and Related Tourism Activities

3.1 Olympic Sports

The Olympic sports comprise all the sports contested in the Summer and Winter Olympic Games. As of 2008, the Summer Olympics include 28 sports with 38 disciplines and about 300 events, and the Winter Olympics include 7 sports with 15 disciplines and about 80 events. The number and kinds of events may change slightly from one Olympiad to another.

Sports, Disciplines and Events

For purposes of Olympic competition, the International Olympic Committee (IOC) makes a distinction between sports and disciplines. A sport, in Olympic terms, is a single or group of disciplines as represented by an international governing body, namely an International Federation. For example, aquatics, represented at the Olympic level by the International Swimming Federation, is a sport at the Summer Olympics that includes the swimming, diving, synchronized swimming and water polo disciplines. Skating, represented by the International Skating Union, is a sport at the Winter Olympics that includes both the figure skating and speed skating disciplines.

Medals are awarded on a per-event basis; there can be one or more events per sport or discipline. For most of the 20th century, demonstration sports have been included in many Olympic Games, usually to promote a non-Olympic sport popular in the host country, or to gauge interest and support for the sport. Some such sports, like curling, were subsequently added to the official Olympic program. This changed when the International Olympic Committee decided in 1989 to eliminate demonstration sports from Olympics Games after 1992. Although no demonstration sports have been included since then, as an alternative, the Beijing Organizing Committee received permission to organize a wushu tournament for the 2008 Summer Olympics.

Changes

Curling was promoted to official Olympic sport at the Nagano 1998 Winter Olympics. A sport or discipline is included in the Olympic program if the IOC determines that it is widely practiced around the world, that is, the number of countries that compete in a given sport is the indicator of the sport's prevalence. The IOC's requirements reflect participation in the Olympic Games as well — more stringent toward men (as they are represented in higher numbers) and Summer sports (as more nations compete in the Summer Olympics). Sports may not depend primarily on mechanical propulsion, though there were power-boating events in the early days of the Olympics.

Previous Olympic Games included sports which are no longer present on the current program, like polo and tug of war. These sports, known as "discontinued sports", were later removed either because of lack of interest or absence of an appropriate governing body. Archery and tennis are examples of sports that were competed at the early Games and were later dropped by the IOC, but managed to return to the Olympic program (in 1972 and 1988, respectively).

The most recent change occurred on July 11, 2005, when the IOC voted to drop baseball and softball from the Olympic program for 2012, a decision that was reaffirmed on February 9, 2006. Softball and baseball are two of seven sports, including golf, rugby, squash, karate and roller sports, that will be considered at the 2009 Olympic Congress in Copenhagen for two openings on the schedule for the 2016 Summer Olympics.

Recognized Sports

Tug of war contested at the 1904 Summer Olympics. It was later dropped from the Olympic program but remains a recognized sport.

Many sports are not included in the Olympic program but are

recognized by the IOC. At any time, a recognized sport may be added to the Olympic program in future Games through a recommendation by the IOC Olympic Programme Commission followed by a voting of the IOC membership. When Olympic demonstration sports were allowed, a sport typically first appeared as such before being officially promoted. An International Federation (IF) is responsible for ensuring that the sport's activities follow the Olympic Charter; from the moment their sport is recognized they become official Olympic federations and can assemble with the IOC and remaining Olympic IFs. Recognized sports that are not part of the competition schedule for an Olympic Games usually become part of the schedule of the World Games.

The following sports, though not contested in the Olympic Games, are recognized as Olympic sports by the IOC:

Air sports	Bandy	Baseball
Billiard sports	Boules	Bowling
Bridge	Chess	Climbing
Cricket	DanceSport	Golf
Karate	Korfball	Lifesaving
Motorcycle sport	Netball	Orienteering
Pelote Basque	Polo	Powerboating
Racquetball	Roller sports	Rugby
Softball	Squash	Sumo
Surfing	Tug of war	Underwater sports
Water skiing	Wushu	

Summer Olympics

At the first Olympic Games, nine sports were contested. Since then, the number of sports contested at the Summer Olympic Games has gradually risen to twenty-eight on the program from 2000—2008. At the 2012 Summer Olympics, however, the number of sports will fall back to twenty-six following an IOC vote in early 2006 deciding the removal of baseball and softball from the Olympic program. These remain Olympic sports nonetheless, with the possibility of a return to the Olympic program at the 2016 games.

In order for a sport or discipline to be in included in the Summer Olympics program (but not necessarily be contested at the Olympics), it must be widely practiced by men and women, in at least 75 and 50 countries, respectively, spread over four continents.

Current Summer Program

The following sports (or disciplines of a sport) make up the current Summer Olympic Games official program and are listed alphabetically according to the name used by the IOC. The figures in each cell indicate the number of events for each sport contested at the respective Games; a bullet (●) denotes that the sport was contested as a demonstration sport.

Five of the 26 sports consist of multiple disciplines. Disciplines from the same sport are grouped shown in table 3.1.

Discontinued Summer Sports

The sports shown in table 3.2, were previously part of the Summer Olympic Games program as official sports, but are no longer on the current program. The numbers in each cell indicate the number of events for each sport that were contested at the respective Games; a bullet denotes that the sport was contested as a demonstration sport.

Demonstration Summer Sports

The following sports or disciplines have been demonstrated at the Summer Olympic Games for the years shown, but have never been included on the official Olympic program:

1. American football (1904 and 1932)
2. Australian rules football (1956)
3. Ballooning (1900)
4. Bowling (1988)
5. Boules (1900)
6. Budo (1964)
7. Finnish baseball (1952)
8. Glima (1912)
9. Gliding (1936)

Table 3.1: Summer Olympic Games.

Sport (Discipline)	Body	1920	1924	1928	1932	1936	1948	1952	1956	1960	1964	1968	1972	1976	1980	1984	1988	1992	1996	2000	2004	2008
Diving		5	5	4	4	4	4	4	4	4	4	4	4	4	4	4	4	4	4	8	8	8
Swimming	FINA	10	11	11	11	11	11	11	13	15	18	29	29	26	26	29	31	31	32	32	32	34
Synchronized swimming																2	2	2	1	2	2	2
Water polo		1	1	1	1	1	1	1	1	1	1	1	1	1	1	1	1	1	1	2	2	2
Archery	FITA	1											2	2	2	2	2	4	4	4	4	4
Athletics (track and field)	IAAF	29	27	27	29	29	33	33	33	34	36	36	38	37	38	41	42	43	44	46	46	47
Badminton	BWF																	4	5	5	5	5
Basketball	FIBA					1	1	1	1	1	1	1	1	2	2	2	2	2	2	2	2	2
Boxing	AIBA	8	8	8	8	8	8	10	10	10	10	11	11	11	11	12	12	12	12	12	11	11
Flatwater canoe/kayak	ICF					9	9	9	9	7	7	7	7	11	11	12	12	12	12	12	12	12
Slalom canoe/kayak													4					4	4	4	4	4
BMX																						2
Mountain biking	UCI																		2	2	2	2
Road cycling		2	2	2	2	2	2	2	2	2	2	2	2	2	2	3	3	3	4	4	4	4
Track cycling		4	4	4	4	4	4	4	4	4	5	5	5	4	4	5	6	7	8	12	12	10
Equestrian	FEI	7	5	6	6	6	6	6	6	5	6	6	6	6	6	6	6	6	6	6	6	6
Fencing	FIE	6	7	7	7	7	7	7	7	8	8	8	8	8	8	8	8	8	10	10	10	10
Field hockey	FIH	1		1	1	1	1	1	1	1	1	1	1	1	2	2	2	2	2	2	2	2
Football (soccer)	FIFA	1	1	1		1	1	1	1	1	1	1	1	1	1	1	1	1	2	2	2	2

(Contd.)

(Contd.)

Sport (Discipline)	Body	1920	1924	1928	1932	1936	1948	1952	1956	1960	1964	1968	1972	1976	1980	1984	1988	1992	1996	2000	2004	2008
Artistic	FIG	4	9	8	11	9	9	15	15	14	14	14	14	14	14	14	14	14	14	14	14	14
Rhythmic																1	1	1	2	2	2	2
Trampoline																				2	2	2
Handball	IHF					1		•					1	2	2	2	2	2	2	2	2	2
Judo	IJF										4		6	6	8	8	7	14	14	14	14	14
Modern pentathlon	UIPM	1	1	1	1	1	1	2	2	2	2	2	2	2	2	2	2	2	1	2	2	2
Rowing	FISA	5	7	7	7	7	7	7	7	7	7	7	7	14	14	14	14	14	14	14	14	14
Sailing	ISAF	14	3	3	4	4	5	5	5	5	5	5	6	6	6	7	8	10	10	11	11	11
Shooting	ISSF	21	10		2	3	4	7	7	6	6	7	8	7	7	11	13	13	15	17	17	15
Table tennis	ITTF																4	4	4	4	4	4
Taekwondo	WTF																•	•		8	8	8
Tennis	ITF	5	5													•	4	4	4	4	4	4
Triathlon	ITU																			2	2	2
Beach volleyball	FIVB																	•	2	2	2	2
Indoor volleyball											2	2	2	2	2	2	2	2	2	2	2	2
Weightlifting	IWF	5	5	5	5	5	6	7	7	7	7	7	9	9	10	10	10	10	10	15	15	15
Wrestling	FILA	10	13	13	14	14	16	16	16	16	16	16	20	20	20	20	20	20	20	16	18	18
Total events		156	126	109	116	129	136	149	151	150	163	172	195	198	203	221	237	257	271	300	301	302

Table 3.2: The sports which were previously part of the Summer Olympic Games program as official sports.

Sport	1920	1924	1928	1932	1936	1940	1944	1948	1952	1956	1960	1964	1968	1972	1976	1980	1984	1988	1992	1996	2000	2004	2008
Baseball					•				•	•		•					•	•	1	1	1	1	1
Basque pelota		•									•								•				
Cricket																							
Croquet																							
Figure skating	3																						
Golf	1																						
Ice hockey	1																						
Jeu de paume		•																					
Lacrosse			•	•		•																	
Polo	1	1			1																		
Rackets	1																							
Roque																								
Rugby union	1	1																						
Softball																				1	1	1	1
Tug of war	1																							
Water motorsports	1																							

10. Kaatsen (1928)
11. Korfball (1920 and 1928)
12. La canne (1924)
13. Surf lifesaving (1900)
14. Longue paume (1900)
15. Motorsport (1900)
16. Roller hockey (1992)
17. Savate (1924)
18. Swedish (Ling) gymnastics (1948)
19. Weight training with dumbbells (1904)
20. Water skiing (1972)

Gliding was promoted from demonstration sport to an official Olympic sport in 1936 in time for the 1940 Summer Olympics, but the Games were cancelled due to the outbreak of World War II.

Winter Olympics

Before 1924, when the first Winter Olympic Games were celebrated, sports held on ice, like figure skating and ice hockey, were contested at the Summer Olympics. These two sports made their debuts at the 1908 and the 1920 Summer Olympics, respectively, but were permanently integrated in the Winter Olympics program as of the first edition. The *International Winter Sports Week*, later dubbed the I Olympic Winter Games and retroactively recognized as such by the IOC, consisted of nine sports. The number of sports contested at the Winter Olympics has since been decreased to seven, comprising a total of fifteen disciplines.

A sport or discipline must be widely practiced in at least 25 countries on three continents in order to be included on the Winter Olympics program.

Current Winter Program

The following sports (or disciplines of a sport) make up the current Winter Olympic Games official program and are listed alphabetically, according to the name used by the IOC (shown in table 3.3). The figures in each cell indicate the number of events for each sport that were contested at the respective Games (the blue cells indicate that those sports were held at the Summer Games); a bullet denotes that the sport was contested as a demonstration sport. On some occasions, both official medal events and demonstration events were contested in the same sport at the same Games.

Three out of the seven sports consist of multiple disciplines:
Bobsleigh — Skating — Skiing

Demonstration Winter Sports

The following sports have been demonstrated at the Winter Olympic Games for the years shown, but have never been included on the official Olympic program:

- ❖ Bandy (1952)
- ❖ Disabled alpine skiing (1984 and 1988)
- ❖ Disabled cross-country skiing (1988)
- ❖ Ice stock sport (1936, 1964)
- ❖ Military patrol (1928, 1936 and 1948)
- ❖ Ski ballet (acroski) (1988 and 1992)
- ❖ Skijoring (1928)
- ❖ Sled-dog racing (1932)
- ❖ Speed skiing (1992)
- ❖ Winter pentathlon (1948)

Military patrol was an official skiing event in 1924 but the IOC currently considers it an event of biathlon in those games, and not as a separate sport. Ski ballet, similarly, was simply a demonstration event falling under the scope of freestyle skiing.

3.2 Olympic Movement

The Olympic Movement encompasses organisations, athletes and other persons who agree to be guided by the Olympic Charter.

- ❖ International Olympic Committee
- ❖ IOC Commissions
- ❖ The Organising Committees of the Olympic Games
- ❖ National Olympic Committees

Table 3.3: The sports (or disciplines of a sport) make up the current Winter Olympic Games official programme, according to the name used by the IOC.

Sport (Discipline)	Body	1908	1920	1924	1928	1932	1936	1948	1952	1956	1960	1964	1968	1972	1976	1980	1984	1988	1992	1994	1998	2002	2006	2010
Biathlon	IBU										1	1	2	2	2	3	3	3	6	6	6	8	10	10
Bobsleigh	FIBT			1	1	2	2	2	2	2		2	2	2	2	2	2	2	2	2	2	3	3	3
Skeleton					1			1														2	2	2
Curling	WCF			1		•												•	•		2	2	2	2
Ice hockey	IIHF		1	1	1	1	1	1	1	1	1	1	1	1	1	1	1	1	1	1	2	2	2	2
Luge	FIL											3	3	3	3	3	3	3	3	3	3	3	3	3
Figure skating		4	3	3	3	3	3	3	3	3	3	3	3	3	4	4	4	4	4	4	4	4	4	4
Short track speed skating	ISU																	•	4	6	6	8	8	8
Speed skating				5	4	4	4	4	4	4	8	8	8	8	9	9	9	10	10	10	10	10	12	12
Alpine skiing							2	6	6	6	6	6	6	6	6	6	6	10	10	10	10	10	10	10
Cross country skiing				2	2	2	3	3	4	6	6	7	7	7	7	7	8	8	10	10	10	12	12	12
Freestyle skiing	FIS																	•	2•	4	4	4	4	6
Nordic combined				1	1	1	1	1	1	1	1	1	1	1	1	1	1	2	2	2	2	3	3	3
Ski jumping				1	1	1	1	1	1	1	1	2	2	2	2	2	2	3	3	3	3	3	3	3
Snowboarding																					4	4	6	6
Total events				16	14	14	17	22	22	24	27	34	35	35	37	38	39	46	57	61	68	78	84	86

- ❖ International Sports Federations
- ❖ Olympic Movement Partners

When he announced in Paris, on a winter's evening in 1892, the forthcoming re-establishment of the Olympic Games, Pierre de Coubertin was applauded, but nobody at the time imagined the scale of the project entailed by reviving the ancient Olympic Games, appointing a committee in charge of organising them and creating an international movement. The IOC was created on 23 June 1894; the 1st Olympic Games of the modern era opened in Athens on 6 April 1896; and the Olympic Movement has not stopped growing ever since.

Olympism is a state of mind based on equality of sports which are international and democratic. It is a philosophy of life, exalting and combining in a balanced whole the qualities of body, will and mind. The goal of the Olympic Movement is to contribute to building a peaceful and better world by educating youth through sport practised without discrimination or any kind, in a spirit of friendship, solidarity and fair play. The Olympic Movement is defined also by the numerous activities in which it engages, such as:

- ❖ Promoting sport and competitions through the intermediary of national and international sports institutions world-wide.
- ❖ Cooperation with public and private organisations to place sport at the service of mankind.
- ❖ Assistance to develop "Sport for All".
- ❖ Advancement of women in sport at all levels and in all structures, with a view to achieving equality between men and women.
- ❖ Opposition to all forms of commercial exploitation of sport and athletes.
- ❖ The fight against doping.
- ❖ Promoting sports ethics and fair play.
- ❖ Raising awareness of environmental problems.
- ❖ Financial and educational support for developing countries through the IOC institution Olympic Solidarity.

"All sports for all people. This is surely a phrase that people will consider foolishly utopian. That prospect troubles me not at all. I have pondered and studied it at length, and know that it is correct and possible", wrote Pierre de Coubertin in 1919. The future proved him right.

3.3 International Olympic Committee

The International Olympic Committee is the supreme authority of the Olympic Movement. The International Olympic Committee was founded on 23 June 1894 by the French educator Baron Pierre de Coubertin who was inspired to revive the Olympic Games of Greek antiquity. The IOC is an international non-governmental non-profit organisation and the creator of the Olympic Movement. The IOC exists to serve as an umbrella organisation of the Olympic Movement. It owns all rights to the Olympic symbols, flag, motto, anthem and Olympic Games. Its primary responsibility is to supervise the organisation of the summer and winter Olympic Games.

President of the IOC from 1894 to 1896

The first President was a Greek. He was born in Ermoupolis, on the island of Syros, on 15 February 1835. The Regulations drawn up by Pierre de Coubertin stipulated that the President of the International Olympic Committee should be chosen from the country where the next Games were to be held. Mr Vikelas was thus President from 1894 to 1896. He had no particular connection with sport when he came from Greece to represent the Pan-Hellenic Gymnastic Club at the Congress in Paris in 1894. The original idea was to stage the first Games in Paris in 1900, but Mr Vikelas was able to convince the Committee that they should be held in Athens in May 1896. After the conclusion of the first Games, he devoted himself to the promotion and popularisation of general education, which he claimed was urgently needed in Greece. With his erudition to which we owe a scholarly work on "Byzantine and Modern Greece", he combined a fertile and whimsical imagination which gave us "Louki Laras" and "Tales from the Aegean". He died in Athens on 20 July 1908.

President of the IOC from 1896 TO 1925

Pierre de Frédy, Baron de Coubertin was born on 1 January 1863 at 20, rue Oudinot in Paris. Very early in life he showed a liking for literature, history and the problems of education and sociology. Giving up the army, abandoning too the political career that was open to him at the age of twenty-four, Pierre de Coubertin decided to launch a vast movement of educational reform, and at twenty-five his life work was started. It is also to him that we owe all the organisation of the Olympic Games, which have benefited from his methodical and precise mind, and from his wide understanding of the aspirations and needs of young people. The Olympic Charter and Protocol, as well as the athletes' oath are his work, together with the ceremonial for the opening and closing of the Games. Furthermore, until 1925 he personally presided over the International Olympic Committee.

The title of Honorary President of the Olympic Games was bestowed on him in 1925 until his death in 1937. It was decided that no other President would ever be granted this honour again. The revival of the Olympic Games represents only a small part of the Baron de Coubertin's work. Apart from numerous publications devoted to the technique and teaching of sport, he was the author of important historial, political and sociological studies. His works total over sixty thousand pages.

He died on 2 September, 1937 in Geneva having spent his entire fortune on his ideals. He is considered one of the great men of the 20th century. In accordance with his last wishes, his heart was interred at Olympia (Greece), in the marble monument commemorating the revival of the Olympic Games.

President of the IOC from 1925 to 1942

Count Henri de Baillet-Latour, born on 1 March 1876, was elected as a member of the International Olympic Committee in Belgium in 1903. One year later he founded the Belgian Olympic Committee which organised Belgian participation in the 1908 and 1912 Games.

After World War I he obtained the celebration of the Games of the VII Olympiad for Antwerp. Although he had only one year in which to prepare these Games, and in spite of the fact that Belgium had suffered badly from the war, Count de Baillet-Latour shouldered all the responsibilities and with great energy took up the management of this huge enterprise.

Among other qualities, the ability he demonstrated at the time of the Games in Antwerp led members of the International Olympic Committee to elect him President when the founder of the Games resigned in 1925. During his presidency, which lasted seventeen years, Count de Baillet-Latour devoted himself untiringly to maintaining the Olympic ideals and aims. He endeavoured continually to keep sport free from all commercialism, and to preserve its nobility and beauty, its "raison d'être". He aimed to acquire an informed personal opinion on all difficult questions and travelled widely throughout the world in order to achieve this object. He was determined, yet diplomatic, and led the Committee with great distinction.

He died on the night of 6 January 1942. A worthy successor to the Baron de Coubertin, he will be remembered as a man of noble character, wholeheartedly devoted to the Olympic cause.

President of the IOC from 1946 to 1952

J. Sigfrid Edström, born on 21 November 1870, was one of the best known personalities in the world of sport. While a student in Gothenburg, Mr Edström went in for athletics and ran the 100 m in 11 seconds. After some years in Zurich, where he attended the Federal Institute of Technology, he was entrusted with important tasks in the sports movement in Sweden.

In the international field, he was one of the organisers of the Olympic Games in Stockholm in 1912, and also participated in the 1908, 1920, 1924, 1928, 1932 and 1936 Games as head of the Swedish delegation. At the 1912 Olympic Games he took the lead in founding the International Amateur Athletics Federation and was elected its first President (1913), an office which he held until 1946.

In 1920 he was elected as a member of the International Olympic Committee in Sweden. One year later he was elected to the Executive Board of the IOC and then as Vice-President (1931-1946). In his capacity as Vice-President he became head of the International Olympic Committee in 1946, on the death of the President, Count de Baillet-Latour. All through the hostilities of the Second World War, since he lived in a neutral country, he managed to keep in contact with the members of the International Olympic Committee, and in 1945 convened the first post-war meeting of the Executive Board, which accepted the invitation from London and selected this city to stage the Games of the XIV Olympiad.

In 1946 he was elected President by acclamation at the first post-war meeting of the IOC in Lausanne. He retired in 1952 at the age of 82 with the title of Life Honorary President of the International Olympic Committee.

President of the IOC From 1952 To 1972

Born in Detroit, Michigan, on 28 September 1887, Mr Avery Brundage graduated from the University of Illinois in 1909 with a degree in civil engineering, magna cum laude. In addition to being a brilliant student, he distinguished himself in athletics. Without neglecting his sports career, he then went into business and in 1915 founded the Avery Brundage Company Builders (1915-1947) which constructed a number of big buildings and skyscrapers around Chicago. He represented his country at the Games of the V Olympiad in Stockholm in 1912, and was three times amateur all-round champion of the United States, a speciality similar to the decathlon. After retiring from active competition, he became interested in the administrative side of sport, occupying the posts of President of the Amateur Athletics Union of the United States (seven terms of office), President of the United States Olympic Committee for twenty-five years (1929-1953), President of the Pan-American Games Association (PASO), etc. After becoming a member of the IOC in 1936, and Vice-President in 1945, in 1952 he was elected President and watched over the destiny of the Olympic Movement until 1972 becoming Life Honorary President from 1972 to 1975. A great advocate of amateurism, he was the author of many articles on amateur sport and the Olympic Movement.

During his frequent journeys all over the world, Mr Avery Brundage amassed one of the finest and largest collections of Asian art in the world. Estimated to be worth 50 million dollars, this collection was donated to the City of San Francisco, which built a museum to house it in the famous Golden Gate Park. Down through the years, Mr Avery Brundage received countless decorations and awards from different countries, towns and organisations wishing to express their appreciation and gratitude. Avery Brundage died on 8 May 1975, in Garmisch-Partenkirchen, Germany.

President of the Ioc From 1972 To 1980

Lord Killanin was born in London, England, on 30 July 1914. During his youth at Eton and later at Magdalene College (Cambridge), he was an accomplished sportsman, taking part in competitions particularly as a boxer, oarsman and rider. A famous journalist on Fleet Street, where he wrote for renowned daily newspapers and magazines, from the age of 22 he experienced enormous success, especially as a war correspondent in China. Enlisted as a volunteer in the British Army for the length of the Second World War, he took part in the Allied landing in Normandy. When he became an IOC member in 1952, he had already headed the Olympic Council of Ireland for two years. Without benefiting from a personal fortune and without ever sacrificing his ideas, passions and major tasks as a leader, he succeeded over the years in forging a comfortable family life as a director or board member of several large companies. At the same time, he became not only the producer but also the chief adviser of many successful films, including "The Quiet Man", on which he worked with his long-standing friend, John Ford.

For eight years, he acted as President of the International Olympic Committee during an extremely difficult period, and was later unanimously elected Honorary Life President. Lord Killanin died in April 1999.

President of the IOC From 1980 To 2001

Seventh President of the International Olympic Committee, Juan Antonio Samaranch was born on 17 July 1920 in Barcelona. An industrialist and President of the "Diputación" of his home province, his ascension to the zenith of the Olympic Movement began by the unusual path of roller-skating: he led the Spanish team to the world title. Elected as an IOC member in 1966, then Chief of Protocol in 1968, his qualities as an untiring worker were soon put to use within various commissions. In 1970, he became a member of the Executive Board, and Vice-President of the IOC from 1974 to 1978. In 1977, Spain restored diplomatic relations with the USSR and Juan Antonio Samaranch was appointed Ambassador to Moscow (1977-1980). He returned to the Executive Board in 1979, as Chief of Protocol. Elected to the presidency of the IOC in the first ballot on 16 July 1980, he succeeded Lord Killanin whose career terminated with the extinction of the Olympic flame on 3 August 1980. From the time he took up office, he tried to give a new direction to the Olympic Movement which was badly shaken by the political difficulties of the XXII Olympiad, and undertook a long voyage around the world to establish numerous contacts with Heads of State and sports leaders and to defend the Olympic cause. He secured the IOC's status as an international non-governmental organisation and restructured its finances (television rights, sponsorship programmes). He kept the Olympic flame alive during the crisis years of boycotts (Moscow 1980 and Los Angeles 1984). It was through his efforts that the Olympic Museum was built in Lausanne (1993).

When the IOC found itself in crisis, because of abuses of trust by some of its members, he undertook major reforms to the structure of the institution. Mr Samaranch's mandate ended on the 16 July 2001, in Moscow, where he was elected Honorary President for Life.

President of the IOC Since 2001

Jacques Rogge is the eighth IOC President, elected on 16 July 2001 at the 112th IOC Session in Moscow. Born on 2 May 1942 in Ghent, Belgium, Jacques Rogge is married and has two children. By profession, he is an orthopaedic surgeon. In the course of his sports career, he competed in the yachting competitions at the Games of the Olympiad in Mexico in 1968, Munich in 1972 and Montreal in 1976. He was also a member of the Belgian national rugby team. Jacques Rogge served as President of the Belgian National Olympic Committee from 1989 to 1992. He became President of the European Olympic Committees in 1989, IOC member in 1991 and Executive Board member in 1998.

The IOC President is elected by the IOC members by secret ballot for an initial term of eight years, renewable once for four additional years. The President presides over all activities of the IOC, acting as its permanent representative. The current President, since 16 July 2001, is Jacques Rogge, of Belgium.

Executive Board

The Executive Board, founded in 1921, consists of the IOC President, four Vice-Presidents and ten other members. All the members of the Executive Board are elected by the Session, by secret ballot, by a majority of votes cast, for a four-year term.

Members

The members of the IOC are individuals who act as the IOC's representatives in their respective countries, not as delegates of their country within the IOC. The members meet once a year at the IOC Session. They retire at the end of the calendar year of which they turn 70 years, unless they were elected before the opening of the 110th Session (11 December 1999). In that case, they must retire when they reach the age of 80. The term of office for all members is eight years, renewable every eight years. The IOC chooses and elects its members from among such persons as its nominations committee considers qualified. All Olympic Movement members have the right to submit nominations.

Administration

The IOC administration is at the service of the needs of the Olympic Movement. It prepares, implements and follows-up on a day-to-day basis the decisions taken by the main organisations of the Olympic Movement.

3.4 Organizing Committees of the Olympic Games

The organization of the Olympic Games is entrusted by the International Olympic Committee (IOC) to the National Olympic Committee (NOC) of the country of the host city as well as to the host city itself. The NOC forms, for that purpose, an Organising Committee for the Olympic Games (OCOG) which, from the time it is constituted, communicates directly with the IOC, from which it receives instructions. The OCOG executive body includes: the IOC member or members in the country; the President and Secretary General of the NOC; and at least one member representing, and designated by, the host city. In addition, it generally includes representatives of the public authorities and other leading figures.

From the time of its constitution to the end of its liquidation, the OCOG must comply with the Olympic Charter, the contract entered into between the IOC, the National Olympic Committee and the host city (Host City Contract) and the instructions of the IOC Executive Board. Nowadays, these Organising Committees have turned into enormous administrative entities employing hundreds of people. The Organising Committee starts its work with a period of planning followed by a period of organisation which culminates in the implementation or operational phase.

A Few Aspects of an Organising Committee's Work:

❖ To give equal treatment to every sport on the programme and ensure that competitions are held according to the rules of the International Sports Federations (IFs);

❖ To ensure that no political demonstration or meeting is held on Olympic sites;

❖ To choose and, if necessary, create the required installations: competition sites, stadiums and training halls; to arrange for the required equipment;

❖ To lodge the athletes, their entourage, the officials;

❖ To organise medical services;

❖ To solve transportation problems;

❖ To meet the requirements of the mass media in order to offer the public the best possible information on the Games;

❖ To organise cultural events that are an essential element of the celebration of the Olympic Games; and

❖ To write the Final Report on the celebration of the Games in the two official languages and distribute it within two years after the end of the Games.

3.5 National Olympic Committees

The National Olympic Committees (NOCs) propagate the fundamental principles of Olympism at a national level within the framework of sports activity. There are currently 205 National Olympic Committees over five continents. Some of these are:

❖ ALB : Albania

- ❖ AND : Andorra
- ❖ ARM : Armenia
- ❖ AUT : Austria
- ❖ AZE : Azerbaijan
- ❖ BLR : Belarus
- ❖ BEL : Belgium
- ❖ BIH : Bosnia and Herzegovina
- ❖ BUL : Bulgaria
- ❖ CRO : Croatia
- ❖ CYP : Cyprus
- ❖ CZE : Czech Republic
- ❖ DEN : Denmark
- ❖ EST : Estonia
- ❖ FIN : Finland
- ❖ MKD : Former Yugoslav Republic of Macedonia
- ❖ FRA : France
- ❖ GEO : Georgia
- ❖ GER : Germany
- ❖ GBR : Great Britain
- ❖ GRE : Greece
- ❖ HUN : Hungary
- ❖ ISL : Iceland
- ❖ IRL : Ireland
- ❖ ISR : Israel
- ❖ ITA : Italy
- ❖ LAT : Latvia
- ❖ LIE : Liechtenstein
- ❖ LTU : Lithuania
- ❖ LUX : Luxembourg
- ❖ MLT : Malta
- ❖ MON : Monaco
- ❖ MNE : Montenegro
- ❖ NED : Netherlands
- ❖ NOR : Norway
- ❖ POL : Poland
- ❖ POR : Portugal
- ❖ MDA : Republic of Moldova
- ❖ ROU : Romania

❖ RUS : Russian Federation
❖ SMR : San Marino
❖ SRB : Serbia
❖ SVK : Slovakia
❖ SLO : Slovenia
❖ ESP : Spain
❖ SWE : Sweden
❖ SUI : Switzerland
❖ TUR : Turkey
❖ UKR : Ukraine

The NOCs come together at least once every two years in the form of the Association of National Olympic Committees (ANOC) to exchange information and experiences in order to consolidate their role within the Olympic Movement. In this way the ANOC helps the NOCs to prepare for their meetings with the IOC Executive Board and Olympic Congresses. The ANOC also makes recommendations to the IOC regarding the use of funds deriving from the television rights intended for the NOCs. These recommendations focus on the implementation of the Olympic Solidarity programmes in particular.

The ANOC is currently made up of the 205 NOCs and is split among five continental associations:

1. AFRICA: ANOCA—Association of National Olympic Committees of Africa.
2. AMERICA: PASO—Pan American Sports Organisation.
3. ASIA: OCA—Olympic Council of Asia
4. EUROPE: EOC—European Olympic Committees.
5. OCEANIA: ONOC—Oceania National Olympic Committees.

The National Olympic Committees (NOCs) promote the fundamental principles of Olympism at a national level within the framework of sports. NOCs are committed to the development of athletes and support the development of sport for all programs and high performance sport in their countries. They also participate in the training of sports administrators by organising educational programs.

Another objective of the National Olympic Committees is to

ensure that athletes from their respective nations attend the Olympic Games. Only a NOC is able to select and send teams and competitors for participation in the Olympic Games.

National Olympic Committees also supervise the preliminary selection of potential bid cities. Before a candidate city can compete against those in other countries, it first must win the selection process by the NOC in its own country. The National Olympic Committee can then name that city to the IOC as a candidate to host the Olympic Games. Although most NOCs are from nations, the IOC also recognises independent territories, commonwealths, protectorates and geographical areas. There are currently 205 NOCs, ranging from Albania to Zimbabwe.

3.6 Discovering the Sports and Disciplines on the Programme of the Next Olympic Games

1.   Aquatics
2.   Archery
3.   Athletics
4.   Badminton
5.   Baseball
6.   Basketball
7.   Biathlon
8.   Bobsleigh
9.   Boxing
10. Canoe/kayak
11. Curling
12. Cycling
13. Equestrian
14. Fencing
15. Football
16. Gymnastics
17. Handball
18. Hockey
19. Ice Hockey
20. Judo
21. Luge
22. Modern pentathlon

23. Olympic sport since 1896
24. Rowing
25. Sailing
26. Shooting
27. Skating
28. Skiing
29. Softball
30. Summer sports:
    - Table tennis
    - Taekwondo
    - Tennis
    - Triathlon
    - Volleyball
    - Weightlifting
31. Winter sports:
    - Wrestling

Recognised Sports

Climbing, bridge, golf, roller skating and surfing are sports that are recognised by the International Olympic Committee (IOC). The International Sports Federations (IFs) that administer these sports must ensure that their statutes, practice and activities conform with the Olympic Charter.

Olympic Sports of the Past

Tug of war, rugby, polo, lacrosse, and golf were once on the Olympic programme. Have a closer look at these sports and discover others that have become a part of Olympic history.

International Sports Federations

The International Sports Federations (IFs) are responsible for the integrity of their sport on the international level.

3.7 Para-Olympic Shooting

Para-Olympic shooting is an adaptation of shooting sports for competitors with disabilities. Shooting is a test of accuracy and control, in which competitors use pistols or rifles to fire a series of shots at a stationary target. Competitions are open to all athletes with a physical disability. Athletes use .22 caliber rifles and air guns (pneumatic, CO_2 gas or spring). Para-Olympic shooting is practiced in at least 51 countries and first appeared in the Summer Para-Olympics at the 1976 Toronto Games.

Athletes compete in rifle and pistol events from distances of 10, 25 and 50 metres, in men's, women's and mixed competitions. Shooting utilizes a functional classification system, which enables athletes from different disability classes to compete together either individually or in teams, with wheelchair users competing on equal level with standing shooters.

Shooting is governed by the International Para-Olympic Committee (IPC) and co-ordinated by the IPC Shooting Technical Committee following the modified rules of the International Shooting Sport Federation (ISSF). These rules consider the differences that exist between shooting for the able-bodied and shooting for persons with a disability.

Classification System

    SH1—Shooters able to support a gun without a stand
    SH2—Shooters requiring a gun support in order to shoot
    SH3—Blind Shooters (sights seek sound-emitting targets)

Sub-classifications A, B and C define wheelchair backrest height depending on back and pelvic strength per athlete.

Equipment Adaptations

Disabled shooters use exactly the same guns and clothing as able-bodied shooters. There are adaptations like the use of a shooting chair for competitors unable to stand, also a shooting table for events like kneeling or prone. A shortened shooting jacket is used for seated competitors, depending on chair height. Rules are covered by ISCD cross-referenced with ISSF rules.

The only additional event is the 10m air rifle prone which is shot with both male and female shooters mixed together. Both sexes shooting

60 shots within 1 hour 30 minutes. Finals are also conducted. For the 10m air rifle prone mixed event, slings are optional for SH1 shooters. SH2 shooters are not allowed to use a sling in this event.

Rifle Events

- ❖ Air Rifle, 10m Range
- ❖ Standing (Standing or seated, no elbow support)
- ❖ Kneeling (Seated, with single elbow support)
- ❖ Prone (Seated, with both elbows supported by a shooting table)
- ❖ .22 Rifle, 50m Range
- ❖ English Match (.22 prone on ground or seated with both elbows supported by a shooting table)
- ❖ Mixed Men and Women, 60 shots.
- ❖ 3 × 20 .22 Rifle (women's event)
- ❖ Standing (Standing or seated, no elbow support)
- ❖ Kneeling (Seated, with single elbow support)
- ❖ Prone (Seated, with both elbows supported by a shooting table)
- ❖ 3 × 40 .22 Rifle (men's event)
- ❖ Standing
- ❖ Kneeling
- ❖ Prone

Pistol Events

- ❖ Air Pistol
- ❖ Men's, Women's events
- ❖ .22 Pistol
- ❖ Men's, Women's events

Competitions

Para-Olympic shooting events are held in competitions across the world, including the Summer Para-Olympics. The ASIAN Games for the Disabled, formerly known as the FESPIC Games, and the Jikji Cup Asian Open Championships in Korea are the biggest Para-Olympic shooting events in Asia. Both of these competitions serve as qualifying events for the Para-Olympic Games.

4

FIFA Confederations and World Cup: A Major Tourist Attraction

4.1 Introduction

The Fédération Internationale de Football Association (French for *International Federation of Association Football*), commonly known by its acronym, FIFA (usually pronounced /fif?/ or/fifæ/), is the international governing body of association football. Its headquarters are in Zürich, Switzerland, and its current president is Sepp Blatter. FIFA is responsible for the organization and governance of football's major international tournaments, most notably the FIFA World Cup, held since 1930.

FIFA has 208 member associations, which is 16 more than the United Nations and 3 more than the International Olympic Committee, though 5 fewer than the International Association of Athletics Federations.

History

The need for a single body to oversee the worldwide game became apparent at the beginning of the 20th century with the increasing popularity of international fixtures. FIFA was founded in Paris on May 21, 1904 — the French name and acronym persist to this day, even outside French-speaking countries. Its first president was Robert Guérin.

FIFA presided over its first international competition in 1906, but this met with little approval or success. This, in combination with economic factors, led to the swift replacement of Guérin with Daniel Burley Woolfall from England, by now a member association. The next tournament staged, the football competition for the 1908 Olympics in London was more successful, despite the presence of professional footballers, contrary to the founding principles of FIFA. Membership of FIFA expanded beyond Europe with the application of South Africa in 1909, Argentina and Chile in 1912, and Canada and the United States in 1913. FIFA, however, floundered during World War I, with many players sent off to war and the possibility of travel for international fixtures severely limited. Post-war, following the death of Woolfall, the organisation was run by Dutchman Carl Hirschmann. It was saved from extinction, but at the cost of the withdrawal of the Home Nations (of the United Kingdom), who cited an unwillingness to participate in international competitions with their recent World War enemies. The Home Nations later resumed their membership. The FIFA collection is held by the National Football Museum in England.

Laws of the Game

The laws that govern football, known officially as the Laws of the Game, are not solely the responsibility of FIFA; they are maintained by a body called the International Football Association Board (IFAB). FIFA has members on its board (four representatives); the other four are provided by the football associations of the United Kingdom: England, Scotland, Wales, and Northern Ireland, in recognition of their unique contribution to the creation and history of the game. Changes to the Laws of the Game must be agreed by at least six of the eight delegates.

Structure

FIFA is an association established under the Laws of Switzerland. Its headquarters are in Zurich. FIFA's supreme body is the FIFA Congress, an assembly made up of a representative from each affiliated national federation. The Congress assembles in ordinary session now once every year, and extraordinary sessions have been held once a year since 1998 & now as and when requested. Only the Congress can pass changes to FIFA's by-laws. Congress elects the President of FIFA, its secretary-general and the other members of FIFA's Executive Committee. The President and secretary-general are the main officeholders of FIFA, and are in charge of its daily administration, carried out by the General Secretariat, with its staff of approximately 280 members.

FIFA's Executive Committee, chaired by the President, is the main decision making body of the organization in the intervals of Congress. FIFA's worldwide organizational structure also consists of several other bodies, under authority of the Executive Committee or created by Congress as Standing Committees. Among those bodies are the Finance Committee, the Disciplinary Committee, the Referee's Committee, etc. Aside from its worldwide institutions (presidency, Executive Board, Congress, etc.) FIFA has created confederations which oversee the game in the different continents and regions of the world. National federations, and not the continental Confederations, are members of FIFA. The continental Confederations are provided for in FIFA's by-laws. National federations must claim membership to both FIFA and the confederation in which their nation is geographically resident for their teams to qualify for entry to FIFA's competitions (with a few geographic exceptions listed below):

- ❖ AFC—Asian Football Confederation in Asia and Australia
- ❖ CAF—Confédération Africaine de Football in Africa
- ❖ CONCACAF—Confederation of North, Central American and Caribbean Association Football in North America and Central America
- ❖ CONMEBOL—Confederación Sudamericana de Fútbol in South America
- ❖ OFC—Oceania Football Confederation in Oceania
- ❖ UEFA—Union Européenne de Football Association in Europe.

Nations straddling the traditional boundary between Europe and Asia have generally had their choice of confederation. As a result, a number of transcontinental nations including Russia, Turkey, Cyprus, Armenia, Azerbaijan and Georgia have chosen to become part of UEFA despite the bulk of their land area being in Asia. Israel, although lying entirely within Asia, joined UEFA in 1994, after decades of its football teams being boycotted by many Arab and predominantly Muslim AFC countries. Kazakhstan moved from AFC to UEFA in 2002. Australia was the latest to move from OFC to AFC in January 2006.

Guyana and Suriname have always been CONCACAF members despite being South American countries. No team from the OFC is offered automatic qualification to the World Cup. In recent World Cup qualifying cycles, the winner of their section had to play a play-off against a CONMEBOL side, a hurdle at which Australia have traditionally fallen. In an effort to improve their national and domestic teams Australia moved to the Asian Federation 2006. This allows Australia to play in Asian tournaments of a much higher standard (as well as being more numerous) such as the AFC Asian Cup and the Asian Champions League. Australia successfully qualified for the 2006 FIFA World Cup by winning just such a playoff in a penalty shootout against Uruguay, just a few months after the clearance to move was granted. Initially, the 2010 FIFA World Cup qualification cycle was planned to provide the winner of OFC qualifying with a place in the final AFC qualification group, but this was scrapped in favour of a playoff between the OFC winner and an AFC team for a World Cup place. In total, FIFA recognises 208 national federations and their associated men's national teams as well as 129 women's national teams; see the list of national football teams and their respective country codes. Curiously, FIFA has more member states than the United Nations, as FIFA recognises several non-sovereign entities as distinct nations, most notably the four Home Nations within the United Kingdom. The FIFA World Rankings are updated monthly and rank each team based on their performance in international competitions, qualifiers, and friendly matches. There is also a world ranking for women's football, updated four times a year.

Recognitions and Awards

FIFA awards, each year, the title of FIFA World Player of the Year to the most prestigious player of the year, as part of its annual awards ceremony which also recognises team and international football achievements. As part of its centennial celebrations in 2004, FIFA organised a "Match of the Century" between France and Brazil

Governance and Game Development

FIFA frequently takes active roles in the running of the sport and developing the game around the world. One of its unique policies is to suspend teams and associated members from international competition when a government interferes in the running of FIFA's associate member organisations or if the associate is not functioning properly.

A recent high-profile suspension was of the Greek Football Federation for political interference. Another recent suspension was on the Kenya Football Federation because it was not running the game in Kenya properly and also of Iraq. The Asia wing of FIFA, the AFC is soon to force 22 leading associations in Asia to increase transparency, competition, quality training and a proper league structure with relegation, promotion and a 2nd division. Suspension will be imposed on any associate which doesn't co-operate with the reform outlines. Notably, one of the associations being targeted is that of Australia, a country whose professional sport leagues are all organised on the model of franchised teams and closed league membership, a system most commonly identified with North America.

A 2007 FIFA ruling that a player can be registered with a maximum of three clubs, and appear in official matches for a maximum of three, in a year measured from 1 July to 30 June has lead to controversy, especially in those countries whose seasons cross that date barrier, as in the case of two former Ireland internationals. The Iraq national team was suspended in May 2008, due to government interference with independent national sports authorities. However the decision was overturned by FIFA on May 29, 2008, since the Iraqi government reversed its earlier decision in dissolving the Iraq Football Association.

FIFA Altitude Ban

FIFA attempted to address the issue of extreme altitude in May 2007, ruling that no future international matches could be played at an altitude over 2500 m (8200 ft). The FIFA altitude ban would most notably have affected the national teams of Andean countries. Under this proposal, Bolivia would no longer be able to play international matches in La Paz (3,600 m), Ecuador would be unable to play in Quito (2,800 m), and Colombia could no longer play in Bogotá (2,640 m).

However, FIFA soon backed away from the proposal after international condemnation, and under political pressure from the CONMEBOL countries, first extending the maximum altitude to 2,800 m (9,190 ft) in June 2007, which made Bogotá and Quito viable international venues once again, and then waiving the restriction for La Paz in July 2007.

Allegations of Financial Irregularities

In May 2006 British investigative reporter Andrew Jennings' book *Foul* (Harper Collins) caused controversy within the football world by detailing an alleged international cash-for-contracts scandal following the collapse of FIFA's marketing partner ISL, and revealed how some football officials have been urged to secretly repay the sweeteners they received. The book also exposed the vote-rigging that went on behind closed doors in the fight for Sepp Blatter's continued control of FIFA. Nearly simultaneous with the release of *Foul* was a BBC television expose by Jennings and BBC producer Roger Corke for the BBC news programme *Panorama*. In this hour-long programme screened on June 11, 2006, Jennings and the *Panorama* team submit that Sepp Blatter is being investigated by Swiss police over his role in a secret deal to repay more than £1m worth of bribes pocketed by football officials.

All testimonies offered in the Panorama expose were provided through a disguised voice, appearance, or both, save one; Mel Brennan, formerly a lecturer at Towson University in the United States (and from 2001-2003 Head of Special Projects for CONCACAF, a liaison to the e-FIFA project and a FIFA World Cup delegate), became the first high-level football insider to go public with substantial allegations of greed, corruption, nonfeasance and malfeasance by CONCACAF and FIFA leadership. During the Panorama expose, Jennings, Brennan and many others exposed allegedly inappropriate allocations of money at CONCACAF, and drew connections between ostensible CONCACAF criminality and similar behaviours at FIFA. Brennan's book, *The Apprentice: Tragicomic Times Among the Men Running—and Ruining—World Football* is due out in late 2008 or early 2009.

FIFA Anthem

Since the 1994 FIFA World Cup like the UEFA Champions League FIFA has adopted an anthem composed by the German composer Franz Lambert. The FIFA Anthem or Hymn is played at the beginning of FIFA structured matches and tournaments such as international friendlies, the FIFA World Cup, FIFA Women's World Cup, and FIFA U-20 World Cup.

4.2 FIFA Confederations Cup

The FIFA Confederations Cup is an association football tournament for national teams, currently held every four years by FIFA. It is contested by the winners of each of the six FIFA confederation championships (CAF, CONMEBOL, UEFA, AFC, OFC, CONCACAF), along with the FIFA World Cup winner and the host country, to bring the number of teams up to eight.

History and Details

When the World champion is also winner of its confederation championship, then the World Cup runner-up also enters the Confederations Cup, ensuring eight teams for the tournament. In the 2005 tournament, however, Brazil, as World champion, and World Cup runner-up Germany, as host, had qualified. When Brazil also won the Copa América, the vacant eighth spot was awarded to Argentina, runner-up in the Copa América.

On three previous occasions teams have declined to participate in the tournament. The UEFA Euro 1996 winner Germany declined to participate in the 1997 FIFA Confederations Cup, and was replaced by the Czech Republic, the runner-up in that tournament. France, 1998 FIFA World Cup winner, declined to participate in the 1999 FIFA Confederations Cup, and was replaced by Brazil, the 1998 World Cup runner-up (and also 1997 Copa America champion). Germany, the runner-up in the 2002 FIFA World Cup, declined to take part in the 2003 FIFA Confederations Cup, and was replaced by Turkey, the third-placed team in the 2002 FIFA World Cup. The first forerunner of the Confederations Cup was the Mundialito, or Copa D'Oro. The Artemio Franchi Trophy, contested in 1985 and 1993 between the winners of the Copa America and European Football Championships, is considered a precursor to the Confederations Cup and was effectively replaced by the tournament in the same way that the Intercontinental Cup club tournament preceded the FIFA Club World Cup.

The tournament was originally organised by and held in Saudi Arabia and called the King Fahd Cup (or Intercontinental Championship), contested in 1992 and 1995 by the Saudi national side and some continental champions. In 1997, FIFA took over the organization of the tournament, named it the *FIFA Confederations Cup* and staged the competition every two years.

From 2005, the Confederations Cup is to be held once in every four years, one year prior to each World Cup in the host country of the forthcoming World Cup. It is now considered a dress-rehearsal for the World Cup it precedes; it uses around half of the stadia intended for use at the following year's World Cup and gives the host nation, who qualify for that tournament automatically, a vital taste of competitive football during two years of friendlies. For the next edition of the tournament, host nation South Africa, Italy (2006 FIFA World Cup winner), Spain (UEFA Euro 2008 winner), the USA (2007 CONCACAF Gold Cup winner), Brazil (Copa América 2007 winner), Iraq (2007 AFC Asian Cup winner) and Egypt (2008 African Cup of Nations winner) have already qualified. Starting with this tournament, however, the South American and European champions will continue to be invited, but will no longer be obliged to take part. It is unclear how the tournament will change should those nations elect not to participate.

Results

Summaries

Year	Host	Final		Third Place Match			
		Winner	Score	Runner-up	3rd Place	Score	4th Place
1992	Saudi Ar.	Argentina	3-1	Saudi Ar.	USA	5-2	Côte d'Ivoire
1995	Saudi Ar.	Denmark	2-0	Argentina	Mexico	1-1 5-4 pens)	Nigeria
1997	Saudi Ar.	Brazil	6-0	Australia	Czech Republic	1-0	Uruguay
1999	Mexico	Mexico	4-3	Brazil	USA	2-0	Saudi Arabia
2001	S. Korea Japan	France	1-0	Japan	Australia	1-0	Brazil
2003	France	France	1-0 gold	Cameroon	Turkey	2-1	Colombia
2005 2009 2013	Germany S. Africa Brazil	Brazil	4-1	Argentina	Germany	4-3 aet	Mexico

NOTE: The 1992 and 1995 tournaments were named the King Fahd Cup. FIFA recognizes them officially as Confederations Cups now.

Successful National Teams

Team	Titles	Runners-up	Third Place
Brazil	2 (1997, 2005)	1 (1999)	—
France	2 (2001, 2003*)	—	—
Argentina	1 (1992)	2 (1995, 2005)	—
Mexico	1 (1999*)	—	1 (1995)
Denmark	1 (1995)	—	—
Australia	—	1 (1997)	1 (2001)
Saudi Arabia	—	1 (1992*)	—
Japan	—	1 (2001*)	—
Cameroon	—	1 (2003)	—
USA	—	—	2 (1992), (1999)
Czech Republic	—	—	1 (1997)
Turkey	—	—	1 (2003)
Germany	—	—	1 (2005)

* = *hosts*

Broadcasting Rights

United Kingdom: Live coverage of selected matches has been shown on terrestrial channel Five, formerly known as Channel 5. Delayed coverage is usually shared between Five and satellite/cable network British Eurosport. Seen as a lower key event, the Confederations Cup has never been shown on main BBC and ITV channels. The rights are generally bought up quietly, around six months before the main event for much less money than the FIFA World Cup.

In *Italy RAI* must, by law, broadcast the *Azzurri* matches, therefore the state broadcaster is very likely to buy part of the rights (if not all of them, since they are cheaper than the World Cup ones) for the Confederations Cup when Italy participates. In the past, the 2003 edition was broadcasted by a syndication of local televisions, the 2005 edition instead, by SKY.

Australia: In the past, Australia frequently qualified for the tournament as champions of Oceania. This meant the tournament was considered quite significant for Australian soccer, and the vast majority of games were shown live on SBS, a public Free-to-air network. Now that Australia has entered the Asian Football Confederation, qualification for this tournament, and therefore transmission of the Cup on Australian television, will be less likely.

Top Scorers

Year	Player	Goals
1992	Gabriel Batistuta	
	Bruce Murray	2
1995	Luis García	3
1997	Romário	7
	Ronaldinho	
1999	Cuauhtémoc Blanco	6
	Marzouq Al-Otaibi	
	Eric Carrière	
	Robert Pirès	
	Patrick Vieira	
2001	Sylvain Wiltord	2
	Shaun Murphy	
	Takayuki Suzuki	
	Hwang Sun-Hong	
2003	Thierry Henry	4
2005	Adriano	5

Overall TopScorers

Player	Country	Goals
Cuauhtémoc Blanco	MEX	9
Ronaldinho	BRA	9
Romário	BRA	7
Adriano	BRA	7
Marzouq Al-Otaibi	KSA	6
Alex	BRA	5
John Aloisi	AUS	5
Vladimír Šmicer	CZE	5
Robert Pirès	FRA	5

Summary

Participations Details

Team	1992	1995	1997	1999	2001	2003	2005	2009	Total
Brazil	—	—	W	F	4°	1R	W	Q	6
Mexico	—	3°	1R	W	1R	—	4°	—	5
Saudi Arabia	F	1R	1R	4°	—	—	—	—	4
Japan	—	1R	—	—	F	1R	1R	—	4
USA	3°	—	—	3°	—	1R	—	Q	4
Argentina	W	F	—	—	—	—	F	—	3

(Contd.)

(*Contd.*)

Team	1992	1995	1997	1999	2001	2003	2005	2009	Total
Australia	—	—	F	—	3°	—	1R	—	3
Cameroon	—	—	—	—	1R	F	—	—	2
France	—	—	—	—	W	W	—	—	2
Germany	—	—	—	1R	—	—	3°	—	2
New Zealand	—	—	—	1R	—	1R	—	Q	2
Egypt	—	—	—	1R	—	—	—	Q	2
South Africa	—	—	1R	—	—	—	—	Q	2
Bolivia	—	—	—	1R	—	—	—	—	1
Canada	—	—	—	—	1R	—	—	—	1
Colombia	—	—	—	—	—	4°	—	—	1
Korea Republic	—	—	—	—	1R	—	—	—	1
Côte d'Ivoire	4°	—	—	—	—	—	—	—	1
Denmark	—	W	—	—	—	—	—	—	1
United Arab Emirates	—	—	1R	—	—	—	—	—	1
Greece	—	—	—	—	—	—	1R	—	1
Italy	—	—	—	—	—	—	—	Q	1
Nigeria	—	4°	—	—	—	—	—	—	1
Czech Republic	—	—	3°	—	—	—	—	—	1
Tunisia	—	—	—	—	—	—	1R	—	1
Turkey	—	—	—	—	—	3°	—	—	1
Uruguay	—	—	4°	—	—	—	—	—	1
Iraq	—	—	—	—	—	—	—	Q	1
Spain	—	—	—	—	—	—	—	Q	1

Note: **1R**: eliminated in the First Round, **F**: Finalist, **W**: Champion, **Q**: Qualified.

General Statistics

	Team	W	D	L	GF	GC	Dif	Pts	Per cent
1.	France	10	9	0	1	24	5	+19	27	90,0
2.	Denmark	3	2	1	0	5	1	+4	7	77,7
3.	Korea Republic	3	2	0	1	3	6	-3	6	66,6
4.	Brazil	23	13	5	5	50	20	+30	44	63,7
5.	Argentina	10	5	3	2	22	14	+18	18	60,0
6.	Uruguay	5	3	0	2	8	6	+2	9	60,0
7.	Nigeria	3	1	2	0	4	1	+3	5	55,5
8.	Germany	8	4	1	3	17	17	0	13	54,1
9.	Cameroon	8	4	1	3	5	5	0	13	54,1
10.	Mexico	19	8	5	6	33	28	+5	29	50,8
11.	Czech Republic	5	2	1	2	10	7	+3	7	46,6
12.	Turkey	5	2	1	2	8	8	0	7	46,6
13.	Japan	13	5	2	6	15	16	-1	17	43,5

(*Contd.*)

(*Contd.*)

	Team	W	D	L	GF	GC	Dif	Pts	Per cent
14.	USA	10	4	1	5	12	11	+1	13	43,3
15.	Australia	13	5	1	7	13	20	-7	16	41,0
16.	Colombia	5	2	0	3	5	5	0	6	40,0
17.	Tunisia	3	1	0	2	3	5	-2	3	33,3
18.	UAE	3	1	0	2	2	8	-6	3	33,3
19.	Saudi Arabia	12	3	1	8	13	31	-18	10	27,7
20.	Bolivia	3	0	2	1	2	3	-1	2	22,2
21.	Egypt	3	0	2	1	5	9	-4	2	22,2
22.	South Africa	3	0	1	2	5	7	-2	1	11,1
23.	Greece	3	0	1	2	0	4	-4	1	11,1
24.	Canada	3	0	1	2	0	5	-5	1	11,1
25.	Côte d'Ivoire	2	0	0	2	2	9	-7	0	0,0
26.	New Zealand	6	0	0	6	2	17	-15	0	0,0

4.4 FIFA U-20 World Cup

The FIFA U-20 World Cup, until 2005 known as the FIFA World Youth Championship, is the world championship of Association football for male players under the age of 20 and is organized by *Fédération Internationale de Football Association* (FIFA). The Championship has been awarded every two years since the first tournament in 1977. In the fifteen tournaments held, only seven nations have won the title. Argentina is the most successful team with six titles, followed by Brazil with four titles. Portugal won two titles, while Germany, Spain, and formerly existing nations Soviet Union and Yugoslavia have won the title once each. A corresponding event for women's teams, the FIFA U-20 Women's World Cup, began in 2002 with the name "FIFA U-19 Women's World Championship" and an age limit of 19. The age limit for the women's competition was changed to 20 beginning with the 2006 FIFA U-20 Women's World Championship, and the competition was renamed as a "World Cup" in 2007 in preparation for the 2008 event. The men's 2007 tournament was played in . The 2009 tournament will be played in Egypt. The 2011 tournament will be played in Colombia

Qualification

This competition, which was also known as the *FIFA Coca-Cola Cup* until 1997, features 24 teams in the final tournament. 23 countries, including the defending champions, have to qualify in the six confederations Youth Championships. The host country automatically qualifies.

Confederation	Championship
AFC (Asia)	AFC Youth Championship
CAF (Africa)	African Youth Championship
CONCACAF (North, Central America and Caribbean)	CONCACAF Under-20 Championship
CONMEBOL (South America)	South American Youth Championship
OFC (Oceania)	OFC Under 20 Qualifying Tournament
UEFA (Europe)	UEFA European Under-19 Football Championship

Results

Summaries

Year	Host	Final			Third Place Match		
		Champion	Score	2nd Place	3rd Place	Score	4th Place
1977	Tunisia	USSR	2-2 a.e.t. (9-8 p.k.)	Mexico	Brazil	4-0	Uruguay
1979	Japan	Argentina	3-1	USSR	Uruguay	1-1 a.e.t. (5-3 p.k.)	Poland
1981	Australia	West Germany	4-0	Qatar	Romania	1-0	England
1983	Mexico	Brazil	1-0	Argentina	Poland	2-1 a.e.t.	Korea Republic
1985	Soviet Union	Brazil	1-0 a.e.t.	Spain	Nigeria	0-0 a.e.t. (3-1 p.k.)	USSR
1987	Chile	Yugoslavia	1-1 a.e.t. (5-4 p.k.)	West Germany	East Germany	2-2 a.e.t. (3-1 p.k.)	Chile
1989	Saudi Arabia	Portugal	2-0	Nigeria	Brazil	2-0	USA
1991	Portugal	Portugal	0-0 a.e.t. (4-2 p.k.)	Brazil	USSR	1-1 a.e.t. (5-4 p.k.)	Australia
1993	Australia	Brazil	2-1	Ghana	England	2-1	Australia
1995	Qatar	Argentina	2-0	Brazil	Portugal	3-2	Spain
1997	Malaysia	Argentina	2-1	Uruguay	Rep. Ireland	2-1	Ghana
1999	Nigeria	Spain	4-0	Japan	Mali	1-0	Uruguay
2001	Argentina	Argentina	3-0	Ghana	Egypt	1-0	Paraguay
2003	United Arab Emirates	Brazil	1-0	Spain	Colombia	2-1	Argentina
2005	Netherlands	Argentina	2-1	Nigeria	Brazil	2-1	Morocco
2007	Canada	Argentina	2-1	Czech Republic	Chile	1-0	Austria
2009	Egypt						
2011	Colombia						

Key: *a.e.t.—after extra time p.k.—match won on penalty kicks.*

Performances by Countries

Below are the 14 nations that have reached the final in the U-20 World Cup finals. Argentina is the most successful nation, leading with six titles and seven appearances in the final.

Team	Titles	Runners-up
Argentina	6 (1979, 1995, 1997, 20011, 2005, 2007)	1 (1983)
Brazil	4 (1983, 1985, 1993, 2003)	2 (1991, 1995)
Portugal	2 (1989, 19911)	
Spain	1 (1999)	2 (1985, 2003)
USSR	1 (1977)	1 (1979)
Germany	1 (19812)	1 (1987)
Yugoslavia	1 (1987)	
Nigeria		2 (1989, 2005)
Ghana		2 (1993, 2001)
Uruguay		1 (1997)
Czech Republic		1 (2007)
Japan		1 (1999)
Mexico		1 (1977)
Qatar		1 (1981)

Note: 1 = host 2 = as West Germany

Performances by Continental Zones

All continents except Oceania had made the appearance in the final match of the tournament. To date, South America leads with ten titles following by Europe with six titles. Africa, Asia, and North America entered the final match seven times, but were disappointed by either one of the two traditional football power continents. Fourth place remains as the best result ever for Oceania, which was achieved in 1993.

Confederation (continent)	Performances
CONMEBOL (South America)	10 titles, won by Argentina (6) and Brazil (4)
UEFA (Europe)	6 titles, won by Portugal (2), Spain (1), USSR (1), Germany (1) and Yugoslavia (1)
CAF (Africa)	Runners-up (Nigeria, 1989 and 2005; Ghana, 1993 and 2001)
AFC (Asia)	Runners-up (Japan, 1999), Runners-up (Qatar, 1981)
CONCACAF (North, Central America and Caribbean)	Runners-up (Mexico, 1977)
OFC (Oceania)	Fourth-place (Australia, 1991 and 1993)

Topscorers

Tournament	Golden Shoe Award	Goals
1977 Tunisia	Guina	4
1979 Japan	Ramón Díaz	8
1981 Australia	Ralf Loose Roland Wohlfarth Taher Amer Mark Koussas	4
1983 Mexico	Geovani	6
1985 Soviet Union	Gérson Balalo Muller Sebastián Losada Fernando Gómez Monday Odiaka Alberto García Aspe	3
1987 Chile	Marcel Witeczek	7
1989 Saudi Arabia	Oleg Salenko	5
1991 Portugal	Sergei Sherbakov	5
1993 Australia	Gian Adriano Ante Milicic Vicente Nieto Chris Faklaris Henry Zambrano	3
1995 Qatar	Joseba Etxeberria	7
1997 Malaysia	Adaílton Martins Bolzan	10
1999 Nigeria	Pablo Mahamadou Dissa	5
2001 Argentina	Javier Saviola	11
2003 United Arab Emirates	Dudu Fernando Cavenaghi Eddie Johnson Daisuke Sakata	4
2005 Netherlands	Lionel Messi	6
2007 Canada	Sergio Agüero	6

Awards

Golden Shoe

The *adidas Golden Shoe* is awarded to the topscorer of the tournament. If more than one players are equal by same goals, the players will be selected based by the most assists during the tournament.

Tournament	Golden Shoe Award	Goals
1977 Tunisia	Guina	4
1979 Japan	Ramón Díaz	8
1981 Australia	Mark Koussas	4
1983 Mexico	Geovani	6
1985 Soviet Union	Sebastián Losada	3
1987 Chile	Marcel Witeczek	7
1989 Saudi Arabia	Oleg Salenko	5
1991 Portugal	Sergei Sherbakov	5
1993 Australia	Henry Zambrano	3
1995 Qatar	Joseba Etxeberria	7
1997 Malaysia	Adaílton Martins Bolzan	10
1999 Nigeria	Pablo Couñago	5
2001 Argentina	Javier Saviola	11
2003 United Arab Emirates	Eddie Johnson	4
2005 Netherlands	Lionel Messi	6
2007 Canada	Sergio Agüero	6

Golden Ball

The *adidas* Golden Ball award is awarded to the player who plays the most outstanding football during the tournament. It is selected by the media poll.

Tournament	Golden Ball Winner
1977 Tunisia	Volodymyr Bessonov
1979 Japan	Diego Maradona
1981 Australia	Romulus Gabor
1983 Mexico	Geovani
1985 USSR	Paulo Silas
1987 Chile	Robert Prosinečki
1989 Saudi Arabia	Bismarck
1991 Portugal	Emílio Peixe
1993 Australia	Adriano
1995 Qatar	Caio
1997 Malaysia	Andrés Nicolás Olivera
1999 Nigeria	Seydou Keita
2001 Argentina	Javier Saviola
2003 United Arab Emirates	Ismail Matar
2005 Netherlands	Lionel Messi
2007 Canada	Sergio Agüero

FIFA Fair Play Award

FIFA *Fair Play Award* is given to the team who has the best fair play record during the tournament with the criteria set by FIFA Fair Play Committee.

Tournament	FIFA Fair Play Award
1977 Tunisia	Brazil
1979 Japan	Poland
1981 Australia	Australia
1983 Mexico	Korea Republic
1985 USSR	Colombia
1987 Chile	West Germany
1989 Saudi Arabia	USA
1991 Portugal	USSR
1993 Australia	England
1995 Qatar	Japan
1997 Malaysia	Argentina
1999 Nigeria	Croatia
2001 Argentina	Argentina
2003 United Arab Emirates	Colombia
2005 Netherlands	Colombia
2007 Canada	Japan

4.5 FIFA U-17 World Cup

The FIFA U-17 World Cup, originally founded as the FIFA U-16 World Championship, later changed to the FIFA U-17 World Championship and known by its current name since 2007, is the world championship of association football for male players under the age of 17 organized by Fédération Internationale de Football Association (FIFA). The first edition was staged in 1985 and tournaments have been played every two years since then. It began as a competition for players under the age of 16 with the age limit raised to 17 from the 1991 edition onwards. The most recent tournament was hosted by South Korea and was won by Nigeria. It has been announced that future editions will be played in Nigeria in 2009 and in Mexico in 2011. Brazil and Nigeria are the most successful nations in the tournament's history, with three wins each. Ghana has won the tournament twice.

A corresponding tournament for female players, the FIFA U-17 Women's World Cup, will begin in 2008.

Structure

Each tournament consists of a group phase, where four teams play against one another and standings in the group table decide which teams advance, followed by a knockout phase of successive matches where the winning team advances through the competition and the losing team is eliminated. This continues until two teams remain to contest the final, which decides the tournament winner. The losing semi-finalists also contest a match to decide third place. From 1985 to 2005 there were 16 teams in the competition, divided into four groups of four teams each in the group phase. Each team played the others in its group and the group winner and runner up qualified for the knockout phase. From 2007 the tournament was expanded to 24 teams, divided into six groups of four teams each. The top 2 places in each group plus the four best third-placed teams advanced to the knockout phase. Competition matches are played in two 40 minute halves (ie 80 minutes in total). In the knockout phase, if the scores are level at the end of 80 minutes an additional 20 minutes of extra time is played. If the scores are still level at the end of extra time, a penalty shoot-out is used to decide the match winner.

Qualification

The host nation of each tournament qualifies automatically. The remaining teams qualify through competitions organised by the six regional confederations. For the first edition of the tournament in 1985, all of the teams from Europe plus Bolivia appeared by invitation of FIFA.

Confederation	Championship
AFC (Asia)	AFC U-17 Championship
CAF (Africa)	African Under-17 Championship
CONCACAF (North, Central America and Caribbean)	CONCACAF Under-17 Championship
CONMEBOL (South America)	South American Under 17 Football Championship
OFC (Oceania)	OFC Under 17 Qualifying Tournament
UEFA (Europe)	UEFA European Under-17 Football Championship

Results

Summaries

Year	Host	Final			Third Place Match		
		Champion	Score	2nd Place	3rd Place	Score	4th Place
1985	China	Nigeria	2-0	West Germany	Brazil	4-1	Guinea
1987	Canada	USSR	1-1 a.e.t. (4-2 p.k.)	Nigeria	Côte d'Ivoire	2-1 a.e.t.	Italy
1989	Scotland	Saudi Arabia	2-2 a.e.t. (5-4 p.k.)	Scotland	Portugal	3-0	Bahrain
1991	Italy	Ghana	1-0	Spain	Argentina	1-1 a.e.t. (4-1 p.k.)	Qatar
1993	Japan	Nigeria	2-1	Ghana	Chile	1-1 a.e.t. (4-2 p.k.)	Poland
1995	Ecuador	Ghana	3-2	Brazil	Argentina	2-0	Oman
1997	Egypt	Brazil	2-1	Ghana	Spain	2-1	Germany
1999	New Zealand	Brazil	0-0 a.e.t. (8-7 p.k.)	Australia	Ghana	2-0	USA
2001	Trinidad & Tobago	France	3-0	Nigeria	Burkina Faso	2-0	Argentina
2003	Finland	Brazil	1-0	Spain	Argentina	1-1 a.e.t. (5-4 p.k.)	Colombia
2005	Peru	Mexico	3-0	Brazil	Netherlands	2-1	Turkey
2007	South Korea	Nigeria	0-0 a.e.t. (3-0 p.k.)	Spain	Germany	2-1	Ghana
2009	Nigeria						
2011	Mexico						

Key: aet—after extra time; pk—match won on penalty kicks

Performances by Countries

Team	Titles	Runners-up	Third-place	Fourth-place
Brazil	3 (1997, 1999, 2003)	2 (1995, 2005)	1 (1985)	
Nigeria	3 (1985, 1993, 2007)	2 (1987, 2001)		
Ghana	2 (1991, 1995)	2 (1993, 1997)	1 (1999)	1 (2007)
France	1 (2001)			
Mexico	1 (2005)			
USSR	1 (1987)			
Saudi Arabia	1 (1989)			

Performances by Continental Zones

Africa is the most successful continental zone with 5 tournament wins (3 for Nigeria, 2 for Ghana) and 4 times as runner up. Notably the 1993 final was contested by two African teams, the only occasion when the final has been contested by two teams from the same confederation. South America has 3 tournament wins and has been runner up twice (all Brazil). Additionally Argentina has finished in third place on 3 occasions but has never appeared in the final. Europe has 2 tournaments wins (1 each for France and USSR) and has been runner up 5 times. Spain has been runner up on 3 occasions. The CONCACAF zone has 1 tournament win (for Mexico in 2005), the only time that a team from this confederation has reached the final.

Asia has 1 tournament win (for Saudi Arabia in 1989), the only time that a team from this confederation has reached the final. (*Australia was runner up in 1999 but at that time was in the Oceania Football Confederation*). Oceania has no tournament wins and 1 occasion as runner up (for Australia in 1999). Australia has since moved to the Asian confederation.

Awards

At every tournament three awards are presented:

- ❖ The Golden Shoe is awarded to the top goalscorer of tournament.
- ❖ The Golden Ball is awarded to the most valuable player of the tournament.
- ❖ The Fair Play Award is presented to the team with the best disciplinary record in the tournament.

Records and Statistics

The United States has appeared in all 12 editions of the competition (1985-2007) and is the only country to do so, Brazil has appeared 11 times and Australia 10 times. Brazil and Nigeria have each appeared in the final on 5 occasions and have each won the tournament 3 times.

France's Florent Sinama-Pongolle holds the record for the most goals scored by a player in a single tournament, scoring 9 goals in the

2001 edition. Spain hold the record for most goals scored by a team in a single tornament with 22 goals in the 1997 tournament.

Tournament	Golden Shoe Award	Goals	Golden Ball	Fair Play Award
1985 China	Marcel Witeczek	8	William	West Germany
1987 Canada	Moussa Traoré	5	Philip Osundu Moussa Traoré	USSR
1989 Scotland	Fode Camara	3	James Will	Bahrain
1991 Italy	Adriano	4	Nii Lamptey	Argentina
1993 Japan	Wilson Oruma	6	Daniel Addo	Nigeria
1995 Ecuador	Daniel Allsopp	5	Mohamed Kathiri	Brazil
1997 Egypt	David	7	Santamaría	Argentina
1999 New Zealand	Ishmael Addo	7	Landon Donovan	Mexico
2001 Trinidad and Tobago	Florent Sinama-Pongolle	9	Florent Sinama-Pongolle	Nigeria
2003 Finland	Cesc Fàbregas	5	Cesc Fàbregas	Costa Rica
2005 Peru	Carlos Vela	5	Anderson	Korea DPR
2007 South Korea	Macauley Chrisantus	7	Toni Kroos	Costa Rica

5

Regional Sports and Related Tourism Activities: Select Case Study

5.1 European Football Tours and Tournaments

Whilst on tour you can choose to play friendly football matches, participate at an International football tournament or have training sessions with a famous Training Academy—on some tours you do everything! We have some wonderful holiday centres with every imaginable facility and hotels in well known holiday resorts making your stay as enjoyable as possible. If you are travelling by coach, we will collect you from your home town and take you directly to your chosen resort. If you are travelling by air, we'll be happy to make your flight arrangements and we'll meet you on arrival and take you directly to your chosen resort. With Sports Tours, you'll be sure that we'll be with you all the way. Your team can gain so much experience by playing football against teams from different Countries. Each year, we hear of 1000's football tournaments taking place throughout UK, Europe & USA. With our extensive UEFA Licensed Match Agents, we can organise friendly football matches in just about any country throughout the World. Please follow the link for further details on our friendlies and international tournaments.

Two European fixture arrangements (per group), which can consist of friendly matches or entry into an International Football Tournament are included in the tour cost. Should you require additional fixtures these can be provided for a small fee, which covers the arrangement fees made by UEFA Licensed Match Agents, additional pitch hire costs (where applicable), referees and other associated costs. If you are travelling to Spain or Italy by air, then additional match transfer costs could be applicable—please call us to discuss your arrangements.

Velling By Air

If you are travelling by air, you must book early to receive the lowest prices. We can arrange for your club to fly from your nearest airport to most of our destinations. On arrival at your destination airport, we will meet you and transfer you to your chosen resort. During your stay, we will provide coach transport to your fixtures and pre arranged excursions. Travelling by coach is the most cost-effective, flexible and convenient way to travel into Europe. We will collect you from your club HQ and take you directly to your chosen resort. Our Club Class Executive coaches have a WC Washroom, reclining seats with a spacious 24" seat pitch, TV/Video/CD/PA entertainments system, Air Conditioning, leg supports, Double glazed and non smoking. Whilst on tour, they will be available to take you to your games and local pre-arranged excursions and places of interest.

We are able to arrange for your club to be coached by famous clubs. A typical itinerary would include:

Day 1: Arrive at resort.
Day 2: *Morning*—2 hour training session including sports lunch.
        Afternoon—Stadium tour of Ajax, Barcelona or Milan.
Day 3: *Morning*—2 hour training session including sports lunch.
        Afternoon—Excursion to the cities of Amsterdam, Barcelona or Milan. *Evening*—Local friendly match.
Day 4: Depart.

Free Places On All European Soccer Tours

Free places are available on all of our European tours depending on the number of people you have travelling and when you pay the deposits. If you were to pay your deposits before 30th November, we will provide you with additional free places. The more people who travel, the more free places you will receive.

5.2 ASEAN Para Games

The ASEAN Para Games is a biannual multi-sport event held after every Southeast Asian Games for athletes with physical disabilities. The games are participated by the 11 countries located in Southeast Asia. The games, patterned after the Para-Olympics, includes mobility disabilities, amputees, visual disabilities and those with cerebral palsy.

The ASEAN Para Games is under the regulation of the ASEAN Para Sports Federation (APSF). The games are hosted by the same country where the SEA Games took place.

History

The 1st ASEAN Para Games, held in Kuala Lumpur, Malaysia on October 25, 2001 to October 30, 2001, was the initial major sports event of the ASEAN Para Sports Federation (APSF). The APSF was conceived in the special meeting of the National Para-Olympic Committees of the ASEAN countries during the 10th Malaysian Paralympiad and the ASEAN Cities Invitational. The ASEAN Para Games, the "parallel" sports event for the disabled after every Southeast Asian Games, was patterned after the Para-Olympics and the FESPIC Games. The 2nd ASEAN Para games was held in Hanoi, Vietnam from December 19, 2003 to December 27, 2003. Timor Leste was formally included in the Games increasing its member countries to eleven. The 3rd ASEAN Para Games was held in Manila, Philippines from December 14, 2005 to December 20, 2005. The 4th ASEAN Para Games was held in Nakhon Ratchasima, Thailand from January, January 20, 2008 to January 26, 2008. The 5th ASEAN Para Games will held in Laos in 2009.

Logo

The design shows the Asean logo positioned with the symbol and image of Para-Olympic and a victory laurel. The design intends to show the emergence of togetherness of Para-Olympic Sports Leaders with One Vision, One Mission and a commitment in the pursuit of equality in sports and in life for persons with a disability in the ASEAN region.

Asean solidarity, working together through APSF with an

unbreakable bond in unity and brotherhood shall display the will and determination to achieve success in sports and in life. The victory laurel signifies this commitment to exccellence.

From this regional image, a sense of cooperation, pride and eternal harmony is unmasked and it is an image that connects us all together in "Mind, Body, Spirit" as in the ideals of the Para-Olympic Movement.

Table 5.1: Participant Countries.

Code	Nation/IOC designation	First use	ISO-code	Notes
BRU	**BRUNEI** (IOC designation: Brunei Darussalam)	1988	BRN	—
CAM	CAMBODIA	1956	KHM	—
INA	INDONESIA	1956	IDN	IHO 1952 FIFA-code IDN
LAO	LAOS (IOC designation: Lao People's Democratic Republic)	1980	LAO	—
MAS	MALAYSIA	1956	MYS	—
MYA	MYANMAR	1996	MMR	BIR 1948-1992
PHI	PHILIPPINES	1924	PHL	—
SIN	SINGAPORE	1948	SGP	—
THA	THAILAND	1952	THA	—
TLS	TIMOR-LESTE	2004	TLS	IOA 2000
VIE	VIETNAM (IOC designation: Viet Nam)	1952	VNM	—

Host Cities of the ASEAN Para Games

1. ASEAN Para Games, Kuala Lumpur, Malaysia, 2001
2. ASEAN Para Games, Hanoi, Vietnam, 2003
3. SEAN Para Games, Manila, Philippines, 2005
4. ASEAN Para Games, Nakhon Ratchasima, Thailand, 2007

Objectives

❖ To promote friendship and solidarity among persons with disabilities in the ASEAN region through sports;
❖ To promote and develop sports for the differently abled;
❖ To rehabilitate and integrate persons with disability into mainstream society through sports.

2005 ASEAN Para Games (3rd ASEAN Para Games)

1.	Nations participating	:	11
2.	Events	:	527 in 10 sports
3.	Opening ceremony	:	December 14, 2005
4.	Closing ceremony	:	December 20, 2005
5.	Officially opened by	:	Jose "Lito" Atienza, Jr. Mayor of Manila
6.	Ceremony venue	:	Fort Santiago, Intramuros

The 3rd ASEAN Para Games was a biannual multi-sport event held after the 2005 Southeast Asian Games for athletes with physical disabilities. It was held in Manila, Philippines from December 14, 2005 to December 20, 2005. Participants came from 11 countries in Southeast Asia. The games, patterned after the Para-Olympics, included athletes with mobility disabilities, amputees, visual disabilities and those with cerebral palsy. The awards and closing ceremonies were held in the walled city of Intramuros, Manila.

Athletes in the said event participated in the 9th FESPIC Games, in Kuala Lumpur 2006.

Medal Tally

Rank	Country	Gold	Silver	Bronze	Total
1.	Thailand	139	64	28	231
2.	Vietnam	80	36	22	138
3.	Malaysia	75	40	26	141
4.	Indonesia	30	26	20	76
5.	Myanmar	29	12	4	45
6.	Philippines	19	39	37	95
7.	Singapore	15	9	9	33
8.	Brunei Darussalam	7	5	5	17
9.	Cambodia	0	3	2	5
10.	Laos	0	2	1	3
11.	Timor Leste	0	0	0	0
	Total	394	236	154	784

Logo, Theme Song and Mascot

Buboy Butanding (Buboy the Whale Shark), Official Mascot of the

3rd ASEAN Para Games. The logo was inspired by previous Para-Olympic Games logos and the 1992 Summer Olympics logo. The four colors represent the four primary colors of the Philippine flag. The three stars symbolize the three main geographical regions of the Philippines as well as the three objectives of the games. The upward position of the arm symbolizes the aspiration for equality and regional unity. The games' theme song was *Power Of My Dream* sung by Broadway actress and Tony Award winner Lea Salonga. The mascot is *Buboy Butanding*, a whale shark, the largest fish in the world, which can be seen in the waters off the eastern coast of the province of Sorsogon.

Sports

1. Athletics (280 events)
2. Badminton
3. Chess
4. Goalball
5. Judo
6. Powerlifting
7. Swimming (247 events)
8. Table tennis
9. Wheelchair basketball
10. Wheelchair tennis

Demonstration Sports

Among the various sports recently introduced during the just concluded 3rd ASEAN Para Games (2005) in Manila, was sailing, using the disability-friendly Access 2.3 Dinghys. This sport is open to those with mobility disabilities, amputees, visual disabilities and those with cerebral palsy as detailed by the International Association For Disabled Sailing rules. The sailing demo introduced the ease of dinghy sailing to disabled guests, as coached by disabled sailors from Malaysia, Singapore and host country Philippines. The subsequent 4-part triangle course race between said representatives from the 3 countries, was also held near Baywalk, Roxas Boulevard and the Manila Yacht Club. Two Access 2.3 dinghys were donated by Sailability Singapore to the Philippine Sailing Association to encourage people with any type of disability, the elderly, the financially and socially disadvantaged to start sailing in the Philippines.

- ❖ Boccia
- ❖ Wheelchair Fencing
- ❖ Sailing
- ❖ Tenpin Bowling

Venues

- ❖ Emilio Aguinaldo College Gymnasium—Powerlifting, Wheelchair Basketball
- ❖ GSIS Hall—Chess
- ❖ Ninoy Aquino Gym—Table tennis
- ❖ PSC Badminton Hall—Badminton
- ❖ Rizal Memorial Coliseum—Judo
- ❖ Rizal Memorial Stadium—Athletics
- ❖ Rizal Memorial Swimming Pool—Swimming
- ❖ Rizal Memorial Tennis Court—Wheelchair Tennis
- ❖ San Andres Gym—Goalball
- ❖ Baywalk, Roxas Blvd, beside the Manila Yacht Club—Sailing demo
- ❖ Participating Countries
- ❖ Brunei
- ❖ Cambodia
- ❖ Indonesia
- ❖ Laos
- ❖ Malaysia
- ❖ Myanmar
- ❖ Philippines
- ❖ Singapore
- ❖ Thailand
- ❖ Timor-Leste
- ❖ Vietnam

2008 ASEAN Para Games

The 4th ASEAN Para Games is a biannual multi-sport event held after every Southeast Asian Games, for athletes with physical disabilities from the Association of Southeast Asian Nations (ASEAN). The games are hosted by the same country where the SEA Games takes place. Nakhon Ratchasima province of Thailand will host the 4th ASEAN Para Games from 20—26 January 2008 under the theme concept: "FRIENDSHIP, EQUALITY, OPPORTUNITY"

4th ASEAN Para Games objectives:

- ❖ Promote friendship and solidarity among persons with disabilities in the Asean Region through sports,
- ❖ Promote and develop sports for the differently abled, and
- ❖ Rehabilitate and integrate persons with disability into mainstream society through sports.

The games, patterned after the Para-Olympics, includes athletes with mobility disabilities, amputees, visual disabilities and those with cerebral palsy. Joining the action are delegations from Southeast Asian countries as well as top ASEAN athletes who've competed in the 9th FESPIC Games, held in Kuala Lumpur 2006. The previous 2005 ASEAN Para Games was held in Manila, Philippines.

In the upcoming 4th ASEAN Para Games, 14 sports will be contested and 186 gold medals will be offered. They include archery, athletics, badminton, boccia, chess, fencing, goalball, judo, powerlifting, shooting, swimming, table tennis, wheelchair basketball and wheelchair tennis. The ASEAN Para Games is subject to the regulations of the ASEAN Para Sports Federation (APSF).

History

The 1st ASEAN Para Games, held in Kuala Lumpur, Malaysia on October 25, 2001 to October 30, 2001, was the initial major sports event of the ASEAN Para Sports Federation (APSF). The APSF was conceived in the special meeting of the National Para-Olympic Committees of the ASEAN countries during the 10th Malaysian Paralympiad and the ASEAN Cities Invitational.

The ASEAN Para Games, the "parallel" sports event for the disabled after every Southeast Asian Games, was patterned after the Para-Olympics and the FESPIC Games. The 2nd ASEAN Para games was held in Hanoi, Vietnam from December 19, 2003 to December

27, 2003. Timor Leste was formally included in the Games increasing its member countries to eleven. The 3rd ASEAN Para Games was held in Manila, Philippines from December 14, 2005 to December 20, 2005. The 4th ASEAN Para Games was held in Nakhon Ratchasima, Thailand from January 20, 2008 to January 26, 2008. The 5th ASEAN Para Games will be held in Laos in January, 2010.

Participating Countries

- ❖ Brunei
- ❖ Cambodia
- ❖ Indonesia
- ❖ Laos
- ❖ Malaysia
- ❖ Myanmar
- ❖ Philippines
- ❖ Singapore
- ❖ Thailand
- ❖ Timor-Leste
- ❖ Vietnam

Emblem and Mascot

The emblem of the ASEAN Para Games is inspired by Chumpol Gate, a historical place in Nakorn Ratchasima, Thailand. Chumpol Gate represents victory. It also denotes the exquisite Thai art and culture. Curvy blue and red lines represent the pageantry of fluttering flags leading eager, excited athletes marching into the stadium. The ASEAN Para Sports Federation logo sits in the center of the emblem, representing friendship and cooperation between participants from ASEAN countries.

Nok-Kao Karom, mascot of the 4th ASEAN Para Games, is a type of dove known locally as *nok khao karom*, recognized as a symbol of Nakhon Ratchasima Province. Karom is wise, cheerful, gentle, and friendly, reflecting the characteristics of Thai people. **K** stands for kind, **A** appreciation, **R** reliable, **O** optimistic, and **M** manners.

- ❖ Sports
- ❖ Archery

❖ Athletics
❖ Badminton
❖ Boccia
❖ Chess
❖ Fencing
❖ Goalball
❖ Judo
❖ Powerlifting
❖ Shooting
❖ Swimming
❖ Table tennis
❖ Wheelchair basketball
❖ Wheelchair tennis

Venues

Opening and Closing Ceremonies

Main Stadium, His Majesty the King's 80th Birthday Anniversary Stadium.

Suranaree University of Technology

1. *Archery*—Football Stadium
2. *Badminton*—Suranareepirom Building
3. *Chess*—Surasammanakan Building
4. *Fencing*—Surapat 3 Building
5. *Shooting*—Shooting Field
6. *Table tennis*—Surapat 2 Building 3rd Floor
7. *Wheelchair basketball*—Keelapirom Building

His Majesty the King's 80th Birthday Anniversary Stadium

1. Athletics—Main Stadium
2. Boccia—Gymnasium
3. Goalball—Gymnasium
4. Swimming—Swimmimg Pool
5. Wheelchair tennis—Tennis Court

Rajamangala of Technology Isan

Judo—Gymnasium

Chanapolkhan Institute of Technology

Powerlifting—Kebkanjana Hall

Medal Tally

Rank	Country	Gold	Silver	Bronze	Total
1.	Thailand	256	109	84	449
2.	Malaysia	81	74	46	201
3.	Vietnam	78	66	43	187
4.	Indonesia	33	25	18	76
5.	Philippines	17	21	21	59
6.	Myanmar	12	11	12	35
7.	Singapore	6	8	5	19
8.	Brunei Darussalam	2	4	10	16
9.	Laos	0	1	3	4
10.	Cambodia	0	1	0	1
11.	Timor Leste	0	0	2	2
	Total	485	320	244	1049

5.3 ASEAN Football Championships

The ASEAN Football Championships (formerly known as Tiger Cup) is a biennial international football competition organised by the ASEAN Football Federation, contested by the national teams of nations in Southeast Asia. Since it was inaugurated in 1996, the cup has been won three times by both Singapore and Thailand. Indonesia has been runner-up three times, but has never won the cup. Malaysia and Vietnam have also been runners-up once each. Singapore-based Asia Pacific Breweries, makers of Tiger Beer, was the sponsor of the competition from its inauguration till 2005, during which the competition was known as the Tiger Cup. The competition was renamed as the ASEAN Football Championship from 2007 as a result of a termination of the sponsorship deal.

Tournaments

1996

The 1996 event was held in Singapore, and was won by the favourites, Thailand, who defeated Malaysia 1-0 in the final.

1998

The 1998 tournament, held in Vietnam. Group A's matches were played in Ho Chi Minh City hosted Indonesia, Thailand, Myanmar, and Philippines. And Group B's matches were played in Hanoi hosted Vietnam, Malaysia, Singapore and Laos.

This tournament was marred by an unsportsmanlike match between Thailand and Indonesia during the group stage of the competition. Both teams were already assured of qualification for the semi-finals, but both teams knew that the winners of the game would face hosts Vietnam in the semi-finals, while the losing team would face Singapore who were perceived to be easier opposition and avoid the fuss of moving training bases from Ho Chi Minh City to Hanoi for the semi-final. The first half saw little action, with both teams barely making an attempt to score. During the second half both teams managed to score, partly thanks to half-hearted defending, resulting in a 2-2 scoreline after 90 minutes.

Then, during injury time, Indonesian defender Mursyid Effendi deliberately kicked the ball into his own goal, despite the Thai's attempts to stop him doing so, thus handing Thailand a 3-2 victory. Both teams were fined for "violating the spirit of the game" and Mursyid Effendi was banned from football for life. In the semi-finals, Thailand lost to Vietnam, and Indonesia also lost to Singapore. In the final, the title was to elude the hosts as they went down 1-0 to unfancied Singapore in one of the competition's biggest shocks to date.

2000

Thailand hosted the Tiger Cup in 2000, and won the tournament as it powered through the competition, ending with a hat-trick by Thai player Worrawoot Srimaka to clinch a decisive 4-1 win over Indonesia. Worrawoot also finished the tournament as a joint top-scorers with Indonesia's Gendut Doni Christiawan with 5 goals each.

2002

In the final match between Thailand and Indonesia, Thailand took a 2-0 lead against hosts Indonesia by the end of the first half. However, the Indonesians battled back to level the score and force the game into a penalty shootout, which was won 4-2 by the Thais.

Therdsak Chaiman was named the Most Valuable Player of this tournament, while Indonesia's Bambang Pamungkas finished as the tournament's top scorer with 8 goals.

2004

The 2004 event was held from 7 December 2004 through 16 January 2005. Matches for Preliminary Group A were held in Vietnam while Preliminary Group B was staged in Malaysia.

The tournament marked the first major football tournament for East Timor after gaining independence in 2000. Despite an unimpressive group stage campaign where Singapore notched draws against Vietnam and Indonesia, the team made it to the final where it clinched a 5-2 win aggregate against Indonesia in the 2-legged match (home and away). In the first leg held in Jakarta, Singapore surprised punters with a 3-1 victory. Singapore won 2-1 on home ground in the return leg 8 days later to claim the country's first international trophy on home soil. In the 3rd-4th place playoff, Malaysia beat Myanmar for the third place.

Lionel Lewis was named the Most Valuable Player of this tournament, while Ilham Jayakesuma of Indonesia won the golden boot with 7 goals in this tournament.

2007

The 2007 Cup was renamed the AFF Football Championship. This was due to the cup's main sponsor, Tiger Beer, not continuing their title sponsorship. This was the last event held at Singapore's National Stadium before its redevelopment. The 2007 AFF Cup was co-hosted by three time champions, Thailand, and defending champions and eventual winners Singapore. The two hosts are the only two teams that have won the championship since its inception in 1996.

The qualifying round for the lower ranked teams in Southeast Asia was held at the Panaad Stadium, in Bacolod City, Philippines from Novermber 12-20 2006. This tournament marks the first time that lower ranked teams were required to participate in the qualifying round (in previous tournaments all teams participated in the final tournament). The teams that competed were host nation (for the qualifying round only) the Philippines, Laos, Cambodia, East Timor and Brunei. They were placed in a single group of five with each team playing each other once. The top two teams in the qualifying round, Philippines and Laos, advanced to the finals joined by automatic qualifiers Thailand, Singapore, Malaysia, Myanmar, Vietnam and Indonesia.

After a group stage with two pools of four the two host nations met in a two game final. In the first leg of the final, a controversial penalty was awarded to Singapore at the 83rd minute of the match, and the Thailand team walked off the pitch as a protest to the referee's decision. The Thailand team returned to the pitch at the 98th minute, and Singapore later won 2-1. In the second leg of the final, Singapore had a goal controversially chalked off for being offside, but finally drew 1-1 to fellow co-host Thailand, with Khairul Amri scoring the decisive goal in the closing stages of the match, thus giving Singapore their 2nd title in succession, winning with an aggregate score of 3-2, and successfully defending the title. While Thailand can point to the controversial penalty for their defeat in the first leg, they failed to defeat Singapore in the Bangkok second-leg. It could have been worse for Thailand had the match officials seen Thai midfielder Datsakorn Thonglao head-butt Singapore's Khairul Amri to vent his anger after the equaliser.

Noh Alam Shah of Singapore was named the tournament's Most Valuable Player and the Golden Boot Award winner for scoring 10 goals, 7 of which came against Laos. Singapore set an AFF Cup record of a 15-match unbeaten run under coach Radojko Avramovic, stretching back to the 2004 Tiger Cup, and 17-match unbeaten run since the 4-0 defeat at home to neighbours Malaysia in the same competition on 18 December 2002.

Results

Summaries

With effect from 2004, the final is played over two legs. However, away goals rule is not applied in this tournament.

Year	Host(s)	Final			Third Place		
		Winner	Score	Runner-up	Third Place	Score	Fourth Place
1996	Singapore	Thailand	1-0	Malaysia	Vietnam	3-2	Indonesia
1998	Vietnam	Singapore	1-0	Vietnam	Indonesia	3-3 after extra time (5-4) on penalties	Thailand
2000	Thailand	Thailand	4-1	Indonesia	Malaysia	3-0	Vietnam
2002	Indonesia Singapore	Thailand	2-2 after extra time (4-2) on penalties	Indonesia	Vietnam	2-1	Malaysia
2004	Malaysia Vietnam	Singapore	3-1* *2-1 won 5-2 on aggregate	Indonesia	Malaysia	2-1	Myanmar
2007	Singapore Thailand	Singapore	*2-1 1-1* won 3-2 on aggregate	Thailand	Malaysia	2-1	Vietnam
2008	Indonesia Thailand						

Note: * = Host; ** = There was no official Third Place match and no official third place was awarded; Malaysia and Vietnam lost in the semi-finals.

Successful National Teams

Team	Titles	Runners-up	Third Place	Fourth Place
Thailand	3 (1996, 2000, 2002)	1 (2007)	—	1 (1998)
Singapore	3 (1998, 2004, 2007)	—	—	—
Indonesia	—	3 (2000, 2002, 2004)	1 (1998)	1 (1996)
Vietnam	—	1 (1998)	3 (1996, 2002, 2007)	1 (2000)
Malaysia	—	1 (1996)	3 (2000, 2004, 2007)	1 (2002)
Myanmar	—	—	—	1 (2004)

5.4 ASEAN Football Federation

ASEAN Football Federation (AFF) is a subset of nations within the Asian Football Confederation from Southeast Asia. ASEAN stands for Association of South East Asian Nations. The AFF was founded in 1984 by the nations of Thailand, Philippines, Brunei, Singapore, Malaysia, Indonesia, Vietnam, Cambodia, Laos and Myanmar. In 1996, the federation ran the first Tiger Cup and since then it has further expanded its role. Today the AFF is still expanding with East Timor joining the organisation in 2004 and Australia, becoming an invitee after it joined the Asian Football Confederation on January 1, 2006. Australia has sent youth squads to the ASEAN Youth Tournaments. On August 7, 2008, AFF formaly announced Suzuki as the new sponsor of their premier international competition, the ASEAN Football Championship:

- ❖ **Formation** : January 31, 1984
- ❖ **Type** : Sports organization
- ❖ **Headquarters** : Petaling Jaya, Selangor, Malaysia
- ❖ **Membership** : 12 member associations
- ❖ **President** : HE Tengku Tan Sri Dato' Seri Ahmad Rithauddeen

Fig. 5.1: AFF logo

Associations

All founding members, unless stated otherwise:

❖   Australia (invitee)
❖   Brunei
❖   Cambodia
❖   Timor-Leste
❖   Indonesia
❖   Laos
❖   Malaysia
❖   Myanmar
❖   Philippines
❖   Singapore
❖   Thailand
❖   Vietnam
❖   Competitions

Men's

❖   ASEAN Football Championship (formerly Tiger Cup)
❖   ASEAN Club Championship
❖   Youth Championships
❖   AFF U20 Youth Championship
❖   AFF U19 Youth Championship
❖   AFF U17 Youth Championship
❖   AFF U16 Youth Championship

Women's

❖   AFF Women's Championship

5.5 Football at All-Africa Games

The men's Association football tournament has been held at every session of the All-Africa Games since 1965. Women's competition was added in 2003

Men's Tournament

Summaries

Year	Host	Final			Third Place Match		
		Gold Medal	Score	Silver Medal	Bronze Medal	Score	Fourth Place
1965	Brazzaville	Congo	0-0 after two extra time (7-2) match won by corner kicks obtained	Mali	Côte d'Ivoire	1-0	Algeria
1969	*Bamako*	*Disrupted by military coup*			*Disrupted by military coup*		
1973	Lagos	Nigeria	2-0	Guinea	UAR	2-1	Ghana
1978	Algiers	Algeria	1-0	Nigeria	Ghana	1-0	Malawi
1987	Nairobi	Egypt	1-0	Kenya	Malawi	3-1	Cameroon
1991	Cairo	Cameroon	1-0	Tunisia	Nigeria	3-0	Zimbabwe
1995	Harare	Egypt	3-1	Zimbabwe	Nigeria	1-1(4-1) on penalties	Guinea
1999	Johannesburg	Cameroon	0-0 after extra time (4-3) on penalties	Zambia	South Africa	2-0	Uganda
2003	Abuja	Cameroon	2-0	Nigeria	Ghana	2-2 (4-1) on penalties	Zambia
2007	Algiers	Cameroon	1-0	Guinea	Tunisia	1-0	Zambia

Medal Table

Team	Gold	Silver	Bronze
Cameroon	4 (1991, 1999, 2003, 2007)		
Egypt	2 (1987, 1995)		1 (1973)
Nigeria	1 (1973*)	2 (1978, 2003*)	2 (1991, 1995)
Algeria	1 (1978*)		
Congo	1 (1965*)		
Guinea		2 (1973, 2007)	
Tunisia		1 (1991)	1 (2007)
Kenya		1 (1987*)	
Mali		1 (1965)	
Zambia		1 (1999)	
Zimbabwe		1 (1995*)	
Ghana			2 (1978, 2003)
Côte d'Ivoire			1 (1965)
Malawi			1 (1987)
South Africa			1 (1999*)

Note: * = host.

Women's Tournament

Year	Host	Final			Third Place Match		
		Gold Medal	Score	Silver Medal	Bronze Medal	Score	Fourth Place
2003	Abuja	Nigeria	1-0	South Africa	Cameroon	1-0	Mali
2007	Algiers	Nigeria	4-0	South Africa	Ghana	3-1	Algeria

Medal Table

Team	Gold	Silver	Bronze
Nigeria	2 (2003*, 2007)	—	—
South Africa		2 (2003, 2007)	—
Cameroon			1 (2003)
Ghana			1 (2007

5.6 Football at Pan American Games

A men's football (soccer) tournament is held at every Pan American Games since the first edition of the multi-sports event in 1951, a women's tournament was only added in 1999.

Men's Tournament

Summaries

The tournament was played in league format from 1951 to 1963, neither final nor bronze medal match hosted. Another format was used in 1971, this time the tournament was played in group format in early stages, but played in league format for final stages. The 1983 tournament saw only 3 teams played in the final group stages, with the first and final time the tournament did not have the fourth place team. Detail has been given in table 5.2.

Medal table

Team	Gold	Silver	Bronze
Argentina	6 (1951*, 1955, 1959, 1971, 1995*, 2003)	1 (1963)	3 (1975, 1979, 1987)
Brazil	4 (1963*, 1975, 1979, 1987)	2 (1959, 2003)	1 (1983)
Mexico	3 (1967, 1975*, 1999)	3 (1955*, 1991, 1995)	2 (2003, 2007)
USA	1 (1991)		2 (1959*, 1999)
Ecuador	1 (2007)		
Uruguay	1 (1983)		
Chile		1 (1987)	2 (1951, 1963)
Cuba		1 (1979)	2 (1971, 1991*)
Colombia		1 (1971*)	1 (1995)
Bermuda		1 (1967)	
Costa Rica		1 (1959)	
Guatemala		1 (1983)	
Honduras		1 (1999)	
Jamaica		1 (2007)	
Netherlands Antilles			1 (1955)
Trinidad and Tobago			1 (1967)

Note: * = host

Table 5.2: Men's Tournament.

Year	Host	Final			Bronze Medal	Third Place Match	
		Gold Medal	Score	Silver Medal		Score	Fourth Place
1951	Buenos Aires, Argentina	Argentina		Costa Rica	Chile		Venezuela
1955	Mexico City, Mexico	Argentina		Mexico	Netherlands Antilles		Venezuela
1959	Chicago, United States	Argentina		Brazil	USA		Haiti
1963	São Paulo, Brazil	Brazil		Argentina	Chile		Uruguay
1967	Winnipeg, Canada	Mexico	4-0 after extra time	Bermuda	Trinidad and Tobago	4-1	Canada
1971	Cali, Colombia	Argentina		Colombia	Cuba		Trinidad & Tobago
1975	Mexico City, Mexico	Mexico Brazil	1-1 after extra time (title shared)		Argentina	2-0	Costa Rica
1979	San Juan, Puerto Rico	Brazil	3-0	Cuba	Argentina	2-0	Costa Rica
1983	Caracas, Venezuela	Uruguay		Guatemala	Brazil		
1987	Indianapolis, United States	Brazil	2-0 after extra time	Chile	Argentina	0-0 (5-4) on penalties	Mexico
1991	Havana, Cuba	USA	2-1 after extra time	Mexico	Cuba	1-0	Honduras
1995	Mar del Plata, Argentina	Argentina	0-0 (5-4) on penalties	Mexico	Colombia	3-0	Honduras
1999	Winnipeg, Canada	Mexico	3-1	Honduras	USA	2-1	Canada
2003	Santo Domingo, Dominican Republic	Argentina	1-0	Brazil	Mexico	0-0 (5-4) on penalties	Colombia
2007	Rio de Janeiro, Brazil	Ecuador	2-1	Jamaica	Mexico	1-0	Bolivia

Women's Tournament

Summaries

Year	Host	Final			Third Place Match		
		Gold Medal	Score	Silver Medal	Bronze Medal	Score	Fourth Place
1999	Winnipeg, Canada	USA	1-0	Mexico	Costa Rica	1-1 (4-3) on penalties	Canada
2003	Santo Domingo, Dominican Republic	Brazil	2-1 after extra time	Canada	Mexico	4-1	Argentina
2007	Rio de Janeiro, Brazil	Brazil	5-0	USA	Canada	2-1	Mexico

Medal Table

Team	Gold	Silver	Bronze
Brazil	2 (2003, 2007*)		
USA	1 (1999)	1 (2007)	
Canada		1 (2003)	1 (2007)
Mexico		1 (1999)	1 (2003)
Costa Rica			1 (1999)

5.7 Football at Island Games

Football has been held since 1989 at the Island Games as a men's competition sport. In 1985 at Isle of Man was played a youth tournament (U-16) won by Frøya

Medalists

Year	Host	Final			Third Place Match		
		Gold Medal	Score	Silver Medal	Bronze Medal	Score	Fourth Place
1989	Faroe Islands	Faroe Islands	Group Stage	Ynys Môn	Åland Islands	Group Stage	Greenland

(Contd.)

(Contd.)

Year	Host	Final			Third Place Match		
		Gold Medal	Score	Silver Medal	Bronze Medal	Score	Fourth Place
1991	Åland	Faroe Islands	2-0	Ynys Môn	Jersey	2-0	Åland Islands
1993	Isle of Wight	Jersey	5-1	Isle of Man	Åland Islands	2-1	Greenland
1995	Gibraltar	Isle of Wight	1-0	Gibraltar	Jersey	6-3	Greenland
1997	Jersey	Jersey	1-0	Ynys Môn	Isle of Wight	3-1	Guernsey
1999	Gotland	Ynys Môn	1-0	Isle of Man	Isle of Wight	2-0	Jersey
2001	Isle of Man	Guernsey	0-0 (3-1)	Ynys Môn	Jersey	2-0	Isle of Wight
2003	Guernsey	Guernsey	3-1	Isle of Man	Jersey	3-0	Isle of Wight
2005	Shetland	Shetland	2-0	Guernsey	Western Isles	4-0	Isle of Man
2007	Rhodes	Gibraltar	4-0	Rhodes	Western Isles	1-0	Bermuda
2009	Åland						

Topscorers

Year	Player	Goals
1989	B. Magnussen	11
1991	Jens Erik Rasmussen	6
1993	Adam Greig	7
1995	Adam Barsdell	4
1997	Eifion Williams	6
1999	Peter Langridge	8
2001	Chris Higgins Daniel Craven	5
2003	?	
2005	Peter Langridge Johnny Myers Martti Pukk	4
2007	?	

Participating Nations

Nation	1989	1991	1993	1995	1997	1999	2001	2003	2005	2007	Participations	Champion	Runner-up	Third	Fourth
Aland Islands	3rd	4th	3rd	7th		6th			7th	7th	7	0	0	2	1
Alderney								11th			1	0	0	0	0
Bermuda										4th	1	0	0	0	1
Falkland Islands							11th		10th		2	0	0	0	0
Faroe Islands	1st	1st									2	2	0	0	0
Frøya			8th	2nd	7th	12th					4	0	1	0	0
Gibraltar			5th	4th	9th	8th	9th	6th		1st	7	1	0	0	0
Gotland						7th		9th		6th	3	0	0	0	0
Greenland	4th	8th	4th	8th	6th	9th	1st	10th	4th		9	1	0	0	3
Guernsey				5th	8th	13th	11th	1st	2nd	8th	7	1	1	0	0
Hitra						14th		13th			2	0	0	0	0
Isle of Man			2nd	6th	3rd	2nd	7th	2nd			6	0	3	1	0
Isle of Wight		7th	6th	1st	1st	3rd	4th	4th			7	2	0	1	2
Jersey		3rd	1st	3rd		4th	3rd	3rd	4th	5th	8	1	0	4	2
Minorca										9th	1	0	0	0	0
Orkney							12th	8th	9th		3	0	0	0	0
Rhodes						5th	6th	15th		2nd	4	0	1	0	0
Saaremaa						14th	10th	12th	6th	10th	5	0	0	0	0
Sark								14th			1	0	0	0	0
Shetland	5th	5th		5th	5th	10th	8th	7th	1st		8	1	0	0	0
Western Isles									3rd	3rd	2	0	0	2	0
Ynys Môn	2nd	2nd	7th	8th	2nd	1st	2nd	5th	5th	11th	10	1	4	0	0

Titles

- ❖ Jersey
- ❖ Guernsey
- ❖ Faroe Islands
- ❖ Ynys Môn
- ❖ Shetland
- ❖ Isle of Wight
- ❖ Gibraltar

6

Commonwealth Games and Related Tourism Activities

6.1 Commonwealth Games Federation

The Role of the CGF

At the heart of the CGF's work is the will to dynamically promote and celebrate a unizue, friendly, world class Games. The Commonwealth is an association of independent sovereign states spread over every continent and ocean. From Africa to Asia, the Paci?c shores to the Caribbean, the Commonwealth's 2 billion people make up 30 per cent of the world's population and are of many faiths, races, languages, cultures and traditions. The Commonwealth Games is a unique, world class, multi-sports event which is held once every four years. It is often referred to as the 'Friendly Games'.

The Commonwealth Games Federation (CGF) is the organisation that is responsible for the direction and control of the Commonwealth Games. As a means of improving society and the general well being of the people of the Commonwealth, the CGF also encourages and assists education via sport development and physical recreation.

Underlying every decision made by the CGF are three core values:—HUMANITY—EQUALITY—DESTINY. These values help to inspire and unite millions of people and symbolise the broad mandate of the CGF within the Commonwealth.

6.2 Commonwealth Games

The Commonwealth Games is a multinational, multi-sport event. Held every four years, it involves the elite athletes of the

Commonwealth of Nations. Attendance at the Commonwealth Games is typically around 5,000 athletes. The Commonwealth Games Federation (CGF) is the organisation that is responsible for the direction and control of the Commonwealth Games. The first such event, then known as the British Empire Games, was held in 1930 in Hamilton, Ontario, Canada. The name changed to British Empire and Commonwealth Games in 1954, to British Commonwealth Games in 1970 and assumed the current name of the Commonwealth Games in 1974. As well as many Olympic sports, the Games also include some sports that are played mainly in Commonwealth countries, such as lawn bowls, rugby sevens and netball. There are currently 53 members of the Commonwealth of Nations, and 71 teams participate in the Games. The four constituent countries of the United Kingdom—England, Scotland, Wales and Northern Ireland—send separate teams to the Commonwealth Games (unlike at the Olympic Games, where the United Kingdom sends a single team), and individual teams are also sent from the British Crown dependencies—Guernsey, Jersey and the Isle of Man—and many of the British overseas territories. The Australian external territory of Norfolk Island also sends its own team, as do the Cook Islands and Niue, two non-sovereign states in free association with New Zealand.

Only six teams have attended every Commonwealth Games: Australia, Canada, England, New Zealand, Scotland and Wales. Australia has been the highest scoring team for ten games, England for seven and Canada for one. At the 1930 games, women competed in Swimming and Diving only. In 1934 women competed in some Athletics events also.

Origins

A sporting competition bringing together the members of the British Empire was first proposed by the Reverend Astley Cooper in 1891 when he wrote an article in *The Times* suggesting a "Pan-Britannic-Pan-Anglican Contest and Festival every four years as a means of increasing the goodwill and good understanding of the British Empire". In 1911, the Festival of the Empire was held in London to celebrate the coronation of King George V. As part of the festival an Inter-Empire Championships was held in which teams from Australia, Canada, South Africa and the United Kingdom competed in events such as boxing, wrestling, swimming and athletics.

In 1928, Melville Marks (Bobby) Robinson of Canada was asked to organise the first British Empire Games. These were held in Hamilton, Ontario two years later.

Opening Ceremony Traditions

From 1930 through 1950, the parade of nations was led by a single flagbearer carrying the Union Flag, symbolising Britain's leading role in the British Empire. Since 1958, there has been a relay of athletes carrying a baton from Buckingham Palace to the Opening Ceremony. This baton has within it the Queen's Message of Greeting to the athletes. The baton's final bearer is usually a famous sporting personage of the host nation. All other nations march in English alphabetical order, except that the first nation marching in the Parade of Athletes is the host nation of the previous games, and the host nation of the current games marches last. In 2006 countries marched in alphabetical order in geographical regions. Three national flags fly from the stadium on the poles that are used for medal ceremonies: Previous host nation, Current host nation, Next host nation. The military is more active in the Opening Ceremony than in the Olympic Games. This is to honour the British Military traditions of the Old Empire.

Boycotts

The Commonwealth Games, like the Olympic Games, has also suffered from political boycotts. Nigeria boycotted the 1978 Games in protest of New Zealand's sporting contacts with apartheid-era South Africa, and 32 of 59 nations from Africa, Asia, and the Caribbean boycotted the 1986 Commonwealth Games due to the Thatcher government's attitude towards South African sporting contacts. Boycotts were also threatened in 1974, 1982, and 1990 because of South Africa.

All Time Medal Table

Rank	Nation	Gold	Silver	Bronze	Total
1.	Australia	643	556	508	1707 [1]
2.	England	579	553	563	1695
3.	Canada	374	402	412	118
4.	New Zealand	124	168	238	525
5.	India	104	90	72	266
6.	South Africa	92	92	96	280
7.	Scotland	82	94	153	329
8.	Kenya	59	47	56	162
9.	Wales	47	71	96	214
10.	Jamaica	40	30	35	105
11.	Nigeria	37	48	57	142
12.	Malaysia/Malaya	36	48	51	135
13.	Pakistan	21	17	16	54
14.	Northern Ireland	17	23	38	78
15.	Sri Lanka/Ceylon	16	19	19	54
16.	Ghana	15	17	187	50
17.	Singapore	13	9	18	40
18.	Uganda	10	12	17	39
19.	Nauru	9	6	11	26
20.	Cameroon	9	5	7	21
21.	Cyprus	9	5	6	20
22.	Trinidad and Tobago	8	13	17	38
23.	Bahamas	8	9	9	26
24.	Tanzania	6	6	9	21
25.	Hong Kong	5	2	7	14
26.	Zimbabwe/Southern Rhodesia	3	6	12	21
27.	Zambia	3	5	14	22
28.	Fiji	3	4	5	12
29.	Namibia	3	2	7	12
30.	Guyana/British Guiana	2	5	6	13
31.	Papua New Guinea	2	4	2	8
32.	Barbados	2	3	4	9
33.	Isle of Man	2	1	4	7
34.	Mozambique	2	1	1	4
35.	Bangladesh	2	1	0	3
36.	Mauritius	1	4	3	8
37.	Northern Rhodesia	1	2	4	7
38.	Bermuda	1	2	2	5
39.	Lesotho	1	1	1	3
40.	Jersey	1	0	3	4

(Contd.)

(Contd.)

Rank	Nation	Gold	Silver	Bronze	Total
41.	Saint Vincent and the Grenadines	1	0	1	2
42.	Saint Kitts and Nevis	1	0	0	1
43.	Botswana	0	3	4	7
44.	Guernsey	0	3	2	5
45.	Rhodesia and Nyasaland	0	2	5	7
46.	Seychelles	0	2	3	5
47.	Samoa	0	1	3	4
47.	Swaziland	0	1	3	4
49.	Rhodesia	0	1	2	3
50.	Grenada	0	1	0	1
51.	Malawi	0	0	3	3
52.	Malta	0	0	2	2
53.	Cayman Islands	0	0	1	1
53.	Gambia	0	0	1	1
53.	Norfolk Island	0	0	1	1
53.	Saint Lucia	0	0	1	1
53.	Tonga	0	0	1	1

Note: [1] Total here lower than total on country page Australia at the Commonwealth Games.

Editions

British Empire Games

1930   British Empire Games—Hamilton, Ontario, Canada

1934   British Empire Games—London, England, United Kingdom

1938   British Empire Games—Sydney, New South Wales, Australia

1950   British Empire Games—Auckland, New Zealand

British Empire and Commonwealth Games

1954   British Empire and Commonwealth Games—Vancouver, British Columbia, Canada

1958   British Empire and Commonwealth Games—Cardiff, Wales, United Kingdom

1962   British Empire and Commonwealth Games—Perth, Western Australia, Australia

1966   British Empire and Commonwealth Games—Kingston, Jamaica

British Commonwealth Games

Fig. 6.1: Flag of the British Commonwealth Games

1970 British Commonwealth Games—Edinburgh, Scotland, United Kingdom

1974 British Commonwealth Games—Christchurch, New Zealand

Commonwealth Games

1978 Commonwealth Games—Edmonton, Alberta, Canada

1982 Commonwealth Games—Brisbane, Queensland, Australia

1986 Commonwealth Games—Edinburgh, Scotland, United Kingdom

1990 Commonwealth Games—Auckland, New Zealand

1994 Commonwealth Games—Victoria, British Columbia, Canada

1998 Commonwealth Games—Kuala Lumpur, Malaysia

2002 Commonwealth Games—Manchester, England, United Kingdom

2006 Commonwealth Games—Melbourne, Victoria, Australia

2010 Commonwealth Games—Delhi, India

2014 Commonwealth Games—Glasgow, Scotland, United Kingdom

2018 Commonwealth Games—TBD

Numbers of Athletes, Sports, and Nations

This list shows the total number of athletes, male and female, the number of sports they were selected to compete in, and the number of nations (including dependencies) competing.

Year	Athletes	Male	Female	Sports	Events	Officials	Nations
2006	4500			16	247		71
2002	3863			17[2]			72
1998	3638			15			70
1994	2669			12			63
1990	2073			10	205		55
1986	1660			10	165		27
1982	1580			12	143		45
1978	1475			11	126		47
1974	1276	977	299	10	121	372	38
1970	1744[1]			10	121		42
1966	1316[1]			10	110		34
1962	863			9		178	35
1958	1122			9		228	35
1954	662			9		127	24
1950	590	495	95	9			12
1938	464			7		43	15
1934	500			6			17
1930	400			6			11

Note: [1]Total including athletes and officials. [2]Includes 3 team sports.

Nations/dependencies that have Competed

1. Aden[1] 1962
2. Anguilla 1982, 1998-
3. Antigua and Barbuda 1966-1970, 1978, 1994-
4. Australia 1930-
5. Bahamas 1954-1970, 1978-1982, 1990-
6. Bangladesh 1978, 1990-
7. Barbados 1954-1966, 1970-1982, 1990-
8. Belize 1978, 1994-
9. Bermuda 1930-1938, 1954-1982, 1990-
10. Botswana 1974, 1982-
11. British Guiana[2] 1930-1938, 1954-1962
12. British Honduras[3] 1962-1966
13. British Virgin Islands 1990-
14. Brunei Darussalam 1958, 1990-
15. Cameroon 1998-
16. Canada 1930-

17. Cayman Islands 1978-
18. Ceylon[4] 1938-1950, 1958-1970
19. Cook Islands 1974-1978, 1986-
20. Cyprus 1978-1982, 1990-
21. Dominica 1958-1962, 1970, 1994-
22. England 1930-
23. Falkland Islands 1982-
24. Fiji 1938, 1954-1986, 1998-
25. The Gambia 1970-1982, 1990-
26. Ghana 1958-1982, 1990-
27. Gibraltar 1958-
28. Gold Coast[5] 1954
29. Grenada 1970-1974, 1994-
30. Guernsey 1970-
31. Guyana 1966-1970, 1978-1982, 1990-
32. Hong Kong[6] 1934, 1954-1962, 1970-1994
33. India 1934-1938, 1954-1958, 1966-1982, 1990-
34. Irish Free State[7] 1934
35. Isle of Man 1958-
36. Jamaica 1934, 1954-1982, 1990-
37. Jersey 1958-
38. Kenya 1954-1982, 1990-
39. Kiribati 1998-
40. Lesotho 1974-
41. Malawi[12] 1970-
42. Malaya[8] 1950, 1958-1962
43. Malaysia 1966-1982, 1990-
44. Maldives 1986-
45. Malta 1958-1962, 1970, 1982—Mauritius 1958, 1966-1982, 1990-
46. Montserrat 1994-
47. Mozambique 1998-
48. Namibia 1994-
49. Nauru 1990-
50. Newfoundland[9] 1930-1934
51. New Zealand 1930-
52. Nigeria 1950-1958, 1966-1974, 1982, 1990-1994, 2002-
53. Niue 2002-

54. Norfolk Island 1986-
55. North Borneo[8] 1958-1962
56. Northern Ireland[7] 1930-1938, 1954-
57. Northern Rhodesia[10] 1954
58. Pakistan 1954-1970, 1990-
59. Papua New Guinea 1962-1982, 1990-
60. Rhodesia[11] 1934-1950
61. Rhodesia and Nyasaland[10] 1958-1962
62. Saint Helena 1982, 1998-
63. Saint Kitts and Nevis (Saint Christopher-Nevis-Anguilla 1978), 1990-
64. Saint Lucia 1962, 1970, 1978, 1994-
65. Saint Vincent and the Grenadines 1958, 1966-1978, 1994-
66. Samoa and Western Samoa 1974-
67. Scotland 1930-
68. Seychelles 1990-
69. Sierra Leone 1966-1970, 1978, 1990-
70. Singapore[8] 1958-
71. Solomon Islands 1982, 1990-
72. South Africa 1930-1958, 1994-
73. South Arabia[1] 1966
74. Southern Rhodesia[10] 1954
75. Sri Lanka 1974-1982, 1990-
76. Swaziland 1970-
77. Tanganyika[13] 1962
78. Tanzania 1966-1982, 1990-
79. Tonga 1974, 1982, 1990-
80. Trinidad and Tobago 1934-1982, 1990-
81. Turks and Caicos Islands 1978, 1998-
82. Tuvalu 1998-
83. Uganda 1954-1982, 1990-
84. Vanuatu 1982-
85. Wales 1930-
86. Zambia[12] 1970-1982, 1990-
87. Zimbabwe[12,14] 1982, 1990-2002

Notes: 1. Aden became South Arabia which left the Commonwealth in 1968.
2. Became Guyana in 1966.
3. Became Belize in 1973.

4. Became Sri Lanka in 1972.
5. Became Ghana in 1957.
6. Left the Commonwealth when handed over to China in 1997.
7. Ireland was represented as the Irish Free State and Northern Ireland in 1934. The Irish Free State, subsequently known in Britain as Eire (1937 to 1948), left the Commonwealth as the Republic of Ireland on January 1 1949.
8. Malaya, North Borneo, Sarawak and Singapore federated as Malaysia in 1963. Singapore left the federation in 1965.
9. Joined Canada in 1949.
10. Southern Rhodesia and Northern Rhodesia federated with Nyasaland from 1953 as Rhodesia and Nyasaland which lasted till 1963.
11. Divided into Southern Rhodesia and Northern Rhodesia in 1953.
12. Competed from 1958-1962 as part of Rhodesia and Nyasaland.
13. Zanzibar and Tanganyika federated to form Tanzania in 1964.
14. Withdrew from the Commonwealth in 2003.

Commonwealth Nations/Dependencies Yet to Send Teams

Very few Commonwealth dependencies and nations have yet to take part. Tokelau is expected to take part in the 2010 Games in Delhi.

The Turkish Republic of Northern Cyprus have made applications to the CGF to send teams. The Pitcairn Islands' tiny population (50 as of July 2007) would appear to prevent the overseas territory from competing. Other states and territories with native populations within the Commonwealth that may be eligible include Christmas Island and the Cocos (Keeling) Islands. It is also conceivable that any future members of the Commonwealth such as applicants Rwanda and Yemen may participate in future games.

List of Sports at the Commonwealth Games

The current regulations state that a minimum of ten and no more than fifteen sports must be included in a Commonwealth Games schedule. There is a list of core sports, which must be included, and a further list of approved sports from which the host nation may choose to include. The host nation may also apply for the inclusion of other team sports to the CGF General Assembly, as the Melbourne organising committee did with basketball for the 2006 Games.

The current core sports consist of athletics, aquatics (swimming, diving and synchronised swimming), lawn bowls, netball (for women) and rugby sevens (for men). These will all remain core sports until at least the 2014 Commonwealth Games.

The approved list of sports also includes archery, badminton, billiards and snooker, boxing, canoeing, cycling, fencing, gymnastics, judo, rowing, sailing, shooting, squash, table tennis, tennis, ten-pin bowling, triathlon, weightlifting, and wrestling. Some of these are often included in the programme, while others, like billiards and sailing, have not yet been included.

In 2002, the CGF introduced the David Dixon Award for the outstanding athlete of the Games.

There is also a requirement to include some events for Elite Athletes with a Disability (EAD). This was introduced in the 2002 Games.

On 18th November 2006, tennis and archery were added to the list of disciplines for the 2010 Games in New Delhi, bringing the total number of sports to 17. Billiards and snooker were considered but not accepted.

Sports Currently Included

The years, in brackets, show when the sports have appeared at the games:

- ❖ Aquatics (1930-)
- ❖ Swimming
- ❖ Synchronised swimming
- ❖ Diving
- ❖ Athletics (men: 1930-, women: 1934-)
- ❖ Badminton (1966-)
- ❖ Basketball (2006-)
- ❖ Boxing (1930-)
- ❖ Cycling (1934-)
- ❖ Gymnastics (1978, 1990-)
- ❖ Rhythmic gymnastics (1994-1998, 2006-)
- ❖ Field hockey (1998-)
- ❖ Lawn bowls (1930-1962, 1972-)

❖ Netball (1998-)
❖ Rugby sevens (1998-)
❖ Shooting (1966, 1974-)
❖ Squash (1998-)
❖ Table tennis (2002-)
❖ Triathlon (2002-)
❖ Weightlifting (1950-)
❖ Events for Athletes with a Disability (2002-)
❖ Athletics
❖ Swimming
❖ Table tennis
❖ Powerlifting
❖ Events on Hiatus
❖ Archery (1982 probably 2010)
❖ Cricket (1998)
❖ Fencing (1950-1970)
❖ Freestyle wrestling (1930-1986, 1994, 2002, back in 2010)
❖ Judo (1990, 2002)
❖ Rowing (1930, 1938-1962, 1986) (may be held in 2014)
❖ Ten-pin bowling (1998)
❖ Events which have not yet been held
❖ Karate
❖ Tennis
❖ Orienteering
❖ Snooker
❖ Yachting
❖ Taekwondo
❖ Water Polo
❖ Lifesaving
❖ Football

6.3 Delhi's Pact for Commonwealth Games: A Case Study

New Delhi: Commonwealth Games 2010 hosts Delhi Tuesday entered into an agreement for strategic alliance with the past hosts of the event—Melbourne. Lord Mayor of Melbourne John So and Chief Minister Shiela Dikshit signed the Delhi-Melbourne Strategic City Alliance Programme, which will focus on sharing experiences in the preparations and management of the event. "The two cities will also promote development of sports, exchange of sporting knowledge, business relating to sports and tourism and cultural activities," a Delhi government official here said. Speaking on this occasion, the chief minister described the agreement as the beginning of a friendship between two prominent cities.

"Melbourne is a beautifully managed city, which hosted the last edition of the Commonwealth Games meticulously in 2006." The agreement provides for the establishment of a joint working group. The group, having equal representation from both the cities, will develop an action plan for promotion of sports, economic activities, sports medicine, and tourism between the two cities. Exchange of information and expertise for hosting the Commonwealth Games will be the prime focus for the first three years of the Delhi-Melbourne Strategic City Alliance Programme. (IANS)

Asian Games and Related Tourism Activities

7.1 Asian Games

The Asian Games, also called the Asiad, is a multi-sport event held every four years among athletes from all over Asia. The games are regulated by the Olympic Council of Asia (OCA) under the supervision of the International Olympic Committee (IOC). Medals are awarded in each event, with gold for first place, silver for second and bronze for third, a tradition which started in 1951.

Competitors are entered by a National Olympic Committee (NOC) to represent their country of citizenship. National anthems and flags accompany the medal ceremonies, and tables showing the number of medals won by each country are widely used. In general only recognised nations are represented, but a few non-sovereign countries are allowed to take part. The special case of Taiwan was handled by having it compete as *Chinese Taipei*, due to the political status of Taiwan.

The 15th Asian Games were held in Doha, Qatar from December 1 to December 15, 2006. The 16th Asian Games will be held in Guangzhou, China from November 12, 2010 to November 27, 2010

History

Far Eastern Championship Games

The Asian Games owes its origins to small Asian multi-sport competitions. The Far Eastern Championship Games were created to show unity and cooperation among three nations: Empire of Japan, the Philippine Islands and the Republic of China. The first games were held in Manila in 1913. Other Asian nations participated after it was organized. It was discontinued in 1938 when Japan invaded China, which led to the expansion of World War II in the Pacific.

Formation of the Asian Games

After World War II, a number of Asian countries became independent. Many of the new independent Asian countries wanted to use a new type of competition where Asian dominance should not be shown by violence and should be strengthened by mutual understanding. In August 1948, during the 14th Olympic Games in London, Indian IOC representative Guru Dutt Sondhi proposed to sports leaders of the Asian teams the idea of having discussions about holding the Asian Games. They agreed to form the Asian Athletic Federation. A preparatory committee was set up to draft the charter for the Asian amateur athletic federation. In February, 1949, the Asian athletic federation was formally formed and used the name Asian Games Federation. It was decided to hold the first Asian Games in 1951 in New Delhi, the capital of India. They added that the Asian Games would be regularly held once every four years.

Reorganization of the Federation

In 1962, the Federation had a disagreement over the inclusion of Republic of China and Israel. Asian Games host Indonesia opposed the participation of Republic of China (due to the existence of People's Republic of China) and Israel. In 1970, South Korea dropped its plan to host the games due to security threats from North Korea, forcing previous host Thailand to administer the games in Bangkok using the funds of South Korea. In 1973, the Federation had another disagreement after U.S. and other countries formally recognized the People's Republic of China and Arab nations' opposition to Israel. In 1977, Pakistan dropped its plan to host the games due to conflicts with Bangladesh and India. Thailand offered to help and the games were held in Bangkok. The Asian NOCs decided to revise the constitution of the Asian Games Federation. A new association, named Olympic Council of Asia, was created in November 1981. India was already scheduled to host the 1982 Games and OCA decided not to drop the old AGF timetable. OCA formally supervised the games starting from the 1986 Asian Games in South Korea.

In the succeeding games, Taiwan (Republic of China) was readmitted but OCA decided to follow the standards of the IOC for Taiwan to use the name *Chinese Taipei*. The OCA also agreed to permanently exclude Israel as its member and requested that the country join European competitions.

Expansion

In the 1994 Asian Games, despite opposition from other nations, OCA admitted the former Soviet republics of Kazakhstan, Kyrgystan, Uzbekistan, Turkmenistan, and Tajikistan. In 2006 Australia was refused entry by OCA President Sheikh Ahmad Al-Fahd Al-Sabah, suggesting that Australia's move from Oceania to Asia would be unfair to the smaller Oceania states. Cricket will be introduced in the 2010 Asian Games.

List of Asian Games

Former or future countries in Asian Games until 2014. Red spot denotes the city of the Games.

Year	Games	Host City	Country	Winner (gold)	2nd (gold)	3rd (gold)
1951	I	New Delhi	India	Japan	India	Iran
1954	II	Manila	Philippines	Japan	Philippines	South Korea
1958	III	Tokyo	Japan	Japan	Philippines	South Korea
1962	IV	Jakarta	Indonesia	Japan	Indonesia	India
1966	V	Bangkok	Thailand	Japan	South Korea	Thailand
1970	VI[1]	Bangkok	Thailand	Japan	South Korea	Thailand
1974	VII	Tehran	Iran	Japan	Iran	China
1978	VIII[2]	Bangkok	Thailand	Japan	China	South Korea
1982	IX	New Delhi	India	China	Japan	South Korea
1986	X	Seoul	South Korea	China	South Korea	Japan
1990	XI	Beijing	China	China	South Korea	Japan
1994	XII	Hiroshima	Japan	China	Japan	South Korea
1998	XIII	Bangkok	Thailand	China	South Korea	Japan
2002	XIV	Busan	South Korea	China	South Korea	Japan
2006	XV	Doha	Qatar	China	South Korea	Japan
2010	XVI	Guangzhou	China	TBA	TBA	TBA
2014	XVII	Incheon	South Korea	TBA	TBA	TBA

Note: [1] Originally to be hosted by South Korea; [2] Originally to be hosted by Pakistan.

List of Sports

These are the sports that have been and will be played at the Asian Games, with the years they played.

- ❖ Archery—since 1978
- ❖ Athletics—All
- ❖ Badminton—since 1962
- ❖ Baseball—since 1994
- ❖ Basketball—All
- ❖ Bodybuilding—2002 to 2006
- ❖ Bowling—1978, since 1986
- ❖ Boxing—since 1954
- ❖ Canoe/Kayak—since 1990
- ❖ Chess—since 2006
- ❖ Cricket—From 2010
- ❖ Cue sports—since 1998
- ❖ Cycling—1951, since 1958
- ❖ Equestrian—1982 to 1986, since 1994
- ❖ Fencing—1974 to 1978, since 1986
- ❖ Football—All
- ❖ Golf—since 1982
- ❖ Gymnastics—since 1974
- ❖ Handball—since 1982
- ❖ Hockey—since 1958
- ❖ Judo—since 1986
- ❖ Kabaddi—since 1990
- ❖ Karate—since 1994
- ❖ Modern pentathlon—1994, 2002
- ❖ Rowing—since 1982
- ❖ Rugby—since 1998
- ❖ Sailing—1970, since 1978
- ❖ Sepaktakraw—since 1990
- ❖ Shooting—since 1954
- ❖ Softball—since 1990
- ❖ Soft tennis—since 1994
- ❖ Squash—since 1998
- ❖ Swimming—All
- ❖ Table tennis—1958 to 1966, since 1974

- ❖ Taekwondo—1986, since 1994
- ❖ Tennis—1958 to 1966, since 1974
- ❖ Triathlon—since 2006
- ❖ Volleyball—since 1958
- ❖ Weightlifting—1951 to 1958, since 1966
- ❖ Wrestling—since 1954
- ❖ Wushu—since 1990

7.2 Asian Football Confederation

The 46 member Asian Football Confederation (AFC) is the governing body of football in Asia, excluding Cyprus and Israel, and including Australia. The AFC was founded in 1954 in Manila, Philippines, and is one of FIFA's six continental confederations. (Nations with both European and Asian territory, such as Turkey, Kazakhstan, Azerbaijan, Armenia, Georgia, and Russia, are instead covered by UEFA; Israel, which lies entirely in Asia, is also a UEFA member.) The main headquarters is located in Bukit Jalil, Kuala Lumpur, Malaysia. The current president is Mohammed Bin Hammam of Qatar.

AFC Competitions

The latest champions of the AFC is Iraq. The AFC runs the Asian Cup, a competition for the national football teams of Asia held every four years, as well as the Asian World Cup Qualifying Tournament and the AFC Challenge Cup. It also runs the Asian Olympics Qualifying Tournament. The AFC also runs three levels of annual international club competitions. The most prestigious (and oldest of the current AFC club competitions) is the AFC Champions League tournament, based on the UEFA Champions League, formed in 2002/03 with the amalgamation of the *Asian Champions Cup* and the *Asian Cup Winners Cup*. (An Asian Super Cup competition between the winners of these two major tournaments ended with the birth of the AFC Champions League.) The other competitions branched off this in 2004 when the 'Vision Asia' blueprint for development was launched. This led to the top fourteen AFC nations, the 'mature nations', sending their best teams to the AFC Champions League. The next 14 nations, the 'developing nations' qualify to send their teams to the AFC Cup.

The rest of the AFC-affiliated countries, the 'emerging nations' send their teams to the AFC President's Cup. The teams which qualify from each country are usually the champions and the cup winners. Currently there is no promotion and relegation between the different levels of nations.

The AFC is going to revamp 22 leagues in Asia, 10 of them by 2009-2012. This is due to the poor performance/absence of Asian teams in the 2006 World Cup. The reforms include: increasing transparency, increase competitiveness, improving training facilities and forcing the leagues to have a system of relegation and promotion.

The 10 leagues marked for reform are: Australia, Japan, China, South Korea, Singapore, India, Iran, United Arab Emirates, Saudi Arabia and Qatar. The proposal would mark a radical change in Australia, where professional leagues in all sports are organised on a model of franchised teams and closed league membership, a system most commonly identified with North America. There are 12 AFC Nations that play in the UAFA organised Arab Nations Cup. These nations are Bahrain, Iraq, Jordan, Kuwait, Lebanon, Qatar, Oman, Palestine, Saudi Arabia, Syria, United Arab Emirates and Yemen.

Women's Football in Asia

The Asian Ladies Football Confederation (ALFC) is the section of the AFC who manage women's football in Asia. The group was independently founded in April 1968 in a meeting involving Taiwan, Hong Kong, Malaysia and Singapore. In 1986 the ALFC merged with the AFC. The Asian Ladies Football Confederation helped organise the AFC Women's Asian Cup, first held in 1975, as well as the AFC's AFC U-19 Women's Championship and the AFC U-17 Women's Championship.

Regions

The AFC is split into four regions. Below shows how the national teams of Asia are split up by region (but are not necessarily part of their regional football federation). As a rule, because of cultural restrictions, only the ASEAN and East Asian regions field equivalent women's teams.

- ❖ ASEAN Football Federation
- ❖ Australia
- ❖ Brunei
- ❖ Cambodia
- ❖ Timor-Leste
- ❖ Indonesia
- ❖ Laos
- ❖ Malaysia
- ❖ Myanmar
- ❖ Philippines
- ❖ Singapore
- ❖ Thailand
- ❖ Vietnam
- ❖ East Asian Football Federation
- ❖ China PR
- ❖ Hong Kong
- ❖ Guam
- ❖ Japan
- ❖ Chinese Taipei (Taiwan)
- ❖ Korea DPR
- ❖ Korea Republic
- ❖ Macau
- ❖ Mongolia
- ❖ Northern Mariana Islands (provisional)
- ❖ West Asian Football Federation
- ❖ Bahrain
- ❖ Iran
- ❖ Iraq
- ❖ Jordan
- ❖ Kuwait
- ❖ Lebanon
- ❖ Oman
- ❖ Palestine
- ❖ Qatar
- ❖ Saudi Arabia
- ❖ Syria
- ❖ United Arab Emirates
- ❖ Yemen
- ❖ Central and South Asian Football Federation

- ❖ Afghanistan
- ❖ Bangladesh
- ❖ Bhutan
- ❖ India
- ❖ Kyrgyzstan
- ❖ Maldives
- ❖ Nepal
- ❖ Pakistan
- ❖ Sri Lanka
- ❖ Tajikistan
- ❖ Turkmenistan
- ❖ Uzbekistan

7.3 Asian Winter Games

The Asian Winter Games is a multi-sport event for members of the Olympic Council of Asia which features winter events. The Japanese Olympic Committee first suggested the idea of holding a winter version of the Asian Games in 1982. Their efforts were rewarded when they were finally given hosting rights for the first edition that was held in Sapporo in 1986, as the city had the infrastructure and expertise gained from hosting of the 1972 Winter Olympics.

From having only seven member nations of the Olympic Council of Asia taking part in the first edition, the number of nations competing in the Winter Asiad has consistently grown. In the most recent Asian Winter Games in Changchun, 27 out of the 45 members fielded a record number of competitors, while all 45 NOCs sent delegations for the first time ever in Winter Asiad history.

List of Asian Winter Games

Year	Games	City	Country
1986	I	Sapporo	Japan
1990	II	Sapporo	Japan
1996	III	Harbin	China
1999	IV	Gangwon	South Korea
2003	V	Aomori	Japan
2007	VI	Changchun	China
2011	VII	Almaty	Kazakhstan

All-time Medal Count

As of the 2007 Asian Winter Games.

Nation	Gold	Silver	Bronze	Total
Japan	101	102	75	278
China	71	71	84	224
Korea	45	53	63	161
Kazakhstan	37	30	27	94
Democratic People's Republic of Korea	1	4	10	15
Uzbekistan	1	2	3	6
Lebanon	1	1	0	2
Mongolia	0	0	2	2

7.4 Asian Indoor Games

The Asian Indoor Games is a multi-sport event held every two years among athletes representing countries from Asia. The games are regulated by the Olympic Council of Asia. The first games were held in 2005 in Bangkok, Thailand. This Games will be composed of sports with TV broadcasting potential and not included in the Asian Games and Winter Asian Games Programs and are not Olympic sports. The sports program will consist of six to eight exciting sports with strong television appeal, including electronic sports, extreme sports, aerobics, acrobatics, indoor athletics, dance sports, futsal, inline hockey, fin swimming, and 25 metres short course swimming.

2005 Asian Indoor Games, Bangkok, Thailand
2007 Asian Indoor Games, Macau, China
2009 Asian Indoor Games, Hanoi, Vietnam
2011 Asian Indoor Games, Doha, Qatar

All-time Medal Count

Rank	Nation	Gold	Silver	Bronze	Total
1.	China	76	44	39	159
2.	Thailand	39	49	55	143

(Contd.)

(*Contd.*)

Rank Nation		Gold	Silver	Bronze	Total
3.	Kazakhstan	32	35	19	86
4.	Hong Kong, China	27	18	16	61
5.	India	16	12	18	46
6.	Korea	15	21	23	59
7.	Japan	14	9	17	40
8.	Chinese Taipei	9	7	9	25
9.	Uzbekistan	8	9	11	28
10.	Iran	7	9	11	27
11.	Macau, China	6	11	10	27
12.	Qatar	6	5	3	14
13.	Indonesia	3	1	6	10
14.	Saudi Arabia	3	1	0	4
15.	Vietnam	2	6	12	20
16.	Philippines	2	2	5	9
17.	United Arab Emirates	2	0	1	3
18.	Singapore	1	8	9	18
19.	Kuwait	1	5	5	11
20.	Malaysia	1	3	6	10
21.	Jordan	1	1	6	8
22.	Laos	0	5	5	10
23.	Iraq	0	3	4	7
24.	Pakistan	0	2	1	3
25.	Myanmar	0	2	0	2
25.	Sri Lanka	0	2	0	2
27.	Mongolia	0	1	4	5
28.	Kyrgyzstan	0	1	1	2
29.	Syria	0	1	0	1
30.	DPR Korea	0	0	2	2
30.	Lebanon	0	0	2	2
32.	Bangladesh	0	0	1	1
32.	Oman	0	0	1	1

7.5 Asian Beach Games

The Asian Beach Games is a multi-sport event to be held every two years among athletes representing countries from Asia. The games are regulated by the Olympic Council of Asia. The first games will be held in 2008 in Bali, Indonesia.

This Games will be composed of sports with strong television appeal such as windsurfing, kiteboarding, swimming, beach volleyball, beach handball, beach soccer, and dragon boat racing.

National Sport

A national sport is a sport or game that is considered to be a intrinsic part of the culture of a nation. In American English the term national pastime is often used. Some sports are *de facto* national sports whilst others are defined by law

National Sports Defined by Law

Country	Sport	Year defined as national sport
Argentina	Pato	1953
Bahamas	Sloop sailing	1993
Bangladesh ("national game")	Kabaddi	1972
Brazil	Capoeira	1972
Canada ("national winter sport")	Ice Hockey	1994
Canada ("national summer sport")	Lacrosse	1859
Chile	Chilean rodeo	1962
Colombia	Tejo	2000
Mexico	Charrería	1933
Korea (Rep.)	Taekwondo	1971
Puerto Rico ("autochthonous sport")	Paso Fino	1966
Sri Lanka	Volleyball	1991
Uruguay	Destrezas criollas ("creole skills": i.e. gaucho skills)	2006

De facto *National Sports*

Country		Sports
Afghanistan	:	buzkashi
Anguilla	:	yacht racing
Antigua and Barbuda	:	cricket

Barbados	:	cricket
Bermuda	:	cricket
Bhutan	:	archery
China (PRC)	:	table tennis
Cuba	:	baseball
Dominican Republic	:	baseball
Finland	:	pesäpallo
Grenada	:	cricket
Guyana	:	cricket
India	:	field hockey
Ireland ("native sports")	:	gaelic football, hurling
Jamaica	:	cricket
Lithuania	:	basketball
New Zealand	:	rugby union
Norway	:	cross-country skiing
Pakistan	:	field hockey
Tokelau	:	kilikiti
United States ("national pastime")	:	baseball
Wales	:	rugby union

8

Adventure Sports Training and Education: Towards Evolving a New Tourism Strategy

8.1 Adventure Sports

India the land yet unexplored can easily be the new millennium's adventure tourism destination. Its vast geographical diversity and the pristine nature of its facilities enables all tastes to be catered for, from the gentlest to the fast paced and for people of every level of competence—the beginner and the expert. From the daunting Himalayan peaks in the North to the azure coastal areas on the South, from the rain forests of the North East to the coral paradise in the South West, it is variety that is as bewildering as it is diverse. What is so fascinating and so compelling almost to the point of addition in adventure sports? It must be the daunting thrill of dashing down the ski slopes or the landscape trekking or pedaling along sheer mountain slopes, white water rafting along the dangerous, roaring waters of great services, hang gliding over enormously deep mountain gorges and climbing serrated glaciers or, mountain summits is believable only through experience. And, yet, these aspects form just a small part of the exhilaration and excitement of the fast developing area, which is increasingly being recognized as adventure tourism.

Wait that is not all. How can one forget the serenity of scuba diving along the coral reefs or floating high above terra firma on hot air balloons, yes, even the slow steady ambling along deserts on the gentle camels or horse riding, elephant riding safaris—all these would have been dismissed as fanciful had it not been true and existing on India. And believe it—India is a perfect destination for adventure tourism because it is as enjoyable, exciting, thrilling and invigorating as one makes it.What helps is the destination which is custom made. In India, the mighty Himalayan and the never, never ending coastline and not to forget the two island territories are open invitations to the fun loving and the adventurous souls.

It is not only India's vast geographical diversity that provides a huge scope for the adventure tourist but also that it is relatively unforayed into and comparatively inexpensive too. Those who want to fancy the wild and see mother—nature in its original form, to see man and nature surviving in each other's arms is rediscovering one's own self. The intrigue of age-old monasteries and temples, the Himalayan peaks and slopes, with its dense tropical forests providing diverse fauna and flora and the 3000km of long-long coastline promises the most exciting of sports and adventure imaginable. The best part is that these facilities exist all year through and in different places with affordable prices. Summer has the spotlight on the mountains in the northern most states with its breath taking, views, winter has the country's coastline to explore and in between the shoulder period is covered with a variety of other sports. Season is not the restriction.

Neither is there a constrain of places to go to. Rock climbing is not restricted to Himalayan foot hills, it can be done in the adventure park at Lado Sarai in Delhi too. Similarly kayaking and canoeing is not merely done in the Himalayan slopes or the sea beaches, but also the Bhulasawa lake on the northern tip of Delhi has a multisports leisure complex for the purpose. So it is with parasailing and paddling, boating and fishing; often such sports are available all over India, details given in table 8.1.

Come learn to fly on one of the best training sites in the country with Nirvana Adventures. We have been in the business of teaching paragliding since 1998 and have introduced hundreds of people to this wonderful sport. We have discovered many flying sites within a close radius of our base that are perfect for training and progressing to higher levels. Our efforts have helped develop this area into a 'Paragliding Stronghold' frequented by pilots of all abilities from all over theworld. Fly with us and discover the freedom of powerless flight and the unspoilt nature of this area:

Table 8.1: List of Flying Clubs.

No.	Name	State	Total No. of Aircraft	Name of C.F.I.	Tele phone No.
1.	Delhi Flying Club, Delhi	Delhi	12	Capt. M.S. Beniwal	4618931
2.	Gujarat Flying Club, Baroda	Gujarat	9	Capt. B.K. Manha	442631
3.	Madras Flying Club, Chennai	Tamil Nadu	7	Capt. N. Jai Prakash	91-44-22561709
4.	Patiala Aviation Club, Patiala	Punjab	6	Capt. G.S. Brar	301823
5.	Haryana Institute of Civil Aviation, Karnal + 2 branches at Hissar & Pinjore	Haryana	6	Capt. Kamal Kishore	0814-252320/250731
6.	Andhra Pradesh Flying Club, Hyderabad.	Andhra Pradesh	8	Capt. G.B. Reddy	7753759
7.	Madhya Pradesh Flying Club, Indore + 1 Branch—Bhopal	Madhya Pradesh	12	Capt. Manoj Chabria	413959
8.	Ludhiana Aviation Club, Ludhiana	Punjab	6	Capt. Rachpal Singh	844539
9.	Bihar Flying Training Institute, Patna	Bihar	5	Capt. N.K. Singh	
10.	Govt. Flying Training School, Bangalore	Karnataka	6	Capt. N. Jai Prakash	332251
11.	Hissar Aviation Club—Branch of Haryana Institute of Civil Aviation	Haryana	5	Capt. M.S. Baniwal	37556
12.	Bombay flying Club, Mumbai	Maharashtra	8	Capt. A.J. Bodas	6185100
13.	Kerala Aviation Training Instt. Thiruvananthapuram.	Kerala	4	Capt. Anil Prakash	
14.*	Nagpur Flying Club, Nagpur	Maharashtra	5	Nil	
15.*	Coimbatore Aviation Training Academy, Coimbatore.	Tamil Nadu	6	Capt. P. Ganpathiappan	
16.	Rajasthan State Flying School, Jaipur	Rajasthan	4	Capt. Mohinder Singh	
17.	Government Aviation Training Institute, Bhubaneshwar	Orissa	4	Capt. B.P.S. Budhiraja	
18.*	Government Flying Training Institute, Calcutta	West Bengal	4	Capt. Bhasker Pandey	
19.	Government Flying Training Centre, Lucknow.	Uttar Pradesh	12	Capt. Anjit singh	

(Contd.)

(Contd.)

No.	Name	State	Total No. of Aircraft	Name of C.F.I.	Tele phone No.
20.*	Assam Flying Club, Guwahati	Assam	2	Nil	
21.	Northern India Flying Club, Jullandhar Cantt. (camp at Patiala)	Punjab	5	Capt. S.S. Kang	
22.	Amritsar Aviation Club, Amritsar	Punjab	6	Capt. Rachpal Singh	
23.	Jamshedpur Co-operative Flying Club, Jamshedpur.	Bihar	3	Capt. Santosh Kumar	
24.*	Bansathali Vidyapith Gliding & Flying Club, Banasthali	Rajasthan	1	Nil	
25.	Pinjore Aviation Club, Pinjore (Distt. Ambala)	Haryana	4	Capt. G.S. Cheema	
26.*	Andaman & Nicobar Flying training Institute, Port Blair	U.T. Andaman & Nicobar Islands	1	Nil	
27.	Ajanta Flying Club, Aurangabad	Maharashtra		Nil	
28.	Kanpur Branch of SCAUPFTC, Lucknow.	U.P.		Capt. K.B. Singh	
29.	Faizabad Branch of SCAUPFTC, Lucknow.	U.P.		Capt S.K. Bhatnagar	
30.	Varanasi Branch of SCAUPFTC, Lucknow.	U.P.		Capt. V.V. Singh	
31.	Bhopal Branch of MP Flying Club, Indore	Madhya Pradesh		Capt. A.K. Singh	
32.	Indira Gandhi Rashtriya Urban Akademi, Fursatganj, under Ministry of Civil Aviation not covered unser subsidy scheme	Uttar Pradesh		Air Cdr. P. Bharadwaj	0535-202808

Note: * These Flying Clubs are not operational.

Table 8.2: List of Private Training Institutes

Sl.No.	Name	State	Total No. of Aircraft	Name of C.F.I.	Telephone Nos.
1.	Orient Flight School, Pondicherry.	(U.T.) Pondicherry	5	Capt. P.S. Guron Chennai, Pondicherry	234041
2.*	Bangalore Aeronotics Technical Services Pvt Ltd., (BATS), Bangalore.	Karnataka	3	Nil	5571566/573900
3.	Tata Nagar Aviation, Jamshedpur	Bihar	6	Capt. T.N. Sridhar	0657-407594/ 407816
4.	Ahmedabad Aviation Academy Ahmedabad.	Gujarat	9	Capt. Jasbir Singh	079-2863468
5.	Garg Aviation Ltd., Kanpur	Uttar Pradesh	3	Capt. Arun Man.	0512-300248
6.	Flytech Aviation Ltd., Hyderabad	Andhra Pradesh	7	Capt. P.D. Rao	040-7800331, 7801109
7.	Rajputana Aviation Academy, Kota.	Rajasthan	4	Capt. Keshari Sing Rathore	91-0141-384200 91-0744-427331
8.*	Udan Research & Flying Institute Pvt Ltd., Indore Renamed Frank Airways (P) Ltd.,	Madhya Pradesh	6		
9.	Academy of Carver Aviation Pvt. Ltd., Balgaum	Karnataka	3	Capt. K.K. Sharma Bombay, Belgaum	3892643 420906
10.	Tetra Aviation Academy, Salem	Tamil Nadu	3	Capt. K.S. Sinha	
11.	Wings Aviation Pvt. Ltd., Hyderabad	Andhra Pradesh	3	Capt. R.K. Kaura	
12.	Teneja Aerospace and Aviation Ltd., Bangalore	Karnataka	5	Capt. M.K. Aggarwal	91(080)5550609 5550610; 5550944

- ❖ *Introductory* (2 day course): great for anyone wondering if paragliding is for them, or for someone just wanting to try out something new and exciting!
- ❖ *Achieving free-flight* (3 day course): Aimed at those who want to achieve their dream of free flight but don't have two weekends to spare.
- ❖ *Beginner Pilot* (P1) (5 day course): For those who are sure they want to fly solwn.

8.2 Sports Tourism: An Overview

Estimates of the size of the sports tourism sector vary, mainly because there is no single, agreed definition of what constitutes "sports tourism". While definitions of tourism are well accepted and fairly consistent throughout the world, definitions of sports tourism range from narrow ones involving travel solely for participation in competitive sporting activity to broader definitions where the "sporting" activity might be more leisure or adventure activity incidental to the main purpose of travel. For the purposes of developing a National Sports Tourism Strategy, a relatively narrow definition has been adopted. It is:

- ❖ *Domestic sports tourism*: any sports-related trip of over 40 kms and involving a stay of at least one night away from home; and
- ❖ *International sports tourism*: any trip to Australia a prime purpose of which is to participate in a sporting activity, either as a spectator, participant or official.

The sport or sporting activity under this definition are organised activities—unstructured activities undertaken by individuals have been excluded, as governments' ability to influence such activities is relatively limited. Under such a definition, it appears that sports tourism in Australia might represent about 5 per cent of the overall tourism market, equating to tourism expenditure of about $3 billion per annum.

Tourism and Sport—The World and Australian Markets

Tourism and travel have grown to become not only one of Australia's, but also one of the world's most significant industries. The World Tourism Organisation predicts that global international tourism, which in 1999 generated, directly and indirectly, 11 per cent of global GDP, will expand by 4.1 per cent per year over the next two decades. Australian international visitor arrivals are predicted to grow more quickly at around 7 per cent per year through to 2008. Based on these predictions, tourism is destined to continue playing a vital role in Australia's economic and social development.

Accompanying the growth in tourism has been a significant expansion in the worldwide sport and recreation industry. These industries come together in the sports tourism sector, and with the emergence of "niche" markets as a major factor in tourism development, the potential for growth in the sector is considerable.

Apart from economic factors, notably increases in disposable income, there is a range of other factors influencing the future growth. These include: continuing increases in the number of sporting events and accompanying media exposure; increased professionalism in sport and consequent demand for training camps; the growth of mass participation events such as Masters Games; and the growth in "manufactured" events—both made for television and made specifically to help promote tourism to a region.

Opportunities for Australia at the International, National and Regional Levels

The hosting of the Sydney 2000 Olympics also provides Australia with a unique opportunity. Apart from showcasing Australia to the world, both as a tourism destination and as a country with the ability to successfully stage major sporting events, the Olympics will leave a legacy of expertise in a range of sports-tourism related fields as well as a legacy of world-class sporting venues. The challenge for sports tourism development is to take advantage of all the opportunities this presents.

Industry Coordination

Sports tourism opportunities, and especially the tourism benefits, are sometimes lost or not maximised because the linkages between the sports and tourism sectors are not well established. Sporting activities, especially events, have historically been organised by sporting organisations for purely sporting purposes. Maximising the tourism potential of the events has often not been a major consideration for the organiser, representing a potential failure of the market. Further, many sporting organisations rely on volunteers, and may not have well developed business or organisational skills or experience. Both of these factors can lead to lost tourism opportunities.

To overcome this, better linkages need to be established between the sporting and tourism groups at all levels—regional, state/territory and national. Regional "sports tourism clusters" provide a model for building these linkages at the local level. Similar groupings at state and national levels would also be beneficial. While the State and Territory events units are working to improve linkages, there may be a role for the Commonwealth to disseminate information and take on a coordination and facilitation role at the national level.

Education and Training

Education and training is critical to the success of both the sports and tourism sectors. For sports tourism, the issue of education and training is especially important in ensuring that sporting bodies in particular have the requisite business skills both to run successful events and to recognise and take advantage of the tourism opportunities which accompany the hosting of those events. While training in this area is certainly available, there may be an issue with ensuring such training is appropriate to the needs of the sector and is affordable and accessible.

Regulatory Issues

Government regulation can and does impact on the sports tourism sector—at the local, State/Territory and Commonwealth levels. This can range from the need to obtain permits for road closures etc at the local level, to visa requirements for international athletes or international visitors generally, involved in a sporting activity. It is important to try to minimise any adverse impacts of such regulation.

A basic problem for many organisers is simply trying to deal with what can seem like a maze of different agencies with differing requirements. While some States/Territories have developed information kits to help address this issue, the Commonwealth could also play a major role in assisting organisers to navigate through this maze.

Infrastructure

Most if not all sporting activities and events rely on there being appropriate infrastructure in place. The most obvious form of infrastructure is the sporting facilities themselves, however other infrastructure is often more important if sports tourism opportunities are to be maximised.

Adequate accommodation and transport are often critical to the success of events where large numbers of people may need to be moved and accommodated. This can provide difficulties in regional areas, where accommodation may be in short supply and where transport links, both to and within a region, may be expensive and/or suffer from inadequate capacity.

A starting point in addressing these issues, and one which the Commonwealth and a number of States and Territories have already embarked on, would be to conduct facilities audits to identify just what sporting facilities and at what standard, are available. A further logical step down this track would be to conduct a broader "asset audit" of all relevant infrastructure, to assist organisers in assessing the ability of a region to support a particular sporting activity or event.

Research and Data Collection

Like many niche tourism sectors, the sports tourism sector suffers from a lack of reliable data on which to base strategic decision-making. Even data which might help measure the size of the sector is not readily available. Indeed, there is no agreed definition of just what constitutes "sports tourism", hence any discussion of research and data needs must start with the need to come to some consensus as to just what "sports tourism" comprises. Limited data is available from the major tourism surveys—the International Visitor Survey and the National Visitor Survey. At best, however, the picture they draw is very partial but does indicate that sports tourism is significant in the overall tourism market.

A further issue is that most of the available research tends to focus on individual events and not on improving our overall understanding of the sports tourism market and how it operates at a national or regional level.

Evaluation of Events

There are numerous "models" employed to evaluate events which can lead to different outcomes and a consequent inability to compare results. A more consistent methodology, and in the case of smaller regional events, a simplified methodology, would be of considerable benefit. The Cooperative Research Centre for Sustainable Tourism, through its events sub-program and its recently established sports tourism "node", may be able to better coordinate activity in this area, and help provide a more "macro level" focus. Australia can learn from international experience in the sports tourism field. The United Kingdom, through the British Tourist Authority, has developed a sports tourism marketing strategy and has recently appointed a sports tourism coordinator in their Sydney office. Canada has been pursuing a program of developing sports tourism "clusters" or networks in regional areas, to bring together relevant players, raise awareness and maximise tourism benefits. South Africa also has identified sports tourism as a growth sector.

Implementation

Successful implementation of a national strategy will require a concerted and coordinated effort from a range of organisations, including governments at all levels (Commonwealth, State/Territory and local), the tourism industry, the sports sector including national and state/territory sporting organisations and researchers.

At the State/Territory level, State departments and events corporations take on much of the responsibility for building these links. At the local level, there may be a greater need for development of networks or "clusters" focussing on sports tourism development. At the national level, there may also be a need for better coordination.

Conclusion

Clearly, sports tourism in Australia has enormous potential. A number of factors, including strong inbound tourism growth, a sporting culture, good sporting and tourism infrastructure, and the catalytic effect of the Sydney 2000 Olympic Games, are combining to make this a key growth area. The challenge is to maximise that growth in a manner that can provide genuine economic and social benefits for Australia and Australians. This draft Strategy poses a number of questions, with the aim of identifying key measures which would need to be implemented to facilitate growth of the sports tourism industry.

Background

The development of the National Sports Tourism Strategy has its genesis in the *National Action Plan for Tourism*. The Plan, released in 1998, provides a policy framework for the future growth of the tourism industry in Australia. It identifies the development of a range of niche tourism products as one of the avenues which will promote strong future growth and diversification of the industry, and identifies sports tourism as one of the sectors showing enormous potential for further development.

In November 1999 the Federal Minister for Sport and Tourism, the Hon Jackie Kelly MP, announced the Government's intention to develop a National Sports Tourism Strategy in recognition of the need for a planned and consistent approach to building a larger sustainable base for the sports tourism sector.

The development of the Strategy to date has involved extensive consultation with a wide range of stakeholders; desk research; the production of a preliminary discussion paper; and the organisation of a series of focus group workshops around Australia. In the past decade tourism has been firmly established as a major industry in Australia, economically, socially and as a job provider for Australians. In 1996-97, tourism directly accounted for 5.8 per cent of expenditure on Gross Domestic Product (GDP). Growth in the tourism industry is forecast to continue well into the next decade, especially for international tourism, with the Tourism Forecasting Council predicting that international visitor arrivals will grow at an average annual rate of 7.3 per cent to 2008 when we will welcome 8.4 million visitors. In 1999, international tourism to Australia generated export earnings of $17 billion and accounted for 14.9 per cent of Australia's total export earnings. Expenditure derived from domestic tourism was $44.8 billion in 1998-99. Sport has always been an integral part of Australian life and it is increasingly being recognised that sporting events and activities have the potential to be a major tourism drawcard. Australia has something of a natural advantage in this niche market given our strong international image as a sporting nation. This reputation is largely based on the achievements of our sports men and women and images from international events held here. It also forms part of the Australian "lifestyle", an experience which is consistently rated as a major motivating factor in bringing international visitors to Australia.

The popularity of sports events, which constitute a significant proportion of all events held in Australia, guarantees that they are a major component of tourism agencies' strategies for destination development. For the Australian Tourist Commission (ATC), the promotion of Australia as a destination for a holiday featuring sports activity is a logical development of Australia's strong sporting image and the ATC has incorporated a "sports" theme in its overseas marketing. Sports tourism, or tourism which is associated with sporting activity, therefore has the potential to develop into a highly significant niche sector which provides Australia with economic and social benefits. The hosting of the Olympic Games in Sydney in 2000 is undeniably a definitive moment for sports tourism in Australia and has the potential to bring significant ongoing benefits to the Australian tourism sector. While mega-events of this ilk are definitely not the "bread and butter" of sports tourism, the Olympics will provide many lessons in organising, running and capitalising on the tourism benefits of sporting events. We need to ensure that Australia obtains every possible advantage from hosting this one-off special event, in order to build a more sustainable base for the long-term future viability of the sports tourism sector in Australia.

The remainder of this document constitutes a draft sports tourism strategy aimed at eliciting comment from interested parties prior to its finalisation.

1. The Key Elements of the Strategy

The aim of the strategy is to facilitate a viable and internationally competitive sports tourism industry and to ensure that the benefits of this niche market are maximised and spread widely throughout Australia. This objective has been identified because of the perception that the tourism benefits which sporting activities and events can provide are not currently being maximised. The strategy identifies *opportunities* for the development of the sports tourism sector as well as identifying and addressing *impediments* to the growth of the industry.

The key elements of the strategy are a range of possible actions which can help to:

- ❖ Improve the coordination and competitiveness of the sports tourism industry ....
- ❖ Identify and address education and training issues for the industry ....
- ❖ Minimise the impact of regulatory issues (*e.g.* visas, customs) on the industry ....
- ❖ Identify and address the infrastructure requirements of the industry ....
- ❖ Identify and address the research and data collection requirements of the industry ....
- ❖ Improve the means of evaluation of the economic benefits of sports tourism........
- ❖ Coordinate the implementation of the strategy ......

2. What is Sports Tourism?

Sports tourism is a niche market which can be broadly described as a tourism activity generated by participation in sporting activity. That activity can be a sporting event or competition, a tour of a sporting facility, or a training camp. Participation might involve being a competitor/participant, official, or spectator. The Australian definitions of international and domestic tourism are well understood and accepted and are used as the basis for the definitions of sports tourism adopted for the development of this Strategy. These are:

- ❖ Domestic sports tourism: any sports-related trip of over 40 kms and involving a stay of at least one night away from home; and
- ❖ International sports tourism: any trip to Australia a prime

purpose of which is to participate in a sporting activity, either as a spectator, participant or official.

As to what constitutes a sporting activity in this context some decisions need to be made in relation to activities that could be seen more as recreational (*e.g.* fishing, golf, skiing, horse-racing) and also to adventure activities (*e.g.* sky surfing, para-sailing, rock-climbing, etc). All of these activities require skill and also offer potential for competition, however they are also frequently pursued by individuals in an unstructured way and maybe entirely incidental to their main reason for travelling.

While this may not matter in some respects, structured, organised sports events, tours, camps and so on arguably offer more potential for industry and governments to target with a view to increasing the tourism potential, than do leisure and adventure activities—important though they are in their own right. It is therefore those activities which can be targeted for further development which are included within the ambit of this Strategy.

3. Tourism and Sport—The World Market

Tourism and travel make up one of the world's largest industries. In 1999 the World Travel and Tourism Council (WTTC) also reports that across the global economy, travel and tourism generates, directly and indirectly:

* ❖   11 per cent of GDP;
* ❖   200 million jobs;
* ❖   8 per cent of total employment; and
* ❖   5.5 million new jobs per year until 2010.

World Tourism Organisation (WTO) data for 1999 show that 663 million people spent at least one night in a foreign country, up 4.1 per cent over the previous year. Spending on international tourism reached US$453 billion — a growth rate of nearly 3 per cent over 1998. These results are in line with WTO's long-term growth forecast *Tourism: 2020 Vision* which predicts that the tourism sector will expand by an average of 4.1 per cent a year over the next two decades. Annual international arrivals are expected to surpass one billion by the year 2010 and reach 1.6 billion by the year 2020.

Reasons for this sustained growth include greater disposable income in tourism generating countries, and, especially in some of the emerging economies of Asia, more leisure time, earlier retirement, improvements in infrastructure and transport (particularly air transport), and changes in consumer spending preferences.

Sport

Sport and active recreation have become very large and successful industries worldwide. A 1994 European Commission Report on the European Community and Sport estimated that the sports industry is responsible for 2.5 per cent of world trade. The factors influencing the growth of sport and recreation are similar to those influencing tourism growth—notably increased disposable income, greater availability of leisure time and changing consumer preferences. An increased awareness of the benefits for all ages of greater physical activity has also been important. In addition, the role of the media in promoting sports has been critical. A number of factors have contributed to this greater international media attention on sport and recreation, especially in western economies:

❖ Increased demand for sports programming from television broadcasters to meet consumer demand, the advent of dedicated sports channels (eg. Fox Sports, ESPN, C7 Sports), and the availability of satellite technology allowing live coverage;

❖ Increased prominence of professional sportspersons across a range of sports, *e.g.* golf, tennis, basketball, baseball, surfing, rugby and soccer;

❖ Large amounts of money being spent by corporations directly and indirectly sponsoring events, teams and individuals for commercial advantage;

❖ Sports associations becoming more like large-scale business enterprises;

❖ Growth of merchandise associated with particular sports, sporting activities and sporting teams;

❖ Significant advertising, promotion, and activity associated with high-profile international sporting events, *e.g.* the Olympic Games, soccer World Cups, Grand Slam tennis, Formula One Grand Prix, and national sporting competitions; and

❖ Increasing opportunities for participation, especially in western economies, through changing leisure patterns, ageing of the population, increased disposable income, and increased awareness of the benefits of physical activity.

Sports Tourism

Having regard to the trends emerging in both the tourism and sports sectors, it is not surprising that significant growth is also occurring in travel for sports related purposes. In fact, this growth is also linked to another trend—that of travelling for specific "niche" purposes, of which sporting activity is one. The British Tourist Authority and English Tourism Board claim as many as 20 per cent of tourists trips are for the prime purpose of sports participation, whilst up to 50 per cent of holidays include incidental sports participation. This level of activity is broadly consistent with Canadian data, with the 1998 Canadian Travel Survey finding that 37 per cent of domestic trips that year were for sports-related purposes. In the case of the United States, the Travel Industry Association of America found that in the past five years, 38 per cent of US adults attended an organised sports event, competition or tournament as either a spectator or participant, while on a trip of 50 miles or more. These figures are based on rather broad definitions of the "sport" in sports tourism.

Significantly, perhaps, the sports market, and hence the sports tourism market, is becoming increasingly internationalised. As previously mentioned, the availability of sports-only TV channels which display sports from numerous countries around the world, as well as increasing coverage of an ever-expanding range of sporting events through more mainstream media outlets, means there is an increasing awareness of the range of sporting activities being pursued around the world, including in countries such as Australia.

4. Tourism and Sport—The Australian Market

Tourism has grown to be one of Australia's most significant industries.

While a small player in terms of world arrivals, Australia is a major tourism destination in terms of tourism receipts, ranking 12th in the world for 1999.

In 1996-97, tourism accounted directly for 5.8 per cent of expenditure on Gross Domestic Product (GDP), and was directly responsible for the employment of over 670 000 persons and indirectly for a further 290 000. This accounts for 11.5 per cent of total Australian employment. In 1998/99, expenditure derived from domestic tourism was $44.8 billion. In 1999, international tourism to Australia generated exports of $17 billion and accounted for 14.9 per cent of Australia's total export earnings.

Tourism is destined to continue playing a vital role in Australia's economic and social development. The Tourism Forecasting Council (TFC) predicts that international visitor arrivals will grow at an annual average rate of 7.3 per cent to 2008 and generate nearly $32 billion in export earnings in 2008. This means international visitor number in excess of 8.4 million in 2008—almost double the current level of tourist visitation to Australia. Much higher levels of growth are predicted from emerging Asian markets including China (21.1 per cent), South Korea (23.7 per cent) and Thailand (18.3 per cent). On the domestic front growth is anticipated to be steady with an average annual growth rate of 1.6 per cent for the period 1998-99 to 2008-09.

Sport

Australia has long been regarded as a sporting nation. Significant interest by the Australian public in sports of one type or another across wide demographic boundaries ensures that the sport industry in Australia assumes a significant economic, social and even political profile.

Involvement in sport and sporting activity not only benefits both the health and general well-being of our nation, it also makes a sizeable contribution to the Australian economy. Precise figures are extremely difficult to find—a problem for sports tourism also, and one which is discussed later in this strategy. What is clear is that the sports sector generates many billions of dollars within the economy and provides employment for tens of thousands of people. Despite its size and significance, many sectors of the industry are not highly commercialised, although some, such as the businesses supplying goods and services which support sporting activities, are very commercially focussed. There is a large "not-for-profit" segment of the sports sector, exemplified by the number of volunteers working within it. In 1994/95 there were 112,877 volunteers working in the sports industries which was almost double the formal employment in sports industries at that time. The majority of these volunteers (89 per cent) worked within the sports, or in the provision of services to sports, sectors.

Structurally, the sports sector is very decentralised. An important part of the sector is the local sporting club—bodies dedicated to the development of single sports run by and for its members. These clubs often affiliate with regional and state associations which, in turn, unite to form National Sporting Organisations (NSOs). Volunteers administer sport at all levels—particularly the club level. At state and national levels professional administrators begin to play a role, although even here volunteers may still make a significant contribution. Professional clubs also exist in parallel with this system in the major sports like the football codes, basketball, cricket and baseball. They belong to state or national leagues and are managed predominantly by full-time professional administrators and coaches.

Special purpose associations exist to promote particular interests such as sports medicine, coaching, school and university competition, physical education, legal issues and professional development for sports workers. These usually affiliate with an umbrella body which operates at the national level. Government involvement in sport occurs at each of the three levels of government—local, state and national, through the various departments dealing with sport and recreation, the Australian Sports Commission, the Australian Institute of Sport, and the State Institutes of Sports and Academies. There are also a range of non-government organisations which administer, coordinate and promote particular interests at both state and national levels.

Within the government sector, there are a number of vehicles for seeking to discuss and coordinate issues relating to sport industry development. The Sport and Recreation Ministers Council (SRMC) is the peak body for discussion between the Commonwealth and State and Territory Governments for issues concerning sport and recreation needs across Australia. It is supported by the Standing Committee on

Recreation and Sport (SCORS), whose members are senior officials in the sports departments of each State and Territory. The Commonwealth Government has also given recognition to the many commercial businesses which service Australian participation in sport, through the development of a strategic plan to facilitate the growth of the commercial sports and leisure services sector. Both the tourism industry and the sports industry in Australia come together in the sports tourism sector. Those involved include sport and tourism departments; major events corporations; sporting bodies; facilities managers; event organisers and promoters; tour operators and accommodation providers; transport operators; retailers; and the full range of organisations providing goods and services to both sporting and tourism operators.

However, not all of these groups necessarily perceive themselves as being part of a broader sports tourism industry, resulting in potential lost opportunities associated with the staging of Australia's many and various sporting events. While it is difficult to establish the size of the industry, some efforts have been made to quantify its value to the Australian economy. For example, during the focus group process forming part of the development of this draft strategy, a number of participants suggested that the sector accounts for about 5 per cent of the total tourism market, based on the relatively narrow definition proposed in the Strategy. If this is the case across both international and domestic tourism, sports tourism in Australia would account for annual expenditure of about $3 billion per annum.

This estimate is consistent with analysis undertaken by the Bureau of Tourism Research and published in the recent paper *Sports Tourism: An Australian Perspective*, which found that 6 per cent of day trips and 5 per cent of overnight trips taken by Australians in Australia, were taken with sport as the primary motivation. This corresponds to expenditure of $1847 million by domestic sports tourists, of which $461 million was on day trips and the remaining $1386 million was spent on overnight trips.

Australian domestic sports tourists appear to generate a higher dollar yield than other domestic travellers, with 31 per cent staying in hotel, resort, motel or motor inn accommodation on their sports trip compared with 23 per cent for all domestic travellers. Consequently, their estimated average daily expenditure of $130 is higher than the $112 estimated for other domestic travellers.

5. Opportunities for Australia at the International, National and Regional Levels

Australia has many competitive advantages in the sports tourism marketplace, including a climate conducive to outdoor activities, a diverse range of sporting activities, access to quality sports facilities, well developed tourism infrastructure and an internationally renowned image as a sporting nation and tourism destination.

Even the fact that our seasons are the reverse of those in the major tourism source markets of the Northern Hemisphere provides a range of opportunities in areas such as pre-season training camps. Similarly, our expertise in areas such as sports science and sports medicine, as well as leading edge facilities such as the Australian Institute of Sport, help to encourage international sporting teams and individuals to travel to Australia.

These assets form the basis for an internationally competitive tourism product. However they have to be managed in a way that delivers the maximum benefits for the country as a whole. While there are numerous opportunities within the broader sports tourism fields, some sectors and some markets appear to have particular potential for Australia to exploit.

International Opportunities

The Olympics

The sport mega-event is the most widely recognised example of sports tourism. And, with mega-events such as the Olympic Games and the World Cup Football it is not surprising that they involve the largest volumes of spectators and the largest revenues of all special events and festivals.

The value of hosting an Olympic Games has been the subject of much research with wide ranging views on the benefits and costs of such an event. A significant increase in tourism is not a guaranteed certainty with many impacts dependent upon the organisation and marketing of the Olympic Games. Regardless, the staging of an Olympic

Games is recognised as being a unique opportunity for the host city and country to engage in high-profile promotion their tourism products at a worldwide level. Development of international standard sporting facilities, and the upgrading of facilities required for pre-Games training, is both an obvious and tangible legacy. High quality facilities combined with a successful hosting of the Olympics will give Australia a head start in bidding for major sporting events in the years immediately following the Games. It is also in these years that the Tourism Forecasting Council predict Australia will receive a major tourism benefit from the Olympic Games with additional international visitor numbers of 342 000 in 2000, 335 000 in 2001 and 350 000 in 2002. If these numbers are realised, and they may well be, Australia will have received an immediate and major dividend from the hosting of the Games. Many of those additional visitors will no doubt participate in sporting activities while in Australia.

Just as importantly perhaps, the lessons that have been learned by governments, sporting bodies and business will play a major role in the further development of the sports tourism sector. The Olympics will also expose Australia's sporting and tourism assets to vast new audiences and markets, providing significant opportunities in the sports tourism field. Australia's traditional international "sports tourism" markets have been North America, Europe and New Zealand. Rugby tests in particular, but also rugby league, cricket and to a lesser extent netball, generate significant trans-Tasman traffic flows. More recently, however there appears to be considerable emerging growth potential from upper middle and high income Asian economies, including Japan, Korea and Taiwan. Other emerging markets (*e.g.* India, Latin America and South Africa) offer similar promise where the distribution of wealth is changing and there is an expanding middle class with an increasing level of disposable income.

National Opportunities

Masters Games

Masters Games provide sports tourism opportunities at the international, national and regional level. They may well prove to be the greatest potential growth area in sports tourism over the next decade. A relatively recent phenomenon, these games have already grown to occupy a central place among sports tourism activities and are keenly fought over and bid for by potential hosts, because of the sheer numbers of participants involved and their demographic profile— ie Masters—which generally equates to high levels of disposable income. At the top of the Masters Games tree—which comprises local, inter-state, national and international events—is the World Masters Games. Recognised as the world's biggest multi-sport festival, the World Masters Games are considered the premier international event for Masters competitors, allowing them to compete regardless of ability, gender, race or religion. In terms of competition, they are twice as big as the Olympic Games.

Held every four years, the World Masters Games are participant focused, with competitors only being required to meet each sports age qualification. In Australia, the first sanctioned Masters Games were held in 1986 in Alice Springs. The first Australian (ie national) Masters Games were held in Tasmania in 1987. Since then the Australian Masters Games have been held in Adelaide (1989), Brisbane (1991), Perth (1993), Melbourne (1995), Canberra (1997) and Adelaide (1999). The eighth Australian Masters Games will be held in Newcastle and the Hunter region in 2001.

The overall philosophy of the Australian Masters Games is to provide an incentive for mature age persons to begin, or continue active participation in sport. It aims to provide a focus for individual sports to develop their own mature age sport events and to maintain mature sports as a continuing aspect of their programs and focus. There is a definite aim of the Games to promote community interest and participation in mature age sport and to thereby contribute to the health of its citizens and the nation. The organisers of the 2001 Australian Masters Games in Newcastle have also identified the potential for the Games to have a significant impact on tourism, sport and culture in the Newcastle and Hunter region and to increase both tourism and brand awareness of the area at a domestic and business level.

"Manufactured" Events

Over the past twenty years or so the interest in sport, especially elite sporting events, has grown at a phenomenal rate. Sport is no longer just about playing the game, it is now perceived to have an obligation to provide public entertainment. This growth has been in parallel with advances in technology and the evolution of the digital age. People now expect to be entertained by worldwide sporting events telecast live direct to their television sets—or perhaps on their home computer.

According to a survey conducted by the Australian Bureau of Statistics in November 1997, sporting programs were the most commonly watched on television after news and current affairs, and were viewed regularly by over half of all Australians aged over 18 (55%). A relatively recent concept is the "manufacture" of sporting events for television—events such as the "One Summer" sporting festival of beach related sporting events is a case in point of what is almost exclusively a television event. There can be a number of tourism-related benefits, including marketing benefits, from events such as these.

Another variation on the "manufactured" event theme is an event which is designed from the outset to promote tourism, rather than being designed as a purely sporting event with the tourism aspect an added extra. The main emphasis in events of this nature, of which there are still relatively few, is on the promotion of tourism to the region where the event is being held, rather than just on the event itself. An excellent example is the Jacobs Creek Tour Down Under in South Australia, which sees cyclists racing through regional South Australia, receiving national and international media coverage and by careful planning and route selection, promoting the region to potential tourists.

One of the major benefits of this type of event is that they can be designed using existing locations, and to suit the capabilities of the region. Examples include cycle races, triathlons, road races, "challenges" such as the Omeo challenge, etc. Critically, these events can be introduced to even out peaks and troughs in tourism activity, and can be tailored to fit into a regional tourism package of events, attractions and activities. They can also spread the accommodation load across a region if necessary. Given that the region which created the event then "owns" the event, they can be conducted on an annual basis which in the longer term reduces the costs associated with their staging.

Regional and Local Opportunities

Masters Games and "manufactured" events can have significant impact at the regional and local level, as well as nationally. Indeed, there are numerous market sectors within sports tourism which lend themselves to regional areas and the lower level of facilities and infrastructure which these areas generally possess.

A key issue for regional areas is to identify the range and level of resources and infrastructure which they do possess, and to use this information as the basis for identifying and pursuing suitable sports tourism opportunities.

Some examples of events which might well lend themselves to hosting by regional or local areas include:

❖ Schools and underage championships, which can vary in size from quite small to very large (*e.g.* Albury has been very active in pursuing this part of the market);

❖ National or indeed international events in "lesser" sports (*e.g.* Corowa has hosted a world parachuting championship recently while Manilla is a world-renowned paragliding centre);

❖ Regional championships in a variety of sports; and

❖ Sports which can be held at a number of locations throughout a region.

Marketing Opportunities

Sports tourism events at the international, national and regional levels have a double-barrelled effect—the direct effect of the attendance of the competitors and/or spectators and accompanying persons, and the indirect effect of the marketing of the destination which will lead to subsequent tourism flows. This indirect effect can be very large—most of the tourism benefits of the Olympics are expected to be of this nature. Even for non-mega events, for example events like the Gold Coast Indy Car Race, the Australian Formula 1 and 500cc Motor Cycle Grand Prix and even events such as the Australian Surf Life Saving Championships, this impact can be very significant.

There is a marketing effect through the word-of-mouth recommendation of attendees at the event, (such as with Masters competitions) but potentially a much greater effect if the event attracts widespread media interest—especially live television coverage.

The marketing spin-offs from sports tourism events can vary enormously depending on a range of factors, including whether the tourism aspects were considered as an integral part of the event and were "built-in" to the development process. For example, the Gold Coast Indy Car race is deliberately designed to showcase Australia's premier beach destination—the Gold Coast—with parts of the track running right beside Surfers Paradise beach.

Given Australia's status as a relatively little known tourism destination in world terms, the marketing benefits from events, particularly from mega-events such as the Olympics, may be greater than for countries which are already well known tourist destinations. This presents a genuine opportunity for better showcasing Australia's tourism assets through sporting events.

6. Industry Coordination

It is clear that major sports events can play a significant role in generating tourism activity on a national and international scale. Such events can have positive economic and social benefits, and have in recent years been increasingly recognised by both national and State governments as a legitimate focus for tourism and general economic development strategies.

One manifestation of governments' support of events-based strategies is the provision of funding for events and infrastructure by Commonwealth, State and Territory sport departments, and the creation in most states of dedicated events corporations. As this investment in events increases, Governments are being increasingly required to justify their expenditure in these areas, with the attendant challenge being how to enhance sporting events as tourism products so as to maximise returns on investment.

Developing a Strategic Approach

The Commonwealth government is currently developing a Strategic National Plan for the Sport and Leisure Services Industry. The plan will articulate a vision for the industry and ways for the industry to become world class in the provision of sport and leisure goods and services. Success in realising this vision will require advanced business networks and better relationships between business, governments, sporting organisations and consumers of leisure activities.

A similar challenge faces the sports tourism sector. The sports tourism focus group discussions identified the need for the sports tourism sector to identify itself as a discrete industry group and to establish the linkages necessary to capture commercial opportunities.

The current lack of an identity and cohesiveness was identified as one of the major impediments to the growth of the sports tourism sector. In addition, the lack of recognition by both government and the private sector of the economic potential of sports tourism has led to many opportunities being overlooked. Some of the key issues which need to be addressed to encourage and enable the growth of sports tourism include *establishing linkages* to enable the raising of awareness of the mutual benefits and advantages of establishing alliances; coordinating planning and the *sharing of resources and information*; and identifying opportunities and mechanisms for *maximising the tourism benefits* of sporting activities.

Establishing Linkages

The fact that most events are organised by sporting bodies as sporting events first and foremost with tourism almost an optional extra, represents a failure of the market. Sporting bodies arguably have little incentive to pursue the tourism benefits which can flow from sporting activities, especially sporting events, because they themselves cannot directly capture many of those benefits. The great majority of those benefits accrue to other parties—tour operators, accommodation providers, transport operators, retail outlets, restaurants and so on. And yet many of these people may not even perceive that they stand to benefit significantly from tourism activity associated with sporting events.

To some extent, States and Territories have moved to address this by establishing major events corporations, to bring together the sports and tourism players and to bid for events. This works very well for some events—most notably the larger, higher profile events on which the events corporations generally focus.

However, the needs of second-tier or regional events are not necessarily adequately met through this process. At a regional level, governments could play a role in facilitating the establishment of "cluster" groups comprising the full range of stakeholders in the sports tourism process. A useful model could be the cluster formed in Cairns following the focus group conducted there—"Sports Tropical North Queensland". Significantly, the Cairns group is being coordinated by the economic development corporation, reflecting the broad benefit which sports tourism events can provide throughout the regional economy.

Sharing of Resources and Information

At the regional level, clusters or networks can play a number of roles to help coordinate activities, assist in the sharing of physical resources and encourage information sharing. For smaller sporting bodies, the level of resources required (eg. signage, barriers, marquees) may be a deterrent to running events, as can be the lack of knowledge for first time organisers. Simply sharing these resources can assist in the planning and running of successful events, with region-wide benefits for both sporting and tourism groups.

At a national level, the Commonwealth could play a role which would largely be one of the provision of information, including providing links and referrals to the enormous range of information already available, much of which has been produced by States and Territories, but which is currently not being accessed by event organisers or tourism groups.

Maximising the Tourism Benefits

There are a number of ways to maximise the returns from investment in events. These include:

- ❖ Improving the yield from existing events;
- ❖ Staging more events;
- ❖ Targeting and supporting events that offer the biggest potential returns in terms of tourism;
- ❖ Spreading the benefits of new and existing events to more regions, rather than just the major metropolitan centres; and
- ❖ Better coordination of sporting events with other tourism related activities to maximise visitor stay and yield.

Success in each of these areas relies on the establishment of alliances between sport and tourism bodies at all levels—national, state/ territory and regional—and greater emphasis on cooperative planning and coordination. This emerged as the top priority in almost every focus group discussion held around Australia.

Recent international experience such as that in the UK (*see* **Appendix 4**) has illustrated that simply bringing the sport and tourism sectors together is not sufficient to encourage the development of working alliances. It will therefore be important to demonstrate clearly to both the sport and tourism sectors the practical advantages of creating and encouraging alliances.

While sporting events continue to be organised purely as sporting events with tourism a secondary consideration, progress towards fully capturing the business opportunities associated with sports tourism will remain difficult. What is required is for events or activities to be seen as sports tourism opportunities and for organisers to give equal weight to the requirement to run a technically and administratively successful sporting event and the opportunity to maximise the visitation and yield by producing an appropriate tourism package.

Possible Commonwealth Facilitation Role

One of the key suggestions arising from the focus group discussions is for the Commonwealth government to play a facilitation role for the development of sports tourism in Australia. In doing so, the Commonwealth government could help address a perceived general lack of coordination between private sector, government, and sport and tourism bodies, and rectify the absence of an effective and appropriate mechanism for the dissemination of information throughout the sports tourism sector. This facilitation role could focus primarily on the provision and dissemination of information, referral to appropriate agencies, and the encouragement of better communication between key sports and tourism players.

Project Facilitation

The Commonwealth government could also play a role in the facilitation of major projects—the so-called mega events—which impact on national interests as well as individual State/Territory interests. A possible model could be the approach adopted for the Olympics, where a coordination unit brought together the many Commonwealth agencies necessary to make the event a success. This role would be undertaken on an "as needs" basis, when events of this magnitude are being considered or planned.

Network Facilitation

More generally, as already mentioned, there is a need to help facilitate the establishment of sports tourism networks or clusters, especially at a regional level, to ensure opportunities are not lost and are indeed maximised. There are existing models in other industries.

By way of example, as part of the Furnishing Industry Action Agenda, which aims to improve the competitiveness of the furnishing industry, the Commonwealth Government has recently announced the establishment of a Furnishing Industry Unit within the Department of Industry, Science and Resources. This unit will act as a focal point within the Commonwealth for issues of concern to the sector, and will aim to improve networking and statistical data collection.

A similar mechanism could be established for sports tourism and might play a similar role, although broader, to that being undertaken by Soar International in Canada. Soar International is a sports information and event management company contracted by the Canadian Tourism Commission to facilitate the development of sports tourism networks in regional areas.

Questions

Should the Commonwealth government facilitate the development of sport tourism in Australia and, if so, in what ways? Some possibilities include:

❖ *Information dissemination*: Development of a website to bring together a range of information relating to international, national, state, regional and local events, funding, planning, management, research and economic evaluation, with links to other relevant websites

❖ *Project facilitation*: Form a "one-stop-shop" for events

organisers to access information and facilitate liaison with other government portfolios and agencies

❖ Establishing networks between sports and tourism organisations and agencies: Develop a database of key stakeholders at national level, and develop a similar model for use by state and regional areas to bring together the relevant organisations and agencies.

❖ *Hosting workshops*: To promote and establish sports tourism "clusters" such as the one formed in Cairns following the Focus Group workshop conducted as part of the development of this Strategy.

❖ *Assessing research needs*: Work with CRC Tourism Events sub-program and researchers to establish, maintain and disseminate a register of research undertaken, and identify research needs

❖ Assessing education and training needs: Work with educational institutions, training bodies and the industry to identify education and training needs and provide information on appropriate courses available to stakeholders.

❖ Providing advice on infrastructure development: Provide advice to government on requirements for facilities and asset audits, disseminate results of audits.

❖ Promoting best practice: Disseminate information on best practice, assist in development of standards, particularly with regard to economic evaluation of events.

❖ Establishing appropriate industry awards: Consider possibility of developing industry "award for excellence" for sports tourism in conjunction with a peak body such as Tourism Council Australia or Sport Industry Australia.

❖ Promoting international competitiveness: Disseminate information and resources which promote competitiveness and assist in capturing international markets (*e.g.* access to Government programs such as the Export Markets Development Grants Scheme)

Is a strategy of encouraging the development of regional sports tourism "clusters" an appropriate way to assist sports tourism development in regional Australia?—if so, whose responsibility is it to undertake this role?

7. Education and Training

There is widespread recognition that a high level of business expertise and management skill is critical if the sports tourism sector is to successfully meet the needs of the increasingly discerning sports tourism consumer. The focus group discussions highlighted the demand for appropriate and accessible education and training, particularly in the area of management, where many not-for-profit sporting organisations rely on part-time staff or volunteers. Equally, tourism organisations would benefit from greater awareness of sports tourism opportunities and some education and training to enable them to maximise the tourism potential of sporting events and activities.

Sport and Recreation

Sport and recreation industry specific education and training is provided through a combination of graduate/post graduate university education, vocational education and training (VET), on the job training (sometimes with a VET component), industry based training and accreditation and a range of short courses. The most common VET providers are the technical and further education (TAFE) institutions, although some sectors, for example the fitness industry, mainly use private training providers. Other training providers include community based organisations, individual businesses and some secondary schools.

A national industry training advisory body, Sport and Recreation Training Australia, which is jointly funded by industry and government with employer and employee representation, provides advice on the range of industry training needs. A National Sport Industry Training package became available in 1999.

Some areas of the industry have introduced training and accreditation systems for instructors, primarily as a result of the threat of litigation in an area of high risk of injury to participants. Employment in these areas is generally dependent on possession of an industry qualification in addition to specific industry skills.

Tourism

As in the sport and recreation sector, the tourism industry has access to industry specific education and training from a combination of graduate/post graduate university education, vocational education and training (VET), on the job training, industry based training and accreditation and a range of short courses.

A national industry training advisory body, Tourism Training Australia (TTA) develops and delivers integrated tourism packages for the tourism industry. Many forms of management and staff training are available, including in-house or on the job training, self paced and distance learning packages, and formal courses offered by TAFE colleges, universities and private tourism training enterprises.

Among the priority areas identified by TTA for future skills development are management and business skills for medium and small enterprises, marketing skills and specific management and operational skills for the meetings, conferences, exhibitions and events sector.

The Sports Tourism Sector

Despite the education and training opportunities available in the sport and recreation and tourism industries, there remains a continuing need for improving workforce and management skills. This is particularly so in areas characterised by volunteers or low wage employees or where there is a predominance of part time jobs and high staff turnover. In particular, organisations relying on government funding find it difficult to attract and retain skilled employees.

In terms of higher education, new courses focussing specifically on sports tourism are starting to emerge. For example, Southern Cross University recently introduced a degree course in Sports Tourism. However, more generally, as was suggested at the focus group discussions, a more comprehensive range of education and training opportunities is needed if the sports tourism sector is to fully realise its growth potential.

This could be achieved through the development of an industry training package that identifies the skill requirements for qualifications in various occupations, and the appropriate training courses to acquire these skills. Development of such a package would require input from industry associations, government sport and tourism bodies, industry training bodies and universities and TAFE institutions. A range of accreditation opportunities could be also developed to enhance professional development opportunities for employees, trainees, and volunteers. Improved access and take-up of management courses would also assist businesses improve their performance. This is particularly so for many not-for-profit sporting organisations whose personnel may have a high degree of technical knowledge about their sport but are less skilled in business management. Volunteers can also pose particular challenges in the take up of management training due to time and resource constraints.

One means of improving management training could be to augment generic management courses with elements tailored to the sports tourism sector, for example, on strategic planning and development of an event calendar, how to create and maintain linkages between sport and tourism organisations, and ways to prepare an appropriate tourism package for a particular sporting market.

One suggestion made in the focus group discussions was for agencies responsible for funding sporting bodies to provide greater recognition for sporting organisations whose executive hold relevant qualifications or undertake appropriate courses or participate in the existing volunteer and management improvement programs. Another suggestion was for State and Territory funding agencies or regional organisations to arrange mobile "in-service" training for regional areas.

Specific sports tourism development courses could also assist in the formation and development of sports tourism clusters, such as the one established in Cairns. There could be a role for regional development and tourism associations to develop and make available 'value adding' packages to regional tourism and sporting organisations that include, for example, checklists and guidelines for organising committees. Such packages could include tourism product marketing material for sporting organisers and information about the event participants for tourism agencies and businesses.

Questions

Does there need to be better dissemination of information to sporting organisations and/or event organisers about the range of relevant training courses available?—if so, whose responsibility is it to undertake this role? Is there a need to develop a specific sports tourism training course or module, for inclusion in existing appropriate management skill programs?—if so, who should do this? Should funding agencies consider making grants to national, state and other sporting organisations contingent on those organisation demonstrating that it has met certain standards regarding the development of business and administrative skills?

8. Regulatory Issues

Governments at all levels can and do impose requirements which impact on sports tourism events and activities. These can be broad requirements such the need for international competitors or spectators to sporting events to obtain a visa or electronic travel authority to enter Australia or they can be specific to a particular event, for example, the closure of roads for the holding of a fun run or triathlon.

Dealing with Commonwealth, State/Territory and Local government departments and agencies can be a daunting prospect for event organisers. This can be especially so for organisers who may be tackling the task of organising their event for the first time or for volunteers in sporting organisations who have neither experience in dealing with regulatory requirements or the time available to deal with these.

During the focus group discussions, the issue of government regulatory requirements was frequently raised as a significant barrier to the successful organisation of sporting events and activities, and the maximisation of tourism opportunities from those activities. It was suggested on numerous occasions that governments could play a role by providing event organisers with a mechanism to help deal with complex regulatory requirements.

A number of State and Territory governments have already developed assistance packages that go some way towards providing just such a service. For example, the Canberra Tourism and Events Corporation (CTEC) has developed a publication entitled *Assistance for Special Events—Information Handbook for Event Organisers*, which contains a section on Government liaison with relevant contact details for organisations such as police, emergency services, roads and traffic bodies, venue hire, litter disposal and so on. The Handbook provides a how-to guide for organising an event, covering issues such as budgeting, sponsorship, media relations, general organisation tips, and evaluating the outcome of the event.

This kind of assistance is not available in all States and Territories. Even where advice is available through Events Corporations, this may not always be available at the local or regional level—ie contact details may not be available for all local government agencies with whom event organisers in regional areas might have to deal. Further, the CTEC publication does not deal with liaison with Commonwealth agencies such as Customs, Immigration and Quarantine for events where there may be international competitors involved.

There is therefore a clear information gap for event organisers in dealing effectively with government agencies—at the local, Commonwealth, and in some instances at least, State/Territory level. There may be a need for Commonwealth, State/Territory and local governments to cooperate more fully in the provision of information to help fill this gap.

Commonwealth Agencies

At the Commonwealth level, a number of agencies oversee regulatory requirements which impact on event organisers, in particular where there are international competitors, spectators or other participants involved.

Visas

Visitors to Australia are required to obtain a visa to enter the country. In the case of most visitors travelling as tourists, this takes the form of an Electronic Travel Authority (ETA) which is, in effect, an "invisible visa".

There are different categories of visas, including business visas and sport visas. The latter are often used by professional sports people who will be staying for some time in Australia pursuing their sporting interests. Depending on the nature and duration of the sporting activity being undertaken, people travelling to Australia who will be participating in some form of sports tourism activity may choose to travel under all of these different visa types.

Two recent innovations by the Department of Immigration and Multicultural Affairs (DIMA) which administers Australia's visa system, will assist organisers and international participants in sporting events in Australia. These are the *International Event Coordinator Network (IECN)*, and *Streamlined Short Term Business Entry*. The IECN is a network of immigration officers located within the DIMA Business Centre in each State and Territory capital city. The role of these officers is to alert event organisers of immigration requirements and to advise Australian posts overseas of details of forthcoming events. The network is potentially of great benefit to event organisers, including organisers of sporting events, who appear not to have utilised its services greatly to this point.

The Streamlined Short Term Business Entry arrangements have been put in place in the lead up to the Olympics, and have enabled sports people to enter Australia on business visas, including the ETA version of the business visa. This is a quicker and more streamlined option for many sports people and will help facilitate travel to Australia to participate in sporting activities. This arrangement may continue following the Olympics.

Customs

The Australian Customs Service maintains Australia's border integrity by ensuring that prohibited goods are not brought into Australia and that other goods brought in either permanently or temporarily, pay the appropriate rate of duty or tax. This may include sporting goods brought in by international visitors for use in competition. As with immigration requirements, the Australian Customs Service can make special arrangements to cater for the needs of teams competing in international events, provided it receives sufficient notice of forthcoming events. For example, special dispensation may be obtained to enable temporary duty-free entry of goods for sporting events.

The special arrangements put in place for the Sydney 2000 Olympic Games will no doubt provide valuable lessons in facilitating the movement of goods and people for future major sporting events.

Quarantine

The Australian Quarantine Inspection Service (AQIS) seeks to protect Australia against the introduction of exotic plant and animal matter which could pose a disease risk for Australia's unique environment and its agricultural industries. For this reason, AQIS inspects goods entering Australia, including sporting equipment, food supplements, and therapeutic substances. Where horses are brought to Australia to compete in races or in equestrian events, a period of quarantine is required. Early contact with AQIS helps minimise any quarantine difficulties which might otherwise impact on a sporting event. AQIS also anticipate that the knowledge and experience gained from the Olympics will help them to adopt best practice approaches to future major sporting events.

Questions

Does government regulation mean that sports tourism opportunities are being lost or not maximised?

Would improved coordination and referral mechanisms for event organisers and/or tourism operators help to overcome some of the difficulties associated with government regulation?

9. Infrastructure

The ability of cities or regions to host successful sports tourism activities and events depends on there being adequate infrastructure in place. This includes sporting facilities, accommodation, air, road and rail transport networks both to and within the region, and other tourism related facilities such as restaurants, retail outlets and entertainment venues.

While the focus of event organisers tends to be on the actual sporting infrastructure, the existence of adequate sporting facilities does not necessarily mean that an event can be held at that location. If accommodation and transport requirements cannot be met or are inadequate, even small regional events will be difficult to host. Accordingly, a strategic approach which considers the adequacy and availability of all relevant infrastructure needs to be adopted when planning sporting events and activities.

Sporting facilities are expensive to provide. For this reason, their funding has almost always been the domain of governments—local, State and Territory and Commonwealth. This can lead to distortions in the provision of facilities, with priorities sometimes influenced by factors other than the perceived benefits to a community. Arguably, this has led to an over-investment in sporting facilities in some areas, and consequent excess capacity. This excess capacity represents a genuine opportunity for sports tourism development—significant benefits can be gained through better facilities utilisation, without the need for further costly investment.

The relationship between facilities and the hosting of events is complex. Investment in facilities can rarely be justified on the basis of being used only for major sporting events. Also, it cannot be assumed that the mere provision of high quality sporting facilities will guarantee a region or a state a flow of major sports tourism opportunities. It is ultimately then incumbent upon a region itself to attract facilities funding, possibly through the hosting of a "catalytic" event, and thereafter to "sell" those facilities effectively to event organisers to help ensure their sustainable use.

Cost-effectiveness is a key consideration in attracting facilities funding. It may be that the costs associated with the construction and maintenance of national or international standard facilities simply cannot be justified for community use alone or even taking into consideration increased use associated with the hosting of national or international events. The commercial viability of facilities can be further reduced when accompanying accommodation and transport infrastructure is inadequate for the hosting of major events.

More recently there has been a trend towards the construction of multi-purpose facilities which can be utilised for a variety of community and entertainment functions as well as the holding of a variety of sporting activities and events. This kind of facility can prove more cost effective than traditional facilities dedicated to a narrow focus on a particular sport or range of sports.

When considering facilities investment, it is also important—both for governments and private investors—to consider the regional facilities environment so as to avoid duplication and maximise the synergies with complementary facilities in nearby regions. The development of regional sporting "hubs" for particular sports can also help reduce the risk of constructing sports specific facilities which are economically unsustainable.

More generally, a strategy by governments and sporting organisations of "sharing" State or national events around regional Australia would help justify the financial investment in regional facilities as well as help ensure a more even distribution of the economic benefits associated with sporting events.

State/Regional Facilities and Asset Audits

Facilities investment and prioritisation of facilities funding would also be enhanced by improved information about the supply and demand for regional sporting infrastructure. This would also help address the difficulties faced by event promoters, organisers or prospective organisers who often lack awareness of just what facilities and of what standard, are available in various regions.

Currently, the Commonwealth is working with the State and Territory governments on undertaking a facilities audit of state, national and international standard facilities. To complement this work regions could benefit if similar audits were conducted at the regional level.

Frequently, events may be organised with little knowledge of, or regard to, other events planned for the same time. This can have serious ramifications for all events staged at that time, with multiple demands on infrastructure and services, which may well exceed the capacity of the region to manage. Data on the utilisation of sporting facilities is therefore important, particularly where there may be strong seasonal variations. In this way, sports tourism activities, along with other events-based tourism activity, can be targeted at low or shoulder season times, to help minimise peaks and troughs.

Accommodation Infrastructure

One of the key issues for maximising the tourism benefits of sporting activity and events is the availability of a range of accessible accommodation, covering the budget to the luxury markets. As part of each region's asset audit, an accommodation directory should be produced detailing the bed numbers in each sector of the market. By identifying the range of accommodation available, local sports tourism organisers can more effectively target particular events, knowing that suitable accommodation for the specific market is available. For example, under age championships may well have quite different accommodation needs from a masters competition.

As part of this accommodation audit, consideration could be given to utilising or upgrading existing facilities such as school dormitories, barracks etc, which may well provide adequate accommodation for the lower end of the market. A vital part of encouraging the development of sports tourism in a region is identifying the benefits which can accrue to the whole community. In particular the businesses directly involved in the provision of services should be made aware of the importance of catering for the needs of their guests to ensure they have a good experience. In the case of accommodation providers, they need to address the particular needs of athletes including bed lengths and adequate and appropriate catering.

Transport Infrastructure

A key issue emerging from the focus group discussions is high cost of transportation in many areas of regional Australia—both to and within regions. An associated issue was lack of transport capacity—the inability to move large numbers of participants in and out of many regions in a short space of time.

Ongoing reforms and deregulation in the transport sector, especially domestic aviation, have the potential to deliver significant benefits to regional Australia, and to help encourage the development of sports tourism and other events based tourism in regional Australia.

Questions

Would regional facilities audits and asset audits assist event organisers to plan for the hosting of sporting events in regional areas?

—if so, whose responsibility should it be do undertake these audits?

Should the funding of sporting infrastructure, including in regional areas, be based on a more rigorous assessment of the potential economic benefits of that infrastructure, including possible tourism benefits?

—what methodologies might be employed to determine those benefits?

10. Research and Data Collection

Sports tourism is a relatively new area of study given its recent rise as a significant niche sector for the Australian tourism industry. A number of Australian researchers have begun to specialise in this field but the current information base available to the industry is still relatively small and a range of research needs to be conducted.

The effects of the Sydney Olympic Games will undoubtedly provide the focus for many research efforts in the coming year but this needs to be complemented by a more grass roots approach to research across a range of sports tourism activities.

A major inhibitor to more and better quality research is the current lack of data available. While some data is collected in relation to individual events, there is no widespread or systematic data series across all sports tourism activities at a state or national level.

The International Visitor Survey (IVS) and National Visitor Survey (NVS) produced by the Bureau of Tourism Research (BTR) currently include limited questions regarding activities undertaken by visitors while travelling throughout Australia. The NVS includes the categories of Sport—Participant or Spectator under Main Purpose of Visit in its survey form. In the IVS 'to participate in or watch an organised sporting event' is a response to a question regarding factors that influenced the decision to visit Australia.

This data provides at best a very partial picture of the level of sports tourism activity in Australia. To improve the available data, there may be some scope to expand the range of questions regarding sports related activities within these surveys or to initiate a stand-alone sports tourism baseline study.

The BTR have also undertaken initial research profiling Australian 'sports tourists'. (Tourism Research Report 3rd edition—*Sports Tourism: An Australian Perspective*) This research extends the definition of sports tourism further than that adopted for this Strategy to include day trips, ie. a round trip of at least 50 kilometres, where the traveller stays away from home for at least 4 hours but does not spend a night away from home as part of that travel. The Survey results showed that 6 per cent of day trips and 5 per cent of overnight trips taken by Australians in Australia, were taken with sport as the primary motivation. (It could be anticipated that a significant further number of trips were undertaken with sport as a secondary motivation.) The paper found that that Australians who travelled to take part in sports, either as spectators, officials or participants (day and overnight) are likely to be male; aged between 15 and 24 years; from an upper income household (earning more than $78 000 per year); and that they generate higher yield per night.

The slightly different definition employed in the BTR study suggests what should probably be the first step in data collection for the sports tourism sector—the establishment of a uniform set of standard definitions for sports tourism. The adoption of standard definitions provides the opportunity for various researchers to produce data which has comparability across the sports tourism sector. An extensive range of agreed definitions should be developed, allowing researchers to choose those required for specific data sets while retaining commonality. The definition adopted in this Strategy might provide the basis for discussion towards such agreement.

Data types which might provide the basis for a range of research in the sports tourism field include (for both domestic and international visitors):

❖ Expenditure on trips involving sporting activities (including expenditure on total trip and on the "sports" component); more detailed questions on motivation for travel, especially for domestic travellers;
❖ Satisfaction information;
❖ Length of stay data (including length of stay for total trip and for the "sports" component);
❖ Demographic information (age, gender, income, occupation);
❖ Type of accommodation used while travelling for sports related purposes; and
❖ Type of transport used while travelling for sports related purposes.

Areas of research which may be useful to the industry include:

❖ Appraisal of potential and proposed sport events;

❖   Estimation of market for new or proposed sport tours;
❖   Identification of infrastructure needed for sports tourism;
❖   Specification of new tourism uses for existing sports infrastructure;
❖   Recommendations for modifications to existing sports infrastructure to enhance tourism value; and
❖   Profiling of sports tourism segments (*e.g.* training camps, tours of facilities).

Other possible areas of research could be:

❖   Measuring the economic impact of sport events at a regional, State/Territory and national level;
❖   Measuring the economic impact of sporting infrastructure;
❖   Measuring the social impact of sports tourism; and
❖   Assessment of the environmental impacts of sport infrastructure and sports tourists.

Work by government bodies such as the Bureau of Tourism Research and the Australian Bureau of Statistics can often provide useful broader contexts for specific research and in the case of BTR often more targeted baseline data. Specific research needs can also be met through academic and industry collaboration. For example, the Cooperative Research Centre for Sustainable Tourism has an events sub-program which potentially can address some of the research and data needs, especially if its activities are focussed towards sports events and activities at the non-micro level. The CRC has also recently established a sports tourism "node", located at the University of Canberra, to provide a focus for its research into the sports tourism market. There is considerable scope for cooperation between industry and research bodies in improving the information available to the sports tourism sector. There is also scope for industry to address its own information needs in terms of local environments and of its specific marketing and development requirements.

Questions

Does there need to be a set of agreed definitions for the sports tourism sector, including definitions of "sports tourism" for both domestic and international travellers?—if so, who should coordinate this work?

Do we need to establish a comprehensive baseline data set on the sports tourism sector to enable research to be undertaken on its economic, social and environmental impacts, as well as trends within the sector?

—if so, who should undertake this work?

Does research into sports tourism need to be better coordinated?—if so, who should coordinate sports tourism research?

Does research into sports tourism need to focus more on the "big picture" issues?—if so, how can this be achieved?

How can we increase industry awareness of available research and statistics to assist operators to make sound business decisions?

8.3 Evaluation of Related Events

Ongoing public sector reform and rationalisation have placed public tourism authorities and sporting organisations under increasing pressure to operate cost-effectively. Government agencies have to be more accountable for policies, programs and funding decisions and this includes funding for sporting events.

Governments lend their support to events on the basis of decisions made regarding benefits and costs ranging from financial to social and cultural. Such events may have the capacity to create income and employment in the short term and generate increased visitation and related investment in the longer term.

Determining the value of sporting events has been a perennially difficult issue for governments to resolve. There are no standard criteria for evaluating the economic significance of staging events. There also appears to be an absence of rigorous and comprehensive criteria for evaluating publicly funded tourism events, with great disparity between States, regions and research companies in their approach, both to the assessment of economic impact and to less tangible cultural and social impacts.

These differing approaches have made it difficult for governments not only to justify expenditure on events, but also to compare the economic success of various events. It is imperative for the credibility of the industry that sound methodologies are used to measure the return on the investment, and that these methodologies are widely accepted.

Development of a commonly accepted framework for evaluation would allow event organisers to compare and predict outcomes for their events with similar sized events. The ability to establish these areas of comparability (as well as differences) is important in gaining an overall view of sports tourism events in Australia and making assessments about the size and characteristics of this industry. This would also facilitate national and international comparisons.

Given the limited budgets of organisations expected to undertake evaluations of events and the often complex methodology, a framework for evaluation is essential for smaller/regional organisations. Several of the State events bodies have developed basic evaluation models which are appropriate but more importantly are financially accessible to the smaller sporting and tourism organisations. It may be appropriate to develop a national standard model for events of this size and nature, possibly based on one of the existing models.

Mega-events such as the 2000 Sydney Olympics Games stand alone in terms of developing methodology to assess their impact—the impact is felt at regional, state and national levels. Much preparatory work has already been completed by researchers in this area leading up to the Games and this will continue post-Games. Notable in this regard is the Federal Government publication *The Olympic Effect* which assesses the likely tourism impact of the Games. A particular challenge will be to ensure that some of the innovative modelling approaches and methodologies developed for, and implemented during, the Games, can filter down to evaluation for smaller events.

Questions

Is it desirable or feasible to develop a standardised methodology for events evaluation or should we seek to develop a range of "best practice" models from which organisations can choose, to assess the impacts of events? If so—

who will progress any activity in this area?

who will determine which model(s) should be endorsed?

12. Implementation

The proposals contained in this strategy will require the concerted efforts of a range of organisations if they are to be successfully implemented and if the sports tourism sector is to achieve its full potential. Those organisations include governments at all levels (Commonwealth, State/Territory and local), the tourism industry, the sports sector including national and state/territory sporting organisations and researchers.

A key theme of the strategy is the need for better coordination between what is a very diverse range of stakeholders involved in the sports tourism sector. Lack of communication and coordination, especially between sporting groups and the tourism sector, has been identified as a major impediment to maximising the tourism potential of sporting activities and events. At the state/territory level, events corporations take on much of the responsibility for building these links. At the local level, there is arguably a greater need for development of networks or "clusters" focussing on sports tourism development. At the national level, there may also be a role for an overarching coordination mechanism of this nature.

Such a national-level group, which could be similar to the Canadian Sports Tourism Coalition (*see* Appendix 4), could be comprised of representatives of key stakeholders across industry and government, and could play a significant role in:

❖ Raising the level of awareness about the sports tourism sector within both industry and government;
❖ Identifying and pursuing specific research needs and priorities;
❖ Identifying and overseeing the role of any facilitation unit which might be established following the release of this strategy; and
❖ Overseeing and reporting on progress in implementing the strategy.

Questions

Is there a need for a group to oversee the implementation of the National Sports Tourism Strategy?

—if so, how should such a group be comprised?

Should the various events organisations across States and Territories identify areas for possible cooperation?

APPENDIX 1

The Strategy Development Process

The development of a National Sports Tourism Strategy has its genesis in the *National Action Plan for Tourism*. The Plan, released in 1998, provides a policy framework for the future development of the tourism industry and identifies the development of a range of niche tourism products as one of the avenues which will promote strong future growth and diversification of the Australian tourism industry. Sports tourism is identified as once of the sectors showing enormous potential for further development.

Against this background, the Minister for Sport and Tourism announced in November 1999 that the Commonwealth would develop a National Sports Tourism Strategy, to examine impediments and opportunities impacting on the development of the sector and to see what role the Commonwealth might play to facilitate its growth.

Given the historical role of the States and Territories in attracting, developing, promoting and hosting major events, including sporting events, consultations were undertaken at an early stage with State and Territory government agencies and a range of other key stakeholders. These included Sport Industry Australia, the Australian Tourist Commission, the Australian Sports Commission, industry associations and academic researchers prominent in sports tourism and/or events research, including the Co-operative Research Centre for Sustainable Tourism.

At the same time, desk research was being undertaken and an inclusion on Sports Tourism was developed for the Commonwealth's Discussion paper, *End Goal 2006—Moving the Sport and Recreation Industry to a Higher Growth Path*. The discussion paper, released in December 1999, was an initial step in the development of a Strategic National Plan for the Sport and Recreation Industry, in fulfilment of an election commitment made by the Government during the 1998 election campaign.

On the basis of the initial consultations and feedback from the *End Goal* Paper, a short discussion paper was developed, drawing together themes and issues associated with sports tourism development. This paper was utilised in a series of focus group discussions convened around Australia in May and June 2000. The group discussions were held in every capital city, as well as two key regional centres, Cairns and Tamworth.

Typically, the focus group discussions brought together industry and government sport, tourism and events representatives. They included representatives of major sporting organisations from each centre or region, managers of major sporting facilities, tour operators with an interest in sporting events or activities, economic development agencies, regional tourism bodies and event organisers.

A number of common themes and issues emerged in many or most groups, but specific issues were also identified impacting on particular regions or States/Territories.

This draft, *"Towards a National Sports Tourism Strategy"* has been prepared on the basis of these consultations and accompanying research. There will be further opportunity for interested parties to comment, following its release in October 2000. Feedback received at that stage will be taken into account in the finalisation of the Strategy.

APPENDIX 2

Summary of Focus Group Outcomes

The focus groups were convened with two primary objectives. Firstly to identify issues of importance to sports tourism stakeholders; and secondly to elicit comment on the discussion paper prepared based on the initial consultations, feedback and research. A number of issues were identified, which were then allocated priority rankings by the group participants. The outcomes of the ten focus groups have been collated and summarised.

Nine common issues have been identified through this process, and the following is a summary of these in priority order and the suggested strategies for addressing each of these.

Issue	Suggested Strategies
1. Strategic Approach Lack of strategic approach to sports tourism development	1. Promote network of sport and tourism organisations to improve communication and coordination. 2. Develop industry profile - establish peak body. 3. Clarify roles of stakeholders. 4. Educate national sporting organisations and tourism organisations on commercial opportunities sports tourism provides. 5. Promote development of business and event management skills in sporting organisations. 6. Encourage coordination of event calendars. 7. Encourage development of events-based tourism strategies.
2. Coordination and Communication Need for better communication at national, State and regional level.	1. Establish national coordination/ communication /facilitation unit to assist the development of sports tourism. 2. Improve information dissemination through web site with links to existing relevant databases. 3. Facilitate access to research findings and resources. 4. Improve lines of communication between stakeholders 5. Maintain project facilitation mechanisms established for Olympics for future major events. 6. Encourage cross-agency linkages to give access to tourism product marketing resources and material.
3. Regional Development Promote the development of sports tourism in regional areas and address impediments to its growth.	1. Develop region specific databases for event managers of stakeholders, services, facilities, accommodation and infrastructure. 2. Encourage sharing of information and expertise – through development of "sports tourism clusters" in regional areas. 3. Target niche events appropriate to area and facilities. 4. Address access issues - transport, sponsorship, media. 5. Encourage coordination to avoid duplication of facilities. 6. Encourage integrated view of sport, tourism and business opportunities at regional level. 7. Encourage rotation of national events throughout all of Australia.
4. Research Need to develop sound research base.	1. Clearly define sports tourism. 2. Coordinated development of research agenda. 3. Conduct further research into economic and social impacts of events, include consideration of both direct and flow-on effects and disseminate findings to stakeholders.

(Contd.)

(Contd.)

Issue	Suggested Strategies
5. Facility development Need coordinated and sound economic approach to development and use of facilities.	4. Conduct accurate market analysis for identification of existing and potential markets. 5. Encourage better understanding of the sports tourism market needs. 6. Undertake post event research - long term tracking of benefits of events. 1. Need to conduct thorough facilities audit, also develop "asset audit" of regional infrastructure to assist in effective planning. 2. Encourage capacity utilisation of existing facilities. 3. Examine cost effectiveness of developing different standards of facilities in regional areas, consider multi-use facilities.
6. Funding Address difficulties in accessing funding for conducting events.	1. Encourage State governments to recognise difficulties faced by State and regional areas in accessing funding and sponsorship for events. 2. Identify funding sources - communicate to organisations, what funding is available and how to access it. 3. Ensure funding is equitable as possible across States and Territories. 4. Assist regional areas to access financial and in-kind sponsorships, possibly as a group. 5. Encourage partnerships between government and private sector - recognise role of private sector in supporting second tier events.
7. Education and Training Identify and address education and training needs in sports tourism sector.	1. Develop profile of the industry to identify opportunities for education, employment and experience. 2. Promote implementation of event management training courses. 3. Develop appropriate sports tourism training modules. 4. Improve business skills through effective training tailored to sector, including volunteers. 5. Encourage development and distribution of manuals and educational resources.
8. Standardised Economic Modelling Need standardised approach to evaluation of events.	1. Develop standardised approach to economic, cultural, social and environmental modelling. 2. Develop standardised evaluation model which is affordable and appropriate for regional areas. 3. Develop methods to deliver meaningful information.
9. Participation	Need to recognise need to provide ongoing support for mass participation in sport.

APPENDIX 3

Discussion of Definitions

The strong linkages between sport and tourism are well recognised, and the literature contains many studies devoted to the topic, however, as discussed earlier, to date there has been no consensus on a definition of sports tourism, and a wide range of definitions have been adopted by different parties.

Definitions used may be influenced by the availability of data, the intent of research being undertaken, current sport and tourism definitions in the country or region concerned, etc.

There is broad agreement about the tourism side of the definition with most countries generally accepting definitions similar to those observed in Australia for international and domestic tourists. (Although there could be some disagreement over whether day trips should be include in a definition of domestic sports tourism—see for example, the article *Sports Tourism: An Australian Perspective* in BTR Tourism Research Report 3rd issue.)

However, there are wide-ranging views on what constitutes sport. Should recreational and adventure activities be included, is sport only sport when it is "organised", are non-competitive events such as fun runs still considered sporting activities? Some other examples of sports tourism definitions are set out below:

Sport Tourist: A temporary visitor staying at least twenty-four hours in the site visited and the purpose of whose journey is to attend sport related events. Specific activity categories are—sports events; sports attractions; sports tours; sports resorts; and sports cruises. (Douvis *et al*, p.2)

Sport: The whole range of competitive and non-competitive active pursuits that involve skill, strategy, and/or chance in which human beings engage, at their own level, simply for enjoyment and training or to raise their performance to levels of publicly acclaimed excellence.

Tourism: The temporary movement of people beyond their own home and work locality involving experience unlike those of everyday life. The experiences might take place as part of a holiday or as an ancillary to business travel. Sport Tourism:— All forms of active and passive involvement in sporting activity, participated in casually or in an organised way for non-commercial or business/commercial reasons that necessitate travel away from home and work locality. (Standeven & DeKnop, p.12)

Sports tourism is a combination of sports activities and travel. From a sport marketing and sport management perspective, it consists of two broad categories of products:

- ❖ sports participation travel (travel for the purpose of participating in a sports, recreation, leisure or fitness activity); and
- ❖ sports spectatorial travel (travel for the purpose of spectating sports, recreation, leisure or fitness activities or events). (Pitts 1997, p. 31)

APPENDIX 4

International Case Studies

Britain

In 1992 the creation of the Department of National Heritage (DNH) pulled together under one roof the leisure sectors of sport, tourism, and the arts. For the first time there appeared to be a formal connection between sport and tourism which might lead to some development of the sports tourism sector. Unfortunately this turned out not to be the case, and for all practical purposes, no significant relationship between sport and tourism was established at either the policy or operational level.

In fact, rather than further integrate sport and tourism, the subsequent policies of the DNH tended to reverse previous policies that allowed greater integration eg. reduction of English Tourist Board core funding and a narrower focus for the Sports Council. (Bull & Weed 1997(1); Standeven & DeKnop)

However, the historical difficulties of linking sport and tourism in Britain may be a thing of the past. The Department of Culture, Media and Sport (formerly DNH) announced in February 1999 the Government's intention to develop innovative niche markets such as sports tourism. The announcement forms part of a 15 point plan for tourism to unlock the full potential of Britain's unique cultural and natural heritage. UK Sport has also created an economic impact "guidance document" to assist with the undertaking of impact studies to determine the value of sports events.

Furthermore, the British Tourist Authority has recently developed a sports tourism marketing strategy which is backed up by three staff in England and a recently appointed staff member in their Sydney office. This innovative move to place a dedicated sports tourism officer in a key source market may place the UK at the forefront of international sport tourism development. While it is very early in the process, the appointment of a dedicated officer in this role may open up a range of opportunities for sports tourism in the UK.

There may be lessons for Australia and in particular, our marketing body the Australian Tourist Commission, should the UK's approach prove to be successful.

Canada

In 1998, 37 per cent of Canada's 73.7 million domestic trips were for sports tourism purposes. In Canada, sport tourists are defined as individuals who travelled and in doing so participated in or attended a sport event during the reference period. Sport tourists account for between 2.5 and 5 million individuals from June to September, July and August being the most popular months for sport tourist activities (15% and 18%). (Statistics Canada—1998 Canadian Travel Survey) (Note that this does not mean that 37 per cent of tourism activity was sports tourism—rather that 37 per cent of travellers travelled at least once for sports purposes).

Since 1996 the Canadian Tourism Commission (CTC) has been involved in a program designed to promote community and tourism industry interest in development of sports tourism as a viable contributor to the economic well-being of local communities. The Canadian Sports Tourism Initiative is a program designed to increase the quality and quantity of sports events hosted in Canada and has a number of objectives:

- ❖ to create a viable sports tourism industry in Canada;
- ❖ to organise Canadian communities to pursue sports tourism by providing them with assistance in organising the appropriate local resources and infrastructures to be effective;
- ❖ to assist communities in developing sports tourism commissions, appropriately organised to recruit sports events;
- ❖ to create linkages with the Canadian national, provincial and local sports system and event hosts to assist in the development of the sports tourism industry;
- ❖ to create new revenue streams and resources for local event organisers, sports friendly businesses and sport in general;
- ❖ to provide effective communication channels to facilitate business to business relationship marketing opportunities between event rights holders and potential host cities; and
- ❖ to create an industry—led, Canadian Sports Tourism Coalition to provide a forum for education, market intelligence and sports tourism marketing for communities and sports involved in the sports tourism business.

Based on positive support demonstrated by communities across Canada, in 1997, a partnership between the CTC, client communities and sport/tourism industry was borne. Soar International, a Vancouver based sports information and event management company was contracted to manage the process.

Communities that have decided to be part of the Sports Tourism Initiative's community planning program participated in a comprehensive planning process. To start the process, a Soar International facilitator presents a half day session to a broad constituency of local sports, tourism and community leaders, covering such topics as what is sports tourism, who are sports tourists, how are sports events organised, where are the opportunities to work together and how a sports tourism commission can be developed. Secondly, using a local project coordinator and a planning tool kit adapted to fit the local community process, data on which to base a sports tourism marketing strategy is gathered.

With this data, Soar International facilitates a workshop which provides sufficient information to prepare a strategic business plan. Using a locally facilitated process, this plan is presented to all the key groups in the community with an interest to ensuring its successful implementation. Soar International then assists the community to refine and implement the strategic plan on an ongoing basis.

By the end of 1999 the regions of Kelowna, Cranbrook, Edmonton, London, Kingston, Hamilton, Moncton, St. John's, Gatineau and Western Newfoundland/Cornerbrook had all undertaken the sports tourism planning process. (Canadian Tourism Commission; Swart 1998)

South Africa

In May 1996 the South African Department of Environmental Affairs and Tourism released a white paper on the development and promotion of tourism in South Africa. The sports tourism sector was specifically identified within this policy document. The intent was both to encourage the development of sports tourism and to encourage the provision of facilities, training, marketing and promotion to give emphasis to the development of this segment of the industry.

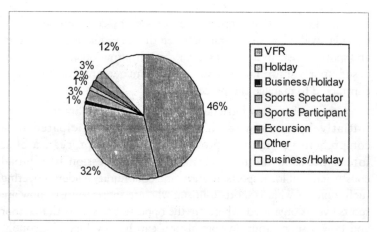

Source: Satour Domestic Tourism Survey

Fig. 8.1: Purpose of Visit for All South African Domestic Trips in 1996

Following the release of the white paper, and in order to capitalise on South Africa's sporting successes and re-entry into the world tourism scene, South Africa Sports Tourism (SAST) was launched jointly by the Ministry of Environmental Affairs and Tourism, and the Ministry of Sport and Recreation in October 1997. (Swart, 1998; Standeven & DeKnop, 1999)

The success of SAST in developing the international market for sport tourism in South Africa is yet to be established. As can be seen in the graph below, Satour figures suggest that Sports Tourism (spectator and participant) makes up four per cent of the domestic tourism market.

APPENDIX 5

Submissions Received

Alvey Reels (Australia), Mr Bruce J Alvey

Athletics Australia, Mr Simon Allatson

Australia Sport International, Mr Stephen Porter

Australian Tourist Commission, Mr John Morse

AV Syntec P/L, Mr Paul Bull

Campsie Sports Physiotherapy & Rehabilitation Centre, Mr Paul James

Classic Sportswear, Mr Tony Magnus

Cox Richardson, Mr John Richardson

CRC for Sustainable Tourism Pty Ltd, Professor Terry De Lacy

Diverse Concepts International, Dr Dion Klein

Emu Oil Therapies Pty Ltd, Mr Neil Duncan

Healthequip, Mr John Bright

Illawarra and Southern Highlands Convention and Sports Bureau, Ms Rachel Preddey

Jim Bradley Speedball Company, Mr Steven Clegg

Jindabyne Winter Sport Academy (NSW), Mr Steve Gibb

Office for Recreation and Sport—Department of Industry and Trade, Mr Simon Forrest

Queensland Events Corporation, Mr Allan Boosey

Queensland Industry of Recreational Fishing, Mr Bruce J Alvey

Racing Solutions, Mr Ian Chivers

Roysen Engineering P/L, Australian Barbell Company, P& J Sporting Products, Mrs Denise Langford

South Australian Thoroughbred Racing Authority, Mr Glen Hardy

Swimplex Pty Limited, Mr Geoffrey Leaver

Tasmanian Office of Sport and Recreation, Mr David Buckingham

Tourism Victoria, Ms Melinda Anderson

University of Tasmania—Virtual Sailing, Professor Norman Saunders

University of Canberra (ACT), Professor Trevor Mules

Victorian Major Events Company Limited, Ms Rosanne Damp.

The intent to watch or participate in an organised sporting event influenced the decision to visit Australia (based on 1998 IVS data)

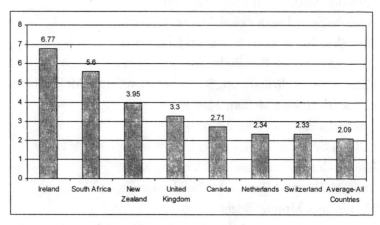

Fig. 8.2: International Visitors.

(a) The Hub represents the main focus of sports tourism around which the respective physical activity be it recreational, competitive or both, evolve.

(b) The Spokes illustrate the five different sports tourism categories according to specific touristic endeavours.

(c) The Spoke Interspaces demonstrate five potential settings in which the sport tourism activity, for the participant or spectator or both, could take place.

THE SPORTS TOURISM PHENOMENON

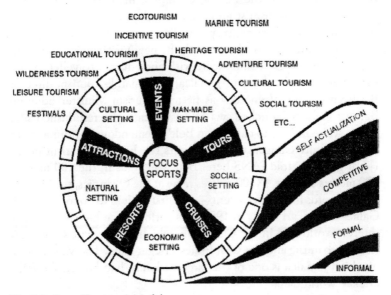

Fig. 8.3: Sport Tourims A Model

(d) The Outer Rim indicates different building blocks that potentially could and do contribute to the overall development of sports tourism.

(e) The Roadway suggests motivation elements which impel tourists, be they participant, spectator or both, in varying degrees and different directions to be involved in specific sports offerings and opportunities.

The Model depicts movement on a Wavy Roadway over time; whereby, each sports tourist can adapt and adjust according to his/her needs, interests and desires. (Kurtzman & Zauhar)

* Note that this model is only one possible interpretation of the way in which the sports tourism market operates. It is included for information only and is not necessarily accepted as valid for the purposes of this Strategy.

8.4 Cashing in on Usain Bolt: Case Study of Jamaica's Unveiling of New Tourism Strategy

New Delhi: Close on the heels of world's fastest human athlete Usain Bolt's dream run at the Beijing Olympics, his native Jamaica has unveiled a new tourism strategy to strengthen its position online to target discerning 21st century travellers, including hi-end visitors from India. "At the most basic level, the new VisitJamaica.com is an improved means to communicate with and educate travellers about the diversity and culture of Jamaica," the island's tourism director Basil Smith said Wednesday as he and Tourism Minister Edmund Bartlett globally launched, via a live webcast, the refurbished site. "Sure, we're hoping to cash in on Bolt's tremendous performance at Beijing," Rajiv Nangia, who represents the Jamaica Tourism Board (JTB) in India, told IANS here. Bolt won golds in the 100 metres, 200 metres and the 4X100 metres relay at the Olympics, setting new world records in all three events—the first athlete to do so in a single Games since Carl Lewis in 1984. His performance has sparked new interest worldwide in the Caribbean, which is otherwise known for its calypso music and the West Indies' cricket team. The West Indies, of which Jamaica is one of the largest islands, had hosted the 2007 cricket World Cup.

"Jamaica is a new destination for discerning and high-end Indian travellers. Last year, 1,008 Indian tourists visited Jamaica, which was a 100 percent ramp up over the previous year. We hope to raise this to between 2,000 and 5,000 by 2009," Nangia added. "The refurbished website will definitely help in this as it has an inbuilt booking facility for travellers who may want to make their plans independent of a travel agent if they wish to," Nangia pointed out, adding that the site also has additional features to enable the travel trade better market the Caribbean nation. The website features a fresh look with a focus on Jamaica's tourism product offerings that go from the "roadside" to the "ritzy". Catering to the needs of the modern and technically savvy global traveller, the website offers a stimulated interactive online experience of the country's diverse attractions, accommodation and indulgences, which many visitors seek before they arrive.

The website is also powered with key features including improved functionality, updated content, quicker response time, GPS tracking of favourite spots and Google Maps. According to Smith, the new site "will be a medium to reach the travel industry and influencers around the world and to maintain Jamaica's position as the premier Caribbean tourism destination". Visitors to the site will be able to explore what Jamaica offers through an engaging experience featuring the country's people, culture, art, music, cuisine, history, attractions and diverse range of accommodation. Greeted with an upbeat version of universal calypso hit "One Love", visitors will be invited to use the "slider" function to navigate through Jamaica's "ritzy" to "roadside" offerings through a flash experience, moving images and videos.

Visitors can also "flip" each image over to learn more and save their favourites in a personalised trip planning page called "My Jamaica". Founded in 1955, the Jamaica Tourist Board is the nation's national tourism agency based in capital Kingston. The JTB was declared the Caribbean's Leading Tourist and Convention Bureau by the World Travel Awards (WTA) for 2006 and 2007, while Jamaica earned the WTA's vote as the World's Leading Cruise Destination, the Caribbean's Leading Destination and the Caribbean's Leading Cruise Destination. (IANS)

8.5 Outdoor Education

Outdoor education usually refers to organized learning that takes place in the outdoors. Outdoor education programs sometimes involve residential or journey-based experiences in which students participate in a variety of adventurous challenges in the form of outdoor activities such as hiking, climbing, canoeing, ropes courses, and group games. Outdoor education draws upon the philosophy, theory, and practices of experiential education and environmental education.

Scope

The term 'outdoor education', however, is used quite broadly to refer to a range of organized activities which take place in a variety of ways in predominantly outdoor environments. Common definitions of outdoor education are difficult to achieve because interpretations vary according to culture, philosophy, and local conditions.

Outdoor education is often mistakenly referred to as synonymous with adventure education, adventure programming, and outdoor learning, outdoor school, adventure therapy, adventure recreation, adventure tourism, expeditionary learning, challenge education, experiential education, environmental education, and wilderness education. Consensus about the meaning of these terms are also difficult to achieve. However, outdoor education often uses or draws upon these related elements and/or informs these areas. The hallmark of outdoor education is its focus on the "outdoor" side of this education; whereas adventure education would focus on the adventure side and environmental education would focus on environmental. For more information, see Outdoor education definitions (Wikibooks).

Aims

Some typical aims of outdoor education are to:

- ❖ Learn how to overcome adversity
- ❖ Enhance personal and social development
- ❖ Develop a deeper relationship with nature.

Outdoor education spans the three domains of self, others, and the natural world. The relative emphasis of these three domains varies from one program to another. An outdoor education program can, for example, emphasize one (or more) of these aims to:

- ❖ Teach outdoor survival skills
- ❖ Improve problem solving skills
- ❖ Reduce recidivism
- ❖ Enhance teamwork
- ❖ Develop leadership skills
- ❖ Understand natural environments
- ❖ Promote spirituality

History

Modern outdoor education owes its beginnings to a number of separate initiatives. Organized camping was evident in the late nineteenth century and early twentieth century in Europe, the UK, the USA,

Australia, and New Zealand. The Scouting movement, established in 1907 by Robert Baden-Powell, employs non-formal education with an emphasis on practical outdoor activities. The first Outward Bound centre at Aberdovey in Wales was established during the Second World War. The Forest Schools of Denmark are examples of European programs with similar aims and objectives.

A key outdoor education pioneer was Kurt Hahn, a German educator who founded schools such as the Schule Schloss Salem in Germany, Gordonstoun School in Scotland, Atlantic College in Wales, the United World Colleges movement, the Duke of Edinburgh Award scheme (which emphasizes community service, craftsmanship skills, physical skill, and outdoor expeditions), and the Outward Bound movement. The second half of the twentieth century saw rapid growth of outdoor education in all sectors (state, voluntary, and commercial) with an ever-widening range of client groups and applications. In this period Outward Bound spread to over 40 countries around the world, including the USA in the 1960s. This, in turn, spawned many offshoot programs, including Project Adventure and the National Outdoor Leadership School, and professional associations such as the Wilderness Education Association and Association for Experiential Education.

A history of outdoor education in the UK has been documented by Lyn Cook (1999). and a history of outdoor education in New Zealand has been published in Pip Lynch's 'Camping in the Curriculum' (2007).

Philosophy and Theory

Philosophy and theory about outdoor education tends to emphasise the effect of natural environments on human beings, the educative role of stress and challenge, and experiential learning. One view is that participants are at their "rawest" level when outdoors because they are "stripped" of many of the conveniences of modern life. Participants can become more aware that they are part of a greater ecosystem and are not as bound by social customs and norms. In essence participants can be true to themselves and more able to see others as people regardless of race, class, religion etc. Outdoor education also helps instill the basic elements of teamwork because participants often need to work together and rely on others. For many people a high ropes course or an outdoor activity may stretch their comfort zone and cause them to challenge themselves physically which in turn can lead to challenging oneself mentally.

The roots of modern outdoor education can be found in the philosophical work of:

* ❖ Comenius
* ❖ John Dewey
* ❖ William James
* ❖ Aldo Leopold
* ❖ John Locke
* ❖ John Muir
* ❖ Jean-Jacques Rousseau
* ❖ Henry David Thoreau
* ❖ Pestalozzi

Foundational work on the philosophy of outdoor education includes work by:

* ❖ Kurt Hahn
* ❖ Willi Unsoeld

A wide range of social science and specific outdoor education theories and models have been applied in an effort to better understand outdoor education. Amongst the key theoretical models or concepts are:

* ❖ Experiential education theories,
* ❖ Group development theories,
* ❖ The Outward Bound Process Model,
* ❖ Stress, optimal arousal, comfort zone, and psychological flow theories, and
* ❖ Psychoevolutionary theory and the Biophilia hypothesis.

Around the World

Outdoor education occurs, in one form or another, in most if not all countries of the world. However, it can be implemented very differently, depending on the cultural context. Some countries, for example, view outdoor education as synonymous with environmental education, whilst other countries treat outdoor education and environmental education as distinct. Modern forms of outdoor education are most prevalent in UK, USA, Australia, New Zealand, Europe and to some extent Asia and Africa. A map is available of locations of outdoor education organisations, facilities, and people.

Research and Critical Views

There is much anecdotal evidence about benefits of outdoor education experiences; teachers, for example, often speak of the improvement they have in relationships with students following a trip. However, hard evidence showing that outdoor education has a demonstrable long-term effect on behaviour or educational achievement is harder to identify; this may be in part because of the difficulty involved in conducting studies which separate out the effects of outdoor education on meaningful outcomes.

A major meta-analysis of 97 empirical outcome studies indicated a moderately positive overall effect of adventure education programs on outcomes such as self-concept, leadership, and communication skills. Interestingly, this study also indicated that there appeared to be ongoing positive effects, unless most educational interventions whose effects tend to fade.

Loynes (1998) has suggested that outdoor education is increasingly an entertainment park consumption experience.

In a controversial paper critiquing the algorithmic paradigm Loynes (2002) has also called for an increase in "creativity, spontaneity and vitality" (p. 124). These dialogues indicate a need for those working in outdoor education to examine assumptions to ensure that their work is educational (Hovelynck & Peeters, 2003).

Trends

There are several important trends and changing circumstances for outdoor education, including:

- ❖ Climate change
- ❖ Environment
- ❖ Nature deficit disorder

- ❖ Physical fitness
- ❖ Rationalization (sociology)
- ❖ Risk aversion
- ❖ Risk management
- ❖ Standards-based education reform

Activities

- ❖ Abseiling
- ❖ Backpacking
- ❖ Camping
- ❖ Canoeing
- ❖ Geocaching
- ❖ Kayaking
- ❖ Nature study
- ❖ Questing
- ❖ Rafting
- ❖ Rock climbing
- ❖ Ropes course
- ❖ Sail training
- ❖ Snowboarding
- ❖ Wayfinding

Associations

- ❖ American Camp Association
- ❖ Association for Experiential Education
- ❖ Association of Outdoor Recreation and Education
- ❖ Wilderness Education Association

Organizations

- ❖ The Duke of Edinburgh's Award—award for personal achievement, including outdoor activities
- ❖ National Outdoor Leadership School
- ❖ Nature's Classroom—environmental education program in the USA
- ❖ Outdoor Education Group—educational organisation in Australia
- ❖ Outward Bound—international educational organization

People

- *Daniel Garvey*—teaches and researches in the area of experiential education
- *Kurt Hahn*—German educator responsible for the creation of Outward Bound.
- *Paul Petzoldt*—mountaineer, founder of NOLS, and co-founder of Wilderness Education Association

Topics

- Adventure recreation
- Adventure therapy
- Adventure travel
- Deep ecology
- Ecopsychology
- Educational progressivism
- Environmental psychology
- Experiential education
- Experiential learning
- Green exercise
- Natural environment

Outbound Management Development Programmes

- Rite of passage
- Summer camp
- Wilderness therapy
- Wood kindergarten

8.6 Frontier Adventure Sports and Training

Frontier Adventure Sports and Training (FAST) is the most established Adventure Race organizer in Canada, in operation since 1997. Frontier Adventure Sports has established an international reputation for solid logistics and challenging racecourses. FAST hosts events under several banners: the Frontier Adventure Challenge, Raid the North and Raid the North Extreme. These non-stop races range in length from 8 hours to six days and require coed teams of three or four to trek, mountain bike, paddle and negotiate fixed ropes, while navigating an unmarked racecourse through the wilderness.

Adventure Racing

Adventure Racing can be defined as a non-stop, multi-day, multi-discipline, team event. In many ways it can be likened to an expedition with a stopwatch. The goal of the competition is to be the first team to get all members across the finish line together. Adventure Racing requires teamwork, perseverance, and strong navigation and wilderness survival skills. The most common disciplines involved in an adventure race are mountain biking, hiking, paddling and rappelling. There are many different lengths and formats of events, ranging from off-road triathlons, to month long expeditions. The course should take competitors through remote wilderness where they must travel without outside assistance. Each team must use strategy to determine the best route, equipment, food and pace to maintain to win.

Raid the North

Since 1997, Raid the North events have been designed to highlight the natural elements of the host region environment. The Raid the North Race Series consists of a national series of 36-hour races in various locations across Canada. Raid the North Events are famous around the world for offering an awe inspiring wilderness challenge amongst the rugged and diverse backcountry in Canada. Teams will cover between 130 and 150 kilometres during the 24-36 hour race event. A Raid the North Team is a co-ed group of four people with a variety of sport, outdoor and wilderness backgrounds. Unlike RTNX, Raid the North events are geared towards the prepared first time adventure racer. All Raid the North Series' races serve as qualifiers for the 3 day Raid the North Series Championship race, held at the end of the season.

Raid the North Extreme

Raid the North Extreme (RTNX) is a 6-day expedition-style adventure race occurring once per year. Strong navigation skills and wilderness experience are paramount as the course covers roughly 450 kilometres of unmarked terrain. Each year the race travels to a different region in Canada that provides rugged wilderness challenges for competitors.

Raid the North Extreme was one of the original founding members of the Adventure Racing World Series and a qualifier race for the AR World Championship. Raid the North Extreme was selected as the Adventure Racing World Championships in 2004. Since that time, RTNX has not participated in the World Series concept. Raid the North Extreme is designed for experienced adventure racers, or those with significant wilderness experience, as there are significantly long sections of remote wilderness where rescue is difficult. Mixed gender teams of four have up to 6 days (non-stop) to cover 450 kilometres by trekking, mountain biking, paddling, and mountaineering. Competitors must navigate their own route through checkpoints throughout the racecourse. It is the only expedition-style event longer than 48 hrs in Canada. Raid the North Extreme competitors come from across Canada and the United States and tend to have a broad multi-sport experience and/or extensive outdoor skills. International race competitors have come from Mexico, Argentina, Spain, France, Finland, New Zealand and Singapore.

Raid the North Extreme has previously been hosted by Elliot Lake, Ontario in 1999, Revelstoke, British Columbia in 2000, Newfoundland & Labrador in 2001, Whitehorse, Yukon Territory in 2002, Atikokan, Ontario in 2003, Newfoundland & Labrador in 2004 and Prince Rupert & Haida Gwaii, British Columbia in 2007. Each race highlights the unique history, untouched wilderness and culture of the host region, including First Nations hunting and trading routes as well as other historic sites.

RTNX Locations & Top 5 Finishers

- ❖ Sole
- ❖ DART-nuun
- ❖ yukonWILD
- ❖ SSS (Spirit, SleepMonsters.ca, Shine-Energy)
- ❖ Playground Bullies

2004: Corner Brook, NL (AR World Championships)

- ❖ Nike ACG/Balance Bar

- ❖ Cross Sportswear
- ❖ Merrel Zanfel Adventures
- ❖ Nokia
- ❖ Mazda

2003: Atikokan, ON

- ❖ EADS
- ❖ Spirit
- ❖ Fudugazi
- ❖ Wild Rose
- ❖ Phoenix

2002: Whitehorse, Yukon

- ❖ Montrail
- ❖ EasternOutdoors.com
- ❖ GoLite
- ❖ Spirit
- ❖ TnT

2001: Corner Brook, NL

- ❖ Salomon/Eco-Internet
- ❖ Nokia Adventure
- ❖ Redbull-Playstation
- ❖ Eastern Outdoors.com-GLAR
- ❖ Spirit

2000: Revelstoke, BC

- ❖ Spirit
- ❖ PHON_NET.COM
- ❖ Old Spice Red Zone
- ❖ Shic Shoc Merrel
- ❖ Olympia

1999: Elliot Lake, ON

- ❖ Salomon/Eco-Internet
- ❖ Olympia
- ❖ Timbuk 2
- ❖ Nomad
- ❖ Lycos

Economic Impact

Raid the North Extreme creates broad tourism promotion for each region it visits, via media coverage and word of mouth. Documentaries on the race have been aired on the Outdoor Life Network, TSN, the Global Television Network, and PBS. RTNX also has a significant economic impact on the host region, creating an estimated local boost of $2.3 million.

Camp Frontier

Frontier Adventure Sports hosts an extensive adventure racing training curriculum focusing on the skills and knowledge required to compete in adventure racing. In partnership with Esprit Rafting, Frontier Adventure Sports offers the Jalcomulco AR Training Week as well as the Pico2Playa Expedition Training Week in Veracruz, Mexico. The Pico2Playa Expedition Week consists of a staged expedition from Pico de Orizaba to the Gulf of Mexico.

History

In 1997, Eco-Challenge competitor Dave Zietsma wanted to bring expedition racing to Canada, and introduced the 36 hour Raid the North race event. Originally known as Frontier Adventure Racing, the company grew to include the 6 day expedition race, Raid the North Extreme, and an 8 hour series, the Salomon Adventure Challenge. In 2002, Frontier was purchased by Geoff Langford, who introduced 14 hour Adventure Challenge events, restructured the company as Frontier Adventure Sports & Training, and created the Camp Frontier brand offering week-long training camps in Mexico.

Since its inception, Frontier has hosted nearly 100 race events in Canada. Frontier is most recognized for its 2007 Raid the North Extreme event held in Haida Gwaii and Prince Rupert, British Columbia, broadcast nationally on the Global Television Network in Canada and on PBS in the US.

Glossary

ABTA: Association of British Travel Agents. Represents the interests of the larger UK tour operators and travel agents (with around 670 members as of 2000), and operates a bonding scheme whereby customers booking with ABTA members have their holidays protected should the operator/agent in question collapse.

Accommodation capacity: The measure of accommodation stock at a defined destination. May be given by various different measures: *e.g.* number of establishments; number of main units within an establishment (*e.g.* rooms, caravan stances); capacity in terms of residents (*e.g.* bedspaces).

Accounting period: Normally one year, the period for which accounts are drawn up

AITO: Association of Independent Tour Operators. Performs a similar function to ABTA, although its membership (and therefore its agenda) differs in comprising some 160 of the smaller UK tour operators.

All-inclusive hotels: Resort facilities that offer all meals, activities and entertainments on site. All holiday expenses at these hotels are covered by one pre-paid price. Caribbean destinations are noted for their high profile brands of all—inclusive hotels which offer unlimited alcoholic drinks, snacks between meals and motorised sports all included in one price.

All-inclusive: A form of package holiday where the majority of services offered at the destination are included in the price paid prior to departure (*e.g.* refreshments, excursions, amenities, gratuities, etc).

Allocentric: Of a minority of tourists—adventurous, outgoing, self-confident, independent, needing little tourist infrastructure. Enjoys high contact with locals.

Alternative tourism: In essence, tourism activities or development that are viewed as non-traditional. It is often defined in opposition to large-scale mass tourism to represent small-scale sustainable tourism developments. AT is also presented as an 'ideal type', that is, an improved model of tourism development that redresses the ills of traditional, mass tourism

Artefact: An object; an item of material culture.

Assets: Something of value that will provide future benefit or utility, can be used to generate revenue. Usually owned, so simply described as 'things we own'.

ATOL: Air Travel Organiser's License. A requirement of the Civil Aviation Authority for all UK tour operators wishing to sell air seats on chartered or scheduled services. Necessitates a financial 'health check' and the putting up of a bond to cover the expense of reimbursing/repatriating tourists in the event of operator failure.

Average Room Rate Achieved: The average of the room rates resulting in room sales which a hotel has experienced for a given time period

Balance of payments: Record of one country's financial transactions with the rest of the world.

Benchmarking: Measuring your performance against that of best in class companies, determining how the best-in-class achieve those performance levels and using this information as a basis for your own company's targets, strategies and implementation..

Benchmarks: Points of reference or comparison, which may include standards, critical success factors, indicators, metrics.

Bureaucracy: An organisation typified by formal processes, standardisation, hierarchic procedures, and written communication

Business travel: Travel for a purpose and to a destination determined by a business, and where all costs are met by that business.

Capacity management: A process that seeks to ensure that their organisations operate at optimum capacity whilst maintaining customer satisfaction levels.

Capital expenditure: The cost of long-term assets; such as computer equipment, vehicles and premises. Importantly these are bought to use over several years and not to resell.

Carrying-capacity analysis: Originally a term applied in ecology referring to the maximum number of animals of a given species that a particular habitat could support. In the context of tourism, it refers to the maximum number of tourists a destination can support.

Case: A case describes a dispute taken to court, and specific cases set legal precedents—a legal principle, created by a court decision, which provides an example or authority for judges deciding similar issues later

Chain of distribution: The means by which products (package holidays in this instance) are distributed from producers (principals) to consumers (tourists), often via wholesalers and retailers (tour operators and travel agents).

Chaos theory: Views organisations/businesses as complex, dynamic, non-linear, co-creative and far-from-equilibrium systems the future performance of which cannot be decided alone by past and present events and actions. In a state of chaos, organisations behave in ways which are simultaneously both unpredictable (chaotic) and patterned (orderly).

Charter: A legal contract between an owner and an organisation for the hire of a means of transport for a particular purpose. An individual traveller will use an intermediary to arrange to be carried on the transport. Often applied to a flight which is the result of a charter.

Class action: A lawsuit filed by a number of people in a similar situation, *e.g.* participants in a particular package holiday might file a class action against the tour operator rather than take action individually..

Code of conduct: Guidelines advising a tourism stakeholder, including tourists, on how to behave in an environmentally responsible manner.

Collaboration: The process of working together in pursuit of common objectives.

Competitive strategies: Offensive or defensive strategies that aim at providing strategic competitive advantage and at increasing the competitiveness of an organisation.

Computer reservation systems (CRS): Computerised Reservation Systems used for inventory management by airlines, hotels and other facilities. CRSs can allow direct access through terminals for intermediaries to check availability, make reservations and print tickets.

Conservation: Can be broadly interpreted as action taken to protect and preserve the natural world from harmful features of tourism, including pollution and overexploitation of resources.

Contract: A legal agreement entered into by two or more parties.

Control: Monitoring and if necessary adjusting the performance of the organisation and its members

Cost-benefit analysis: Full analysis of public and private costs and benefits of project.

Cost-plus pricing: A method of pricing where an amount, to cover profit, is added to costs to establish the selling price, this is an internally orientated pricing method.

Critical incident point (CIP): A critical incident point or 'moment of truth' is any event which occurs when the customer has (or even perceives that he has) contact with a service organisation.

Cultural: See 'culture'

Culture: A set of shared norms and values which establish a sense of identity for those who share them. Typically applied at the level of nation and/or race.

Customer: "An organization or a person that receives a product"..

Decision-making unit (DMU): The combination of inputs to a purchasing decision

Delegation: The assignment to others of the authority for particular functions, tasks, and decisions.

Dependency theory: This theory maintains that developing countries are kept in a position of dependency and underdevelopment due to existing economic and institutional power structures sustained by leading Western nations. Dependency theorists argue that the policies and activities of multinational corporations, national bilateral and multinational aid agencies such as the World Bank and the International Monetary Fund (IMF) tend to widen the gap between rich and poor countries and perpetuate the dependency of developing nations.

Designation: The act of conferring a legal status on a building which requires compliance with specific legislation on conservation and preservation.

Discretionary income: Money received from employment or other sources which can be freely spent on leisure pursuits (such as travel and tourism) after general living costs, taxation etc. are taken into consideration.

Discrimination: Unequal treatment of persons on grounds which are not justifiable in law, *e.g.* in the UK, discrimination on the grounds of sex or race.

Disintermediation: A process by which the consumer 'bypasses' the services of an intermediary or intermediaries in the chain of distribution, in order to purchase products direct from those who supply them. In the travel industry, examples of disintermediation include airlines selling tickets direct to the public over the internet, thus cutting out the travel agent in the selling process.

Distribution: The process employed to provide customers access to the product. For travel products distribution focuses largely on the ways in which the customer can reserve or purchase the product.

Diversification: The process of developing new products for new markets, in order to achieve business growth.

Due diligence: Taking what is considered in law to be reasonable care.

eCommerce: Internet facilitated commerce, using electronic means for promoting, selling, distributing, and servicing products.

Economic growth: An increase in real output per capita.

e-mediaries: Electronic booking systems (usually web-based) which combine commerce and the traditional intermediary role of travel agents. Products and services are usually sourced from a range of other product providers allowing customers to book a range of different tourism and travel services from one website, and may enable price/product comparisons between competing suppliers.

Employee Relations: Covers communications, employee participation in management decisions, conflict and grievance resolution, trade unions and collective bargaining.

Environmental auditing: Inspection of a tourism organisation to assess the environmental impact of its activities.

Environmental management systems: Systems established by tourism organisations with the aim of mitigating negative environmental impacts.

Environmental scanning: The process of collecting information to carry out a systematic analysis of the forces effecting the organisation and identifying potential threats and opportunities with view to generating future strategies.

Evolutionary theories: Theories of tourism which see destinations evolving, in the sense that the types of tourists change, or evolve, over time.

Exclusion clause: This is a term in a contract that tries to exclude or limit the liability of one of the parties if there is a breach. Such clauses often take the form of "small print" in the standard terms and conditions of the dominant partner in the contract *e.g.* tour operators.

Externalities: Those costs or benefits arising from production or consumption of goods and services which are not reflected in market prices.

Familiarisation trips: (Fam trips) Visits to tourism destinations made in order to experience and learn more about the destination. Such trips are usually organised either by tour operators or by destination managers to improve knowledge of the destination. When travel agents are taken on such trips it is expected that their increased knowledge will lead to greater level of sales of holidays to that destination.

Force majeure: This is an unforeseeable or uncontrollable situation or train of events that would excuse a breach of contract.

Global Distribution System (GDS): The reservation network which links bookers such as travel agencies to travel suppliers' booking systems.

Globalisation: Generally defined as the network of connections of organisations and peoples are across national, geographic and cultural borders and boundaries. These global networks are creating a shrinking world where local differences and national boundaries are being subsumed into global identities. Within the field of tourism, globalisation is also viewed in terms of the revolutions in telecommunications, finance and transport that are key factors currently influencing the nature and pace of growth of tourism in developing nations.

Group norms: Informal standards of behaviour and performance that develop from the interaction of the group

Heritage: Today's perception of a pattern of events in the past.

History: A pattern of events in the past.

HRM: Human Resource Management, concerned with the strategic management of human resources to achieve a competitive advantage.

Impacts: Effects, which may be either positive or negative, felt as a result of tourism-associated activity. Tourists have at least three kinds of impacts on a destination: economic, sociocultural and environmental. Tourism also has effects on tourists, in terms of possible attitude and behaviour changes.

Industry structure: An explanation of the functions, form and interrelationships of individual elements, organisations and activities within a defined industrial sector (such as tourism).

info-mediaries: Organisations which provide websites/electronic guides as an information resource, sharing other resources such as web links to organisations that sell tourism/travel. The infomediary may be an organisation or company in its own right, or may form part of an individual company's or organisation's customer service

Information systems: Systems that use information technology to capture, transmit, store, retrieve, manipulate, or display information.

Infrastructure: Construction needed to support economic development.

Inseparability: The characteristic of service consumption being inseparable from its production, meaning that any errors made in production are seen by the consumer

Institutions: Institutions are 'an established law, custom, usage, practice, organisation, or other element in the political or social life of a people; a regulative principle or convention subservient to the needs of an organized community or the general needs of civilization' (Scrutton 1982: 225, in Hall and Jenkins 1995).

Intangibility: The characteristic of not being touchable—a good is tangible whereas a service is intangible

Integration: The linking (through changes of ownership such as mergers, acquisitions and takeovers) of different stages of the chain of distribution to form larger, more powerful organisations. Integration can be vertical (where links are developed with suppliers and distributors) or horizontal (where links are at the same stage of the distribution chain).

Intermediary: An organisation within the chain of distribution whose function is to facilitate the supply of a given product from producers to consumers. In the travel industry examples are travel agencies and tourism information offices.

Interpretation: An educational process that is intended to stimulate and facilitate people's understanding of place, so that empathy towards, conservation, heritage, culture and landscape is developed.

Invisible trade: Trade in services.

Labour market: The pool of employees from which an employer can fill vacancies.

Leadership: Influencing and directing the performance of group members towards the achievement of organisational goals

Leisure travel: Travel undertaken for pleasure and unrelated to paid work time.

Liabilities: An obligation to pay money or provide service in the future. Simply described as 'things we owe'.

Lifecycle: The particular pattern through which a destination evolves.

Limits of acceptable change: Environmental indicators that can monitor changes over time as a consequence of tourism.

Litigation: Legal action to resolve an issue before a court.

Luxury sports tourism: Active or passive sports tourism serviced by high quality facilities and luxuriant accommodation and attendant services.

Marginal or contribution pricing: A method of cost plus pricing which focuses on the variable or marginal cost only and thus establishes the lowest possible selling price.

Market orientated pricing: A method of pricing that benchmarks prices against competitors when deciding on price.

Market segmentation: Market segmentation is a marketing approach that encompasses the identification of different groups of customers with different needs or responses to marketing activity. The market segmentation process also considers which of these segments to target.

Mass tourism: Traditional, large scale tourism commonly, but loosely used to refer to popular forms of leisure tourism pioneered in southern Europe, the Caribbean, and North America in the 1960s and 1970s.

Mature market: A market in which a wide range of substitutable products or services are available to consumers who exhibit a sophisticated approach to consumer decision making.

MAVERICS: Characterisation of tourists of the future as multi-holidaying, autonomous, variegated, energised, restless, irresponsible, constrained and segmented.

Mediation: An attempt to settle a dispute using a neutral third party

Merit good: One with public as well as private benefits

Midcentric: Of the majority of tourists—displaying a mix of allocentric and psychcentric characteristics. Prefers to be cushioned from contact with locals.

Mode of travel: The type of transport used to make a journey between an origin and a destination, and can include walking and cycling as well as all forms of mechanical transport.

Modernisation theory: The socioeconomic development and process that evolves from a traditional society to modern economies such as the United States and Western Europe. Harrison (1992) argues that modernisation is a process of westernisation where developing countries emulate Western development patterns.

Motivation: Internal and external forces and influences that drive an individual to achieving certain goals.

Mystery shoppers: These researchers investigate companies through using their services, whilst pretending to be customers (or potential customers). They usually monitor such areas as the level of customer service and product knowledge.

National income: A measure of the total level of economic activity which takes place in an economy over a year.

Negligence: Failing to exercise what is legally considered to be reasonable care.

Net worth/Total net assets: The net value of all operational assets and liabilities, shows the amount of money invested in operational capacity of the business. Calculated by deducting current and long-term liabilities from the value of Fixed assets and Current assets

Niche tourism: Small specialised sector of tourism which appeals to a correspondingly tightly-defined market segment

No-frills: A low-cost scheduled travel package based on minimising operator service and costs, which are passed to the consumer as a low price.

Non-profit: Non-profit organisations are those which are driven by non-financial organisational objectives, *i.e.* other than for profit or shareholder return.

Occupancy rate: The measure of capacity utilised within an accommodation unit for a given time period (*e.g.* day, week, month or year)

Online agency: Travel agencies who operate using the World Wide Web to provide information to potential customers as well as allowing the customer to book travel and related products without the necessity of speaking to a salesperson.

Operations management: "The ongoing activities of designing, reviewing and using the operating system, to achieve service outputs as determined by the organization for customers".

OPODO: A web based booking site linking the reservation systems of co-operating airlines, allowing bookers to compare times and prices for particular journeys

Organisation: A deliberate arrangement of people to achieve a particular purpose

Other recruitment difficulties: Includes poor recruitment/retention practices, poor image, low remuneration, poor employment conditions which arise despite sufficient skilled individuals.

Owners' equity: Combines the original investment and any retained profit to show the total value of the owners' interest in the business.

Package holiday: Also known as an inclusive tour. Defined in law as 'the pre-arranged combination of at least two of the following components when sold or offered for sale at an inclusive price and when the service covers a period of more than 24 hours or includes overnight accommodation: (a) transport; (b) accommodation; and (c) other tourist services not ancillary to transport or accommodation', as set out in Section 2(1) of the European Union's Package Travel Regulations, 1992.

Perishability: The characteristic of being perishable. In tourism the term is used to describe, for example, a particular hotel room on a specific night or a particular seat on a specific flight—they cannot be 'stored' and sold later, so they are perishable.

Personal disposable income: The amount an individual has left over for personal expenditure on goods and services, after payment of personal direct taxes, national insurance and pension contributions.

Personnel: Concerned with the practical management and administration of people at work.

PESTEL analysis: Examines the political, economic, socio-cultural, technological, (physical) environmental and legal forces within which businesses operate and which act on them

Physical evidence: The tangible evidence of a service, including everything which can be seen, touched, smelt and heard.

Politics: Politics has been defined in many ways. According to Heywood, politics is 'The activity through which people make, preserve and amend the general rules under which they live'. According to Davis *et al.*, 'Politics is the process by which the structure, process and institutions are brought to a decision [including non-decisions] or outcome. It is an endless activity; while politics operates, all decisions [and non-decisions and actions] are provisional'. So politics means no decision or action is final. All decisions and actions of a government or institution of the state is open to question and is up for debate and argument and is, ultimately, subject to change.

Pollution: Harmful effects on the environment as a by-product of tourism activity. Types include: air; noise; water; and aesthetic.

Porter's forces: A model which suggests that the profit potential for companies is influenced by the interaction of five competitive forces: rivalry in the market place; the threat of substitutes; buyer power; supplier power; and barriers to entry into the market for new players.

Positioning: The process of ensuring potential customers have a desired perception of a product or service, relative to the competition. Price elasticity of demand: A relationship between the changes in prices charged for a good or service (here taken as hotel rooms) and the change in the amount demanded. Price elasticity of demand: A measure of the variability that can be expected in sales when prices are changed. Unity elasticity would see equal increase in sales to in reaction to a decrease in price. Inelastic demand would not change when prices went down or up.

Principal: A term that encompasses accommodation providers, carriers, ground handlers and any other provider of services to tourists, except for those whose primary function is to package and distribute tourism products (*i.e.* tour operators and travel agents).

Process control: A systematic use of tools to identify significant variations in operational performance and output quality, determine root causes, make corrections and verify results.

Process design: Involves specifying all practices needed, flowcharting, rationalisation and error prevention.

Process improvement: A proactive task of management aimed at continual monitoring of a process and its outcome and developing ways to enhance its future performance .

Process management: Planning and administering the activities necessary to achieve a high level of performance in a process and identifying opportunities for improving quality, operational performance and ultimately customer satisfaction. It involves design, control and improvement of key business processes.

Process: "A set of interrelated or interacting activities which transforms inputs into outputs".

Product: "The result of a process" (*i.e.* output), which may be either a service, or a good (hardware or processed materials) or software (*e.g.* information) or their combination.

Profit: The excess of revenue over expenses, if expenses exceed revenues in a given period the organisation will make a loss.

Psychocentric: Of a minority of tourists—preferring 'away' to be like 'home'; requiring appropriate tourism infrastructure.

Public policy: Is whatever governments choose to do or not to do . Such a definition covers government action, inaction, decisions and non-decisions as it implies a very deliberate choice between alternatives.

Quality: The degree to which a set of inherent characteristics of a product fulfils customer requirements.

Regulation: Control through formalised processes.

Relationship marketing: Relationship marketing is a business philosophy which aims to develop strong relationships with a range of stakeholders, such as suppliers, media, intermediaries and public organisations, as well as with customers.

Requirements: Stated, generally implied (as a custom or common practice for the organisation, its customers and other interested parties) or obligatory needs.

Responsible tourism: Type of tourism which is practised by tourists who make responsible choices when choosing their holidays. These choices reflect reponsible attitudes to the limiting of the extent of the sociological and environmental impacts their holiday may cause.

Retained profit: The profit left in the business at the end of the accounting period after all deductions and appropriations have been made.

Revenue expenditure: The cost of resources consumed or used up in the process of generating revenue, generally referred to as expenses.

Revenue management: Revenue management is a management approach to optimising revenue, often based on managing revenues around capacity and timing (yield management), for different market segments or from different sources of funding.

Sales: Revenue from ordinary activities—not necessarily cash.

Seasonality: A phenomenon created by either tourism supply or demand (or both) changing according to the time of the year.

Service encounter: The moments of interface between customer and supplier

Service marketing mix: The addition of People, Physical Evidence and Process to the four areas of activity more usually associated with marketing products,—Price, Place, Promotion and Product.

Servicescape: The location in which the service encounter takes place

Skills gaps: Employers perceive existing employees have lower skill levels than needed to achieve business objectives, or where new, apparently trained and qualified for specific occupations, entrants still lack requisite skills.

Skills shortages: Lack of adequately skilled individuals in the labour market due to low unemployment, sufficiently skilled people in the labour market but not easily geographically accessible or insufficient appropriately-skilled individuals.

Small business: A small business is one which has a small number of employees, profit and/or revenue. Often these are owner-managed, with few specialist managers. Some definitions of small businesses distinguish between businesses with under 10 employees, which are micro-businesses, and those with 10-49 employees, which are classified as small businesses.

Social: Relating to human society and interaction between its members.

Sports event tourism: Tourism where the prime purpose of the trip is to take part in sports events as either a participant or spectator

Sports participation tourism: Active participation in sports that is the prime purpose of the tourism trip

Sports tourism: A social, cultural and economic phenomenon arising from the unique interaction of activity, people and place.

Sports training tourism: Sports tourism trips where the prime purpose is sports instruction or training.

Sport-tourism link: Not just sports holidays, but all areas in which a link between sport and tourism might be of mutual benefit (*e.g.* joint facility development, marketing and information provision).

Stakeholder: Any person, group or organisation with an interest in, or who may be affected by, the activities of another organisation.

'The State': 'The state' is a set of officials with their own preferences and capacities to effect public policy, or in more structural terms a relatively permanent set of political institutions operating in relation to civil society' (Nordlinger 1981, in Hall and Jenkins 1995). The state includes elected politicians, interest or pressure groups, law enforcement agencies, the bureaucracy, and a plethora of rules, regulations, laws, conventions and policies.

Statute: The law as made by parliament, *e.g.* in the UK, the Disability Discrimination Act (1995). A statute is made up of many parts called 'sections' or 'provisions'.

Statutory instrument: The vast majority of delegated legislation in the UK is in the form of statutory instruments governed by the Statutory Instruments Act 1946

Strategic information systems: Systems designed to support the strategic management decision processes and implementation.

Strategy pyramid: A visual way of representing the different levels of the strategy conceptualisation and implementation process. The most general assumptions are shown at the apex and the practical, implementation actions are at the base.

Suppliers: Individuals, companies or other organisations which provide goods or services to a recognisable customer or consumer.

Sustainable tourism: Tourism that is economically, socioculturally and environmentally sustainable. With sustainable tourism, sociocultural and environmental impacts are neither permanent nor irreversible.

SWOT analysis: Brings together the internal and external environmental scanning to identify the business's internal strengths and weaknesses and external opportunities and threats.

Tort: A civil wrong.

Tour operator: An individual or organisation in the business of (bulk) buying, and subsequently bundling, the various components that make up a package holiday (see above), for sale via a travel agent or direct to the consumer.

Tourism flows: The major movements of tourists from specific home areas to destinations.

Tourism income multiplier (TIM): Exaggerated effect of a change in tourism expenditure on an area's income.

Tourism satellite account: System of accounting at national or regional level which reveals the total direct impact of tourism on the economy.

Tourism System: A framework that identifies tourism as being made up of a number of components, often taken to include the tourist, the tourist generating region, the transit route region, the tourist destination and the tourism industry.

Tourism with sports content: Tourism products that include participation in sport that is not the prime purpose of the trip.

Tourist attractions: Tourist attractions are defined as being destinations for visitors' excursions which are routinely accessible to visitors during opening hours. Visitors can include local residents, day-trippers or people who are travelling for business or leisure purposes. Formal definitions exclude shops, sports stadia, theatres and cinemas, as these meet a wider purpose, although in practice tourists may consider the excluded categories to be tourist attractions.

TOWS matrix: Uses a SWOT analysis to develop strategies by matching strengths with opportunities, using opportunities to reduce weaknesses, using strengths to overcome threats, and reducing weaknesses and avoiding threats.

Travel agent: The retailer of travel and related products. Whilst this refers to the sales person employed to sell travel products, the term is often applied in reference to the business that is established to sell travel products (the travel agency).

Variability: Because the production and the consumption of a tourism experience are inseparable and because differing circumstances and people will affect each experience, those experiences are prone to variance and create a challenge for tourism managers to achieve consistency of standards.

Virtual organisation: Organisation in which major processes are outsourced to partners.

Working Capital: Operational assets and liabilities needed for everyday operation, *e.g.* cash or bank overdraft, stock and trade creditors, known as net current assets/liabilities.

Yield Management: "A revenue maximization technique which aims to increase net yield through the predicted allocation of available ... capacity to predetermined market segments at optimal price" (Donaghy *et al.*, 1997a).

Zoning: Different eco-systems may be zoned in terms of their robustness to pressures from tourism in an attempt to mitigate environmental damage.

Word	*Sport*	*Definition*
Abadaca	BMX	Where a rider goes straight up the ramp, touches the back tire to the coping, then goes down the ramp fakie.
Abec	SKT	The tolerance rating system for bearing that designates the level for stress resistance of the bushing. The lower the rating the looser the bearing, the higher the rating the tighter the bearing.
Abec 1	SKT	The standard rating for Chinese and Russian bearings.
Abec 3	SKT	The standard rating for German and Swiss bearing, with Swiss considered the best. This is due to the fact that a skater has the options to rebuild these bearings, because they have a C-ring that allows the bearing to be taken apart.
Abs (acrylonitrile butadien)	SNB	A hard tough lightweight plastic that remains flexible and maintains a shape memory when heated. Used in contraction for a tip-tail sidewalls and any area which needs reinforcement.
Acid	INL	Street term, when a skater has his front foot outside of grindplate, with his back foot on soul.
Acid drop	SKT	To ride straight off of something and freefall to the ground.
Aerials	ETC	With specialized big air ramps and landings, original moves were upright moves; spread eagles and back scratches and helicopters. Later complicated inverted maneuvers began to dominate, quadruple flips and multiple front and back flips with twists.
Air to fakie	SNB	Any trick where the wall is approached riding forwards, no rotation is made, and the snowboarder lands riding backwards.

Word	*Sport*	*Definition*
Alley-oop (2)	SNB	A term used to describe any maneuver in the halfpipe where one rotates 180 or more degrees in the uphill direction; that is, rotating backside on the frontside wall or rotating frontside on the backside wall.
Alley-oop	SKT	When a trick is performed in the opposite direction of which the skater is moving.
Alley-oop soul	INL	A backwards soul grind in which the skater turns his body in the air hopping on the rail.
Andrecht	SNB	A rear handed backside handplant with a front-handed grab.
Axle	SKT	The metal rod running through the hanger, with the ends being where the wheels are screwed on.
Back Flip	BMX	Done in the air with the rider still on the bike. In vert, and occasionally in street, the rider will land in fakie position on the same ramp. In dirt and street, the rider will do a back flip from jump to jump.
Backside	MULTI	When a turn or trick is executed in a direction that the back of the body is facing the arc of the trick.
Backside air	SNB	Any air performed on the backside wall of halfpipe.
Backside rodeo	SNB	Coming off a jump and turning your back down the hill, flipping 540 and landing fakie or rotating a total of 720 and landing regular.
Backside rotation		MULTI Rotating clockwise for a regular-footer and rotating counter-clockwise for a goofy-footer. When riding switchstance the exact reverse applies and a regular footer will rotate counter-clockwise and a goofy footer will rotate clockwise.
Backside wall	SNB	When standing at the top of the halfpipe

Word	Sport	Definition
		and looking down towards the bottom, the backside wall is the left wall for regular footers and the right wall for goofy footers. If you ride straight down the center of the halfpipe, your backside wall is behind
Backslide	INL	A soul grind variation in which the skater has front foot grabbed, back foot on outside plate.
Bar Spin	BMX	While a rider is in the air, he spins the handlebars a full rotaion or more, grabbing them again before landing. Bar spins are thrown in combination with other tricks, such as back flips, to make them more difficult and earn more points with the judges.
Base plate	SKT	The flat part of the truck that fixes to the board via four drilled holes for truck bolts.
Bearings	SKT	Bearings have an inner and outer part, which the balls ride on, allowing the wheel to turn.
Bevel	SNB	The degree of angle to which the edges of a board can be tuned. Snowboards used for racing and carving should have a greater bevel than say a board used in the halfpipe.
Bi-axial fiberglass	SNB	A reinforcing cloth used in the production of snowboards. It provides excellent torsional stiffness compared to regular fiberglass weaves.
Bio grab	INL	To grab the outside of the skate with the hand of the same side.
Blindside	MULTI	A term given to any rotation where the rider has oriented him/herself "blind" to his/her takeoff or landing and must stretch to look over their shoulder. Such a technique usually increases the difficulty.

Word	*Sport*	*Definition*
Blunt	SKT	When a trick is performed, the contact spot of the board with the obstacle is the area of the tail behind the back trucks. The wheels are also on top of the object.
Board	SKT	Also called a deck. The platform that the hardware is mounted to, usually maple laminate.
Board length	SNB	The measurement from the tip to the tail.
Boardslide/ railslide	SKT	To slide on an obstacle or lip with the contact point being the underside of the board.
Boned out	MULTI	A term used to explain the emphasis of style in a trick. In other words, if someone "boned out a indy" they would grab hard and create an emphasis of the maneuver such that his/ her legs may appear extended or stretched to a maximum degree.
Bonk	SNB	The act of hitting an object with the snowboard.
Box Jump	BMX	Jump used in street competitions consisting of two ramps on either side of an approximately 10-foot deck.
Brainless	INL	A backflip with 540 degree turn on a ramp.
Budget variation	INL	A variation where on only the position of one skate is changes during the trick.
Bushing	SKT	Urethane spacers found in between the base plate and truck that cushions the sleeve of the truck when it's turning.
Butter slide	MULTI	Rider approaches wake or snow, then hops the board and lands on the edge of the wake or on the snow with the board sideways (perpendicular to the direction of travel) and slides the board on top.

Word	*Sport*	*Definition*
Cab	INL	Short for Caballerial.
Camber	SNB	The arched shape that is designed into the boards construction, creating a high point that lies on or near the midpoint of the boards running surface. To create spring or rebound in the flex of a board.
Camber	ETC	The arch built into a ski so that the ski can distribute the skier's weight over the entire length of the ski.
Camel	INL	A toe-tap upon re-entry onto a ramp or obstacle.
Can-Can	BMX	When a rider takes one foot off a pedal and stretches their leg over the frame between his legs so both legs are on the same side of the bike, then returns the foot to the pedal before landing.
Canting	ETC	Wedges placed underneath ski boots to properly position skier's knees over the ski at the proper angle.
Canyon	BMX	The sunken area between ramps in dirt and the empty space between two ramps in street. The big danger in dirt and street is when a rider may not go far enough or may have trouble with a maneuver and doesn't make the second ramp, landing in the canyon.
Cap construc tion	SNB	A form of integrated structural design that used the outermost material or skin to bear the load of strength of an object. Much like the shell of crab. To reduce weight and enhance torsional rigidity and edge responsiveness and eliminate the need for sepa.
Carbon fiber material	SNB	A fiber woven material produced from the mineral carbon. To stiffen and strengthen a board with a minimum of added weighted.

Word	*Sport*	*Definition*
Carve	SKT	To make a long, curving arc while skating.
Carved turn	ETC	A turned arc by a skier with little or no slipping or skidding.
Cased	MULTI	To land short or miss a landing.
Chatter	SKI	The tendency of skis not to grip on snow or ice when pout on edge, caused either by the inability of the ski to dampen vibration or by the skier not weighting the ski properly and sufficiently.
Chicken salad air	SNB	The rear hand reaches behind the front leg, grabs the heel side between the bindings while the front leg is boned. Also, the wrist is rotated inwards to complete the grab.
Cliffhanger	MTX	Rider hooks his feet under the bars and riases his hands in the air
Closed mold	SNB	A mold that holds all the pre-shaped components of a board in a sealed chamber which eliminates additional shaping after pressing. To mass producer snowboards more rapidly by containing the board shape and minimizing finishing and shaping steps.
Concave	SKT	The contour given to decks. The concave will dip down from the left to right and should be asymmetrical. Provides strength to the board and aids the skater when performing tricks.
Construct flex	SNB	Q uniform flex pattern from nose to center to tail. To balance the overall flex patter of the board from the tip and tail to the center.
Continuous edge	SKT	Edges designed without small "cracks" in the outmost contact area. To add strength and at times, stiffness to the edges.
Coping	MULTI	A rounded lip at the top of a ramp or

Word	*Sport*	*Definition*
		obstacle, usually made of metal, cement, or PVC pipe.
Corkscrew 540	SNB	Sideways backside 540, also called a barrel roll.
Cowboy	INL	Skater has front foot on outside plate, back foot on outside plate. Trick is also known as the Cab Driver and it resembles a mix of a Torque and a Backside. The Cowboy comes from the bowed shape of the legs when doing this trick.
Crail air	SNB	The rear hand grabs the toe edge in the front of the front foot while the rear leg is behind.
Crippler	SNB	An inverted aerial where the rider performs a 180 degree flip. The athlete approaches the wall riding forward, becomes airborne, rotates 90 degrees, flips over in the air, rotates another 90 degrees, and lands riding forward.
Crooked cop air	SNB	Tuck kneed backside grab
Crooked grind	SKT	Nosegrind with nose sliding at the same time.
Crossed	INL	A grab with the opposite hand of the skate.
Crossed up	INL	When the skater's legs are crossed while performing a trick.
Curb grind	INL	A grind performed on a sidewalk curb.
Dampening	ETC	The quality in a ski which absorbs vibration.
Dampening	SKT	To control and minimize the amount of resonance of vibration created by the energy separated by board flex and surface of the snow. Any material like rubber sheer, built into the edges, or core that keep the board quiet and more responsive.
Directional board and flex	SNB	A board designed to provide excellent characteristics when being ridden forward

Word	*Sport*	*Definition*
		as opposed to backwards. Bindings are usually mounted farther back and the flex and sidecuts are altered accordingly, with the tail being a little stiffer.
Directional twin	SNB	A board that features designs of directions and twin tips to allow for a wider range of use, for example freeriding and halfpipe.
Disaster	SNB	A lip trick where one gets "hung up " on the coping, most often with the board perpendicular to the coping.
Double Can Can	MTX	Rider moves one leg to other side of bike, then brings other leg up to meet it, elevating his butt off the seat.
Double grab	SNB	Basically, doing two separate tricks while in the air. One goes off of a jump, grabs the board one way, then grabs it in another way, then lands.
Downhill ski	SKI	The lower ski or the one that will become the lower ski in any ski turn.
Drop in	MULTI	To enter the ramp or obstacle from the top.
Duck Foot	SNB	A term used to describe stance angles with toes pointing outward.
Durometer	MULTI	A measurement of the resiliency, or hardness, of a urethane wheel.
Edges	MULTI	The strips of metal usually made hard steel, on the outer edges of the running surface of skis or snowboards.
Effective edge	SNB	The length of metal edge on the snowboards which touches the ground; it is the effective part which is used to make a turn. It does not include the edge of the tip and tail.
Effective edge	SKT	The difference between the two contact areas beneath the tip and tail when the

Word	Sport	Definition
		camber is depressed. A measurement used to define the actual length of the surface area that comes into contact on a perfectly flat surface.
Eggflip	SNB	An eggplant where the rider chooses to flip over in order to re-enter the pipe instead or rotating 180 degrees. This trick is performed forward to fakie or switchstance (fakie to forward).
Eggplant	SNB	A one-handed 180 degree invert in which the front hand is planted on the lip of the wall and the rotation is backside.
Electra base	SNB	An extremely hard sintered base material contracted with graphite to reduce friction. Generally black in color. Used on high-speed boards on colder snow/ice conditions.
Elgeurial (bfm)	SNB	An invert where the halfpipe wall is approached fakie, the rear hand is planted, a 360 degree backside rotation is made, and the rider lands going forward. Named after Eddie Elguera.
Elliptical flex	SNB	A flex pattern which is softer towards tip and tail. To create a smoother flex pattern than the mid-section of the board.
Enduro	MTX	Long distance, cross-country motocross race. Example: Baja 1,000.
Eurocarve	SNB	A term used to describe a certain mode of riding in which the rider makes large and hard cutting turns; usually getting way up on the edge and leaning the body parallel to the ground.
Extruded base	SNB	Particles of base materials are compressed and pushed out through a flat form to create a sheet of base material. This quality of base

Word	Sport	Definition
		material is used for average temperature snow conditions and for easy base repair.
Fall line	MULTI	The path of least resistance down and given slope.
Farfernugan	INL	See Torque.
Farside	INL	When a trick is performed on the outside or away edge of a ramp or obstacle.
Fast slide	INL	A grind on one skate on which the skater rides the front foot on the inside of the grindplate and the back foot is grabbed.
Feeble grind	SKT	The back truck is grinding, front of body facing edge with toe-side rail grinding edge also.
Fiberglass	SKT	A fabric of woven glass fibers which is available in different weave patterns and weights for a variety of applications. To strengthen board construction and control the flex attributes in a board.
Fifty fifty	SKT	A double axle grind (on both trucks).
Flat bottom	MULTI	The area in a halfpipe between the two opposing transitional walls.
Flat spin	INL	The trick that turned heads in 1997/98. A skater gets air, turns the axis of his body nearly horizontal to the ground or ramp, spins, rights himself and lands.
Flatland	SNB	Term used to describe tricks performed on the flat slope with obstacles (e.g. nose slide, blunt slide, tail wheelie).
Flex pattern	SNB	The relative softness and stiffness of a board along its length. To allow for the proper distribution of energy to be transfer to the board in the proper location also its running length for more effective edge control.

Word	Sport	Definition
Floating edge	SKT	When a board is constructed with a rubber strip separating the edge material and core material. To act as a shock absorber to smooth out the ride and a board to enhance its responsiveness.
Foam	SKT	Polyurethane (PU) A synthetic resin material which is comprised of a base and a catalyst. When combined, expand to fill the cavity of a closed mold and bond. Used as a core and sometimes a bonding material in the construction of a snowboard.
Frame	INL	The component that attaches to the base of the skate and holds the wheels.
Free skiing	ETC	Skiing for fun, not competing or training.
Freeriding	SNB	Snowboarding on all types of terrain for fun, no contest, no halfpipe, no gates, no rules.
Freestyle	SNB	The kind of snowboarding which is mostly associated with riding the halfpipe, but may also be used to describe any type of snowboarding which includes tricks and maneuvers.
Freestyle	MTX	Expression contest in which riders are given a time allotment to hit a variety of jumps, performing aerial maneuvers for a judged score. Have also been called Freeride Competitions.
Fresh fish air	SNB	The backside version of the Stale Fish.
Front foot	SNB	The foot mounted closet to the nose. A regular footers left foot and a goofy footers right foot.
Front hand	SNB	The hand closet to the nose of the snowboards. The left hand for regular footers and the right hand for goofy footers.
Frontside	MULTI	When a turn or trick is executed in a

Word	*Sport*	*Definition*
		direction that the front of the body is facing toward the outside of the arc of the trick.
Frontside air	SNB	The trick is best described for its grab. The frontside grab is with the rear hand between the bindings on the toe edge; in this particular maneuver the front leg is boned. It can also be any air performed on the frontside wall of the halfpipe.
Frontside turn	SNB	A turn where the toe edge faces to the outside of the turn while the snowboard is riding on the heel edge. A left for a regular footer and right turn for a goofy footer.
Fun Box	BMX	A four-sided box jump (ramp on every side) that is included in street courses.
Gap	MULTI	The space between ramps or obstacles. Separates obstacles and is often jumped over from one obstacle to the other, making for more creative airs. (also called the Canyon)
Gay twist	SKT	While riding fakie, usually at the lip of a ramp, to complete a 360 in the air while grabbing and head back down the ramp forwards.
Gay twist	SNB	Halfpipe fakie to regular 360 spin with a grab.
Giant slalom	MULTI	A form of Alpine racing in which the racer passes through a series of gates, similar to slalom but faster and more open.
Grasser	SNB	A variation on the method air performed with the front hand grabbing the heel edge and twisting the board so it faces down hill. The back leg is also boned out. Named after a group of riders from Grass Valley in CA.
Grind plate	INL	A piece of metal or plastic that attaches to the frame and creates a better grind spot than the frame alone.

Word	Sport	Definition
Grip tape	SKT	Adhesive backed sandpaper material fixed to the top of the board to provide traction.
Haakon flip	SNB	A halfpipe trick named after freestyle legend Teje Haakonsen of Norway. Haakon Flip is like a switch rodeo performed in a halfpipe.
Half cab	SKT	A 180 degree Caballerial.
Half cab	SNB	It is the freeriding version of the Caballerial in which one rotates 180 degrees from fakie to forward off of a straight jump.
Half pipe	MULTI	A type of ramp that is shaped like a "U" and used for vert skating.
Half pipe	MULTI	A snow structure that consists of opposing radial transition walls of the same height and size. Used to catch air and perform tricks by traveling back and forth from wall to wall while moving do
Hand plant	MULTI	A type of trick where one hand grabs the skate while doing a one handed handstand on a ramp, or obstacle.
Handplant (backside)	MULTI	A 180 degree handplant in which both hands or the rear hand may be planted on the lip of the wall and the rotation is backside.
Handplant (frontside)	MULTI	A 180 degree handplant in which the front hand is planted on the lip of the wall and the rotation is frontside.
Handplant (layback)	SNB	A 180 degree handplant in which the rear hand is planted on the lip of the wall and the rotation is frontside.
Hang up	SKT	When either the back or front truck catches on an obstacle, usually causing a fall.
Hang up	INL	To catch one or both skates on the lip of a ramp or obstacle during re-entry.

Word	Sport	Definition
Hanger	SKT	Part of the truck that gets the most abuse. When grinding it is done along the top of the hanger. Contained inside the hanger is the axle.
Heel Clicker	MTX	Rider brings both feet off the pegs and touches them together over the handlebars.
Heel out	INL	A skater grinds with front foot on heel, back foot on outside plate toes turned out. Known as the "Tom Fry trick" and can only be done backside. Somewhat like a Royale but front foot is on the heel.
Heelflip	SKT	While performing on Ollie, the heel pushed down on the edge of the board causing it to flip over.
Hip	MULTI	The spot where a ramp or obstacle comes to a point. Tricks are done while flying over or off of it.
Ho ho	MULTI	A general term given to any two handed handplant.
Horizontal lamination	SNB	Layers a component, most commonly wood, that are bonded together on top of each other to form a strong material from otherwise weak elements. Used as either the full deck material or the core in the construction of a board.
Hucker	SNB	One who throws himself/herself wildly through the air and does not land on his/her feet.
Iguana air	SNB	The rear hand grabs the toe edge near the tail.
Indy air	SNB	A true "Indy Air" is performed backside with the rear hand grabbing between the bindings on the toe edge while the rear leg is boned. The term "Indy" may also be used to simple describe the location of the grab.

Word	*Sport*	*Definition*
Insert	SNB	A small cylinder, which is threaded on the inside, that is install reinforcement to attach bindings to. Used to reinforce the area of a snowboard where the screws for attaching the bindings go into the board.
Inside ski	SKI	The ski which is on the inside of the turn will become the inside ski in any turn.
Interlock system	SNB	The tip and tail sections, usually made of plastic, are mechanically locked to the core using a jigsaw puzzle type arrangement. Spreads out the stress at the junctions of these materials.
Invert	MULTI	Another name for a hand plant.
Inverted 180	MULTI	To get upside down while perfroming a 180.
Inverted 540	SNB	To get upside down while spinning a 540.
Inverted 720	SNB	An inverted aerial where the rider performs a 720 degree rotational flip. The rider approaches the wall riding forward, becomes airborne, rotates 720 degree in a backside direction while performing a front flip, and lands riding fakie.
Inverted aerial	SNB	A maneuvers where the rider becomes airborne and upside down at any given moment.
Japan	MULTI	The front hand grabs the toe edge, the front knee is tucked and the board is pulled up and the back is arched.
Jib	SNB	Riding which closely resembles street skating. "Jibbers" commonly slide rails, bonk trees and perform flatland tricks.
Jump ramp	SKT	A small ramp used to give the skater some air to perform a trick.
Kevlar	SNB	A man-made fibrous material that has a high strength to weight ratio. To strengthen a

Word	Sport	Definition
		snowboard without adding weight and to enhance the performance of the flex action.
Kick turn	SKT	When pressure is applied to the tail of the board, lifting the front and turning it in another direction.
Kicker	MULTI	A name for a jump ramp. Kickers usually have the property of throwing you up into the air rather than giving you distance.
Kickflip	SKT	The same as a Heelflip except the toe pushes down to flip the board.
Kingpin	SKT	The bolt that holds the hanger and base plate together.
Knee pad	MULTI	A type of protective padding worn on the knees.
Knee slide	MULTI	A way of controlling a fall by sliding on plastic caps on the knee pads.
Late	MULTI	A term used to describe incorporating something into a trick just before its completion and landing.
Lazy boy	MTX	Rider hooks his feet underneath the bars and lies back on the seat with his hands in the air.
Leash	SNB	A retention device used to attach the snowboard to the front foot so that it doesn't run away-completely useless.
Lien air	MULTI	The front hand grabs the heel edge and the body leans out over the nose. Essentially a method on the frontside wall. Named after Neil Blender.
Lip	MULTI	The top edge portion of the halfpipe wall.
Lip trick	MULTI	Any trick performed on or near the lip of the wall of the halfpipe.
Lipslide	MULTI	To force the tail over the lip and slide on the surface before re-entry.

Word	*Sport*	*Definition*
Look Back	BMX	Where the rider in the air turns the handlebars and his body backwards, looking to the back of his bike.
Makio	INL	Skater riders with front foot soul, back foot grabbed. Created by a Japanese skater name Makio. The topside variation is called Fishbrain, created in 1995 by Tom Fry.
Manual	BMX	Where a rider does a wheelie across the top deck before returning to the ramp.
Manual	SKT	Another name for Wheelie.
Mcegg	SNB	An invert where the rider plants the front hand on the wall, rotated 540 degrees in a backside direction and lands riding forward.
McMetz	MTX	Double, simultaneous Saran wraps. Both legs pass through the arms simultaneously and both arms release at the same time to allow the legs to pass back through to the foot pegs.
Mctwist	SKT	A 540 degree turn performed on a ramp. Named after Mike McGill.
Mctwist	SNB	An inverted aerial where the rider performs a 540 degree rotational flip. The rider approaches the halfpipe wall riding forward, becomes airborne, rotates 540 degrees in a backside directions while performing a front flip and lands riding forward.
Melonchollie	SNB	The front hand reaches behind the front leg and grabs the heel edge in-between the bindings while the front leg is boned.
Method	SNB	The front hand grabs the heel edge, both knees are bent, and the board is pulled up behind the rider. In the halfpipe, the rider's body can become almost parallel with the ground.

Word	Sport	Definition
Michalchuk	SNB	Mike Michalchuk's signature halfpipe trick, self-described as my backside flip—sort of like an inverted backside 540 or a backflip backside 540". Essentially a backside rodeo.
Miller flip	SNB	An invert where the halfpipe wall is approached riding forward, the front hand is planted, a 360 degree frontside rotation is made, and the rider lands riding fakie.
Miller flip	INL	A backflip with 360 turn degree turn.
Mistrial	INL	A skater rides with the front foot soul, back foot on the outside plate with toes turning out. The topside variation is called an Overpuss for the exposure it gives to the skaters pelvic area, the reverse topside variation is called Misfit.
Misty	SNB	Can also be used as an adjective to describe a spin that gets a bit sideways (somewhere between upright and inverted).
Misty flip	SNB	Partially inverted bacside spin. Named by Ali Goulet.
Misty flip	INL	A move first popularized by Ryan Jacklone. The move involves a front somersault with a 540 spin.
Miszou	INL	A grind with the front skate in the soul position, and the back skate perpendicular to the rail or obstacle. A few years ago, the Miszou was the trick of choice for transferring from one rail to another, usually to frontside. Miszou is Japanese for water.
Moguls	ETC	Skiers are judged on how they ski a mogul run, including two mandatory air offs which skiers perform tricks. Pro mogul competitions have racers competing head to head in an elimination format.

Word	*Sport*	*Definition*
Monocoque	SNB	A form of integrated structural design that used the outermost material or skin to bear the load of strength of an object. To reduce weight and enhance torsional rigidity and edge responsiveness and eliminate the need for separate sidewall material.
Mute	SNB	The front hand grabs the toe edge either between the toes, and front leg is boned out.
Mute	INL	A crossed-grab air.
Nac Nac	MTX	Rider brings one leg over the rear fender to the other side of the bike, as if he's dismounting in mid-air.
Natural	INL	The direction that the skater feels best performing a trick, right skate forward or left skate forward.
No Hander Lander	MTX	Landing a jump with no hands on the bars.
No-Footer/ No-Hander	BMX	Any air pulled without feet/hands touching the bike.
Nollie	MULTI	Much like an Ollie only you spring off of your nose instead of your tail.
Nollie frontflip	SNB	Springing off of the nose while going off a jump and leaning forward, allows you to do a frontflip.
Nose bonk	SNB	To hit an object with the nose of the board.
Nose grab	SNB	The front hand grabs the nose of the board.
Nose poke	SNB	Any maneuver where you bone your front leg and "poke" the nose of the board in a direction away from your body. Usually while grabbing.
Nose slide	MULTI	Sliding on the nose of board on the edge of an obstacle like a handrail, ledge, or ramp lip.

Word	*Sport*	*Definition*
Nose Wheelie	BMX	Where a rider rides the front wheel while the back wheel is in the air.
Nosegrind	SKT	Just the front truck is grinding.
Nothing	BMX	When a rider fully lets go of his bike with his hands and feet in the air so that no part of his body is touching the bike.
Nuclear air	SNB	The rear hand reaches across the front of the body and grabs the heel edge in front of the front foot.
Ole	ETC	A rider rotates with the handle over head.
Ollie	SNB	A method to obtain air by first lifting the front foot then lifting the rear foot as you spring off of the tail.
Ollie	SKT	A no handed air performed by tapping the tail of the board on the ground or ramp surface. Named after Alan Gelfend.
One-Footer/ One-Hander	BMX	Any air pulled with one foot/hand off of the bike.
One-Handed Superman	MTX	Superman with one hand off the handlebars and grabbing the rear fender.
Open mold	SNB	A form that is used to assemble and hold the parts of a snowboard during the pressing process that allows the expansion and bleeding of the bonding.
Palmer	SNB	A kind of method where the grab is near the nose, the board is pulled across the front of the body, and the nose is pointed downward. Named after Shaun Palmer.
Parabolic	ETC	A super sidecut ski intended to make skiing easier for beginners.
Phillips 66	SNB	An invert where the rider approaches the halfpipe wall riding fakie, plants the rear hand on the lip of the wall while doing a

Word	Sport	Definition
		"front flip " and lands on the transition riding forward.
Pick	BMX	Where a rider balances one part of his bike on their coping, stalling for a moment before returning to the ramp. Usually involves stalling on the front tire (Nose) or either front or back or both pegs.
Ply	SNB	Short for plywood. The most commonly used material for the deck. Usually seven layer ply.
Poptart	SNB	Airing from fakie to forward in the halfpipe without rotation.
Pornstar	INL	Skater riders with the front foot soul, back foot on outside of grindplate with toes pointing in. This trick was purportedly named by Brooke HOward Smityh and is probably the only trick that Brooke has not named after a Mortal Kombat character.
Pre-jump	ETC	A maneuver in which the skier jumps before reaching the crest of a bump so that his trajectory follows the contour of the bump, resulting in less air and more speed.
Pre-peg fiberglass	SNB	A stiff sheet of fiberglass previously treated with epoxy resin. Used as an alternative to fiberglass. Generally a matter of manufacturer's production progress.
Ptex	SNB	One of several names for the plastic base material used on boards.
Quadratic sidecut	SKT	To soften the transition from the entrance to the exit of a turn and provide a more forgiving feel.
Rail	SKT	The edge of the board. Also refers to plastic strips attached to the underside of the board.
Rail	SNB	There are tow rails on a snowboard; each comprised of a sidewall and an edge.

Word	Sport	Definition
Railslide	MULTI	Also called boardslide. To slide on an obstacle or lip with the contact point being the underside of the board.
Ramp boards	SKT	Large deck and firm wheels mounted on wide trucks to make the board as stable as possible.
Rear foot	SNB	The foot mounted closest to the rail.
Rear hand	SNB	The hand closet to the tail of the board.
Regular foot	MULTI	To ride with the left foot forward.
Retainer	SKT	Keep the ball bearings spaced correctly.
Revert	SNB	To switch from riding fakie to forward, or from forward to fakie, usually while the board is still touching the ground.
Rewind	SNB	A term used to describe any maneuver where a rotation is initiated, stopped and its momentum reversed.
Rewind	INL	To complete the arc that a skater begins when coming off a grind or stall by spinning.
Rippey flip	SNB	Straight back flipping frontside 360, with a method grab (Jim Rippey).
Riser	SKT	Plastic piece under the base of the truck to raise it for better wheel clearance. Often used with larger wheels.
Roast beef	SNB	The rear hand reaches between the legs and grabs the heel edge between the bindings while the front leg is boned. Also, the wrist is rotated inward to complete the grab.
Rock and roll	MULTI	A trick where the underside of the board and wheels are tapped on the lip before a kickturn to reenter.
Rocket Air	INL	A trick were you grab both skates with both hands, while skates are straight in front of the skater.

Word	Sport	Definition
Rocket Air	BMX	When a rider takes both feet off the pedals in the air and places them on the back pegs, then returns them to the pedals before landing. Can be landed in this position also.
Rodeo	SNB	Turning frontside 180 while completing an inverted 360 rotation for a total of 540. A rodeo 720 is when you would turn frontside 360 while completing an inverted 360 rotation for a total 720.
Rodeo flip	SNB	Partially inverted 360 with a back flip.
Roll-in	BMX	A portion at the top of a ramp that riders can use to roll into the ramp rather than dropping in over the vertical section of the ramp. Often used to gain more speed entering the ramp and as a gap to air over depending on where it lies on the ramp.
Rolling down the windows	SNB	A phrase used to describe when someone is caught off balance, and they rotate their arms wildly in the air to try and recover.
Royale	INL	Skater riders with the front foot on inside plate, back foot on the outside plate, toes pointed in. Brooke Howard Smith was the founder of the Royale. He 'royaled' the big rail on the first X Games.
Rubber dampening systems	SNB	Incorporating rubber into the construction of the board to dampen vibrations and provide certain performance characteristics.
Run	MULTI	A series of tricks in a sequence.
Sad plant	SNB	A term used to describe any handplant where the front leg is boned for style.
Sandwich construction	SNB	Layers of materials, on top of each other, with additional components for sidewall strength and torisional flex patterning. Used

Word	*Sport*	*Definition*
		to construct a board with different layers of materials on top of each other.
Saran Wrap	MTX	Rider passes one foot between his hands and back to the peg, removing one hand from the bars to let it pass through.
Sato flip	SNB	Halfpipe trick done by Rob Kingwill (Sato—Japanese for "sugar"). Kind of like a frontside McTwist. Rider drops in fast, riders up the transition as if doing frontside 540, pops in the air and grabs frontside, then throws head, shoulders, and hips downs
Seabelt	SNB	The frontside reaches across the body and grabs the tail while the front leg is boned.
S-bend	ETC	A rider performs an Air raley while rotating his body 360 degrees while inverted.
Session	MULTI	A period of skating.
Shifty	SNB	A grabless trick where the upper torso and lower body are twisted in opposite directions and then returned to normal.
Shove it	SKT	A trick performed by spinning the board beneath the feet.
Shovel	SKT	The front of the board that rises up off the snow. Design is usually a result of boards intended use, powder boards have lots of shovel, race boards have very little.
Shovel	ETC	Area near the tip of the ski.
Shovel	SNB	The lifted or upward curved sections of a snowboard at the tip and tail.
Side cut	SNB	The curve built into the sidewalls and edges of a board to enhance turning characteristics. To create a curve on the turning surface that is characteristic of the boards riding style.
Side wall	SNB	The area between the topsheet and the base,

Word	Sport	Definition
		and above the edges on a snowboard. Holds the core and other materials from shifting during the manufacturing process, and to protect them as a finished product.
Sidewall	ETC	Refers to the side of the ski.
Sintered base	SNB	A form of polymer plastic that is compress into a long shape, set on a roller and sliced into sheets of base material. A slightly harder more porous from of base material used on performance snowboards.
Slalom	MULTI	A form of Alpine racing in which the racer must run a course designated by a series of gates set in various combination as to test technique, speed, and agility. Failure to pass through the gate properly results in disqualification.
Slick	SKT	A board that has a layer of slippery plastic bonded to the bottom for extra slide/ strength. They are usually heavier than plain wood boards. Most serious skaters prefer wood.
Slob air	SNB	The frontside air where the front hand grabs mute, the back leg is boned and the board is kept parallel with the ground.
Smith grind	SKT	A type of grind trick where the back truck is grinding, while the rail of the board is also grinding the lip of the ramp or obstacle. Frontside Smith Grind: the toe-side edge is involved; Backside Smith Grind: the heel-side edge is involved.
Soul grind	INL	A grind where the leading skate is parallel with the rail or obstacle and the rear skate is perpendicular to it.
Spaghetti air	SNB	The front hand reaches between the legs and behind the front legs to grab the toe edge in

Word	Sport	Definition
		front of the front foot while the back leg is boned.
Spine ramp	MULTI	Two half pipes placed back to back creating a double U shape.
Stain	SKT	Normal deck without a slick bottom.
Stale	INL	Any trick in which the skater reaches behind his body to grab the wheels or frame.
Stale egg	SNB	An eggplant with a stalefish grab.
Stalefish air	SKT	The frontside trick where the rear hand grabs the heel edge behind the rear between the bindings while the front leg is boned.
Stalemasky air	SNB	When a maneuver is performed such that the point of emphasis in the maneuver is held or "stalled" for an extended period of time.
Stall	INL	To land on a lip and stop for a second and then re-enter.
Stall	BMX	When a rider pauses briefly on the coping before dropping back into the ramp.
Stance	SNB	The position of one's feet on the ground.
Stiffy air	SNB	Any maneuver in which both legs are boned and a grab is incorporated.
Stinky	SNB	Riding with the legs spread open.
Street	BMX	An event consisting of different types and styles of ramps positioined so that they can be approached in many different ways. Competitors plan out their runs through these ramps according to individual style.
Street boards	SKT	Shorter and narrower than ramp boards. Usually has a shorter wheelbase than a ramp board.
Sub Box	BMX	Street course jump consisting of two ramps, one on either side of a platform that is topped

Word	Sport	Definition
		by an approximately 3-foot high box, with a 2-foot deck on top. The height and small surface of the box make it easy for a rider to clip a back wheel.
Sublimated top sheet	SNB	Topsheets that have had the graphics added through the sublimation process. Provides very durable graphics because they are cooked right into the plastic.
Super g	ETC	A faster more open version of the giant slalom, kind of a cross between GS and downhill.
Superman	BMX	Where a rider takes bolth feet off the pedals in the air and stretches his legs as far behind the bike as possible. Looks like Superman flying holding on the handlebars, hence the name.
Superman	MTX	Rider releases both legs from pegs and throws his legs back, elevating himself over the bike.
Swing weight	SKT	The distribution of weight from the tip and tail to the center of the board. To balance a board and control its ability to initiate rotation or to stop rotation in relationship to its overall weight.
Swiss cheese air	SNB	The rear hand reaches between the legs and grabs the heel edge in front of the front foot while the back left is boned.
Switch stance	SKT	When the feet are placed in the opposite of the normal stance and you are going forward with a slightly different balance point than in your normal stance. Not the same as fakie where you ride backwards with your normal balance and stance.
Switch take off	SNB	Going into a jump backwards.

Word	Sport	Definition
Symmetrical design	SNB	When all the design components of the side cut and shape are parallel in design. The opposite of Asymmetrical. To position a rider on a board when less angulation or opposing angulation is necessary.
Table Top	BMX	When a rider flattens his bike out into the horizontal plane in the air, then straightens it back out to land.
Tabletop	MULTI	Type of jump—with a ramp going up, flat on top, and a landing ramp on the far side.
Tail	MULTI	The rear tip of the board or ski.
Tail bonk	SNB	To hit an object with the tail of the snowboard.
Tail grab	SNB	The rear hand grabs the tail of the snowboard.
Tail poke	SNB	Any maneuver where you bone your rear leg and "poke" the tail of the snowboard in a direction away from your body usually while grabbing.
Tail protector/ tip protector	SNB	Usually a metal plate built into the tail or tip of the board. To protect the tail or tip from damage and to control swing weight.
Tail slide	SKT	Sliding on the tail of the board.
Tail slide	SNB	To slide along the ground or an object solely on the tail of the snowboard.
Tail tap	SNB	See Tail Bonk.
Tail wheelie	SNB	To ride solely on the tail of the snowboard with the nose in the air.
Tailwhip	BMX	Where a rider whips his bike around the axis of the handlebars, while keeping the handlebars and his body stationary, and landing back on the bike before hitting the

Word	Sport	Definition
		ground. Double Tailwhips (two bike rotations) are also popular, but extremely difficult.
Taipan air	SNB	The front hand reaches behind the front foot and grabs the toe edge between the bindings. The front knee is then bent to touch the board tuck knee style.
T-bolt	SNB	A small metal inside threaded cylinder with a disk attached to the bottom, to prevent it from pulling up and out of the board. To repair or substitute the area of binding attachment to a board.
Tip	SKT	Top end of the ski.
Tire Tap	BMX	Where a rider's back wheel is on the deck and the front wheel is in the air, balancing for a moment before dropping back in to the ramp.
Toe edge	SNB	A snowboard has two different edges. The toe edge is the one at which the toes rest.
Toeside	SNB	The frontside of the board is the side where the toes rest. And the frontside of the board is the side to which his/her chest faces.
Toeside rotation	SNB	Rotating counter-clockwise for a regular footer, and rotating clockwise for a goofy footer.
Tombstone	BMX	A vertical portion of a ramp that rises above the rest of the top of the ramp to add more vert. Resembles a rectangular tombstone on top of the ramp.
Top sheet	SNB	Usually a form of flexible plastic that sits on top of the laminated or foam core. Also the material that is used as the cap in Monocoque Construction. To protect the core materials of the boards, and to act as a material for graphics applications.

Word	Sport	Definition
Torque	INL	Skater rides with the front foot on the outside of the grindplate, toes turned in, back foot on inside of grindplate. Also called Farfernugan.
Torque slide	INL	Skater rides with front foot on the outside of grindplate, back foot grabbed. This is one of the toughest grinds to master. Some people call it a Suicide because of its difficulty.
Torsion box construction	SNB	When the core material is fully wrapped with a strength enhancing material like fiberglass. To manipulate the flex and torsional rigidity of a snowboard from the core construction.
Torsional flex	SNB	The actual resistance to twisting a boards from side to side. To define the flex of a board from side to side. Its resistance to twisting and its responsiveness to initiating a turn and hold an edge.
Traditional skis	ETC	Describes skis with shapes typical of all skis of the past 50 years, these skis have a straighter shape than modern skis.
Transition	MULTI	The curved part of the terrain between 0 and 90 degrees.
Transition	BMX	The point where a ramp or jump goes from the horizontal plane to the vertical plane.
Transition (tranny)	SNB	The radial curved section of a halfpipe wall between the flat bottom and the vertical. A snowboarder pumps and rides the transition to gain speed, catch air, and land.
Traverse	MULTI	Skiing across the slope at an angle to fall line.
Traverse	SNB	To ride perpendicular to the fall line. Halfpipe rider traverses from wall to wall in the halfpipe.

Word	Sport	Definition
Truck	SKT	The hardware that is comprised of the axle and base plate mounted to the underside of the board.
Truck Driver	BMX	A regular 360 while simultaneously spinning the handlebars 360 degrees. A double Truck Driver would be spinning the bars 720 degrees.
Tuck knee	SNB	A technique where one knee is bent, and the ankle is bent sideways in order to touch the knee to the snowboard between the bindings.
Turndown	BMX	Where a rider turns the handlebars and his body down towards the ground while the rest of the bike stays facing straight up.
Tweaked	SNB	A term used to describe the emphasis of style in a trick.
Twin tip	SNB	A type of snowboard designed for freestyle snowboarding. It has an identical tip and tail so that the board may be ridden similarly in both directions.
Unity	INL	Skater rides with front foot on outside of grindplate and places foot in the front of back foot which is on outside of its grindplate. When skater performs a Unity, it looks as though they're sitting Indian style.
Uphill ski	ETC	The ski higher on the fall, or the one that will become the upper ski in any ski turn.
Variable flex	SNB	When the tip, tail and middle of a board each have varying degrees of flex. To vary the overall flex of a board from the tip to the middle to the tail.
Variable radius	SNB	A side cut design that incorporates a changing radius size along the length of the board. To adjust a side cut design of a board

Word	*˙Sport*	*Definition*
		by using many intersecting radius sizes, to enhance its turning characteristics.
Varial	SKT	An aerial where the board is spun from backwards to forwards beneath the feet.
Variation	INL	To change from one type of grind or grab to another while doing long trick such a handrail.
Vert	INL	Short for vertical, meaning a 90 degree ramp, pool, or wall.
Vert	BMX	The half-pipe event. A half-pipe is like a big "U" with two transition areas at either end that extend to vertical stands, separated by the flat bottom in between.
Vertical	SNB	The vertical top portion of a wall in a halfpipe which allows the snowboarder to fly straight up into the air and not' out of the pipe or into the pipe.
Vertically laminated wood core	SNB	Pretty much the industry standard. Strips of wood ranging from 1/8" to 3/4" are bonded together side to side with the joints running vertical. This allows for several different woods to be used in each core to optimize performance characteristics.
Waist	SNB	The width measurement taken at the narrowest part of the board which is near the middle of its length.
Wall	MULTI	Any bank that is at or above 90 degrees.
Wallride	MULTI	To ride on a wall that has no transition.
Wax	INL	The substance skaters spread on the curbs and obstacles to make them more slippery.
Wheels	SKT	Attached to the truck—rolling devices which are usually made of urethane. In addition to the standard wheels, there are

Word	*Sport*	*Definition*
		now those which have a nylon or high-tech plastic on the interior part of the wheel.
Whip	MTX	Classic Motocross move where rider turns and lays the machine flat in mid air.
Wood core	MULTI	Various type of wood used to provide the shape and thickness of a board.
World cup	ETC	An annual series featuring the best freestyle and alpine skiers.
X-Up	BMX	While in the air a rider turns the handlebars as far as they will go in one direction without releasing the grip, then turns them back in the other direction before landing.

Bibliography

"A Short History of Lacrosse in Canada". Canadian Lacrosse Association. Retrieved on 2008-07-14.

"About Finland: General information: Sports". Embassy of Finland, Washington (2007-06-11). Retrieved on 2008-07-21. "the national sport, "pesäpallo"

"About Ireland: Culture and Sport". Government of Ireland. Retrieved on 2008-07-21. "Gaelic Football and Hurling, as Ireland's native sports are the most popular."

"airports & tourists". Global Culture (2007).

"Antiguans and Barbudans". everyculture.com. Retrieved on 2008-07-10. "Cricket, a left-over from the British rule, is the national sport of Antigua and Barbuda."

"Argentina Decree No. 17468 of 16/09/1953". Global Legal Information Network. Retrieved on 2008-07-14.

"Banglapedia: Kabadi". Asiatic Society of Bangladesh. Retrieved on 2008-07-21. "Ha-du-du was given the name kabadi and the status of National Game in 1972."

"Barbados: Sports". Government of Barbados. Retrieved on 2008-07-21. "The national sport of Barbados is cricket"

"BOAT RACING SEASON OFFICIALLY OPENS", *The Anguillian* (2007-03-03). Retrieved on 2008-07-21. "Director of Sports, Alkins Rogers, [..] reported that the Government recognizes boat racing as the national sport of Anguilla and was giving financial resources for its development."

"Buzkashi: the national game of Afghanist [sic]". Embassy of Afghanistan, Canberra. Retrieved on 2008-07-21.

"Citizens: Sports: Hockey". *National Portrait of India*. Government of

India. Retrieved on 2008-07-22. "Hockey, the National Sport of the Country is one of the most religiously followed games in India."

"Citypaper online". Retrieved on 2007-11-10.

"Colombia Law 613 of 4 September 2000". Global Legal Information Network. Retrieved on 2008-07-14.

"Games". Guyana Tourism Authority. Retrieved on 2008-07-21. "Cricket lovely Cricket! One cannot miss out on Guyana's national sport without participating in a game of cricket while in Guyana."

"History of Jamaica". Jamaican Embassy, Washington. Retrieved on 2008-07-21. "The legacy of Britain also lives on in Jamaica in many ways [..] the game of cricket is the national sport."

"History of Tae Kwon Do". North American Tae Kwon Do Schools. Retrieved on 2008-07-14.

"La Charrería "Nuestro Deporte Nacional"" (in Spanish). Mexican Department of Tourism. Retrieved on 2008-07-14. "El año de 1933 fue muy importante, ya que el general Abelardo L. Rodríguez, emite un decreto presidencial, dando a la Charrería el título de único Deporte Nacional."

"Long-term Prospects: Tourism 2020 Vision". World Tourism (2004).

"Monthly Market Report: Germany". Tourism Australia (February 2008).

"National Sports of Canada Act". Retrieved on 2008-07-09.

"National Symbols". *Bhutan Portal*. Government of Bhutan. Retrieved on 2008-07-21. "National Game: The national sport of Bhutan is archery."

"Number One Tourist Destination is Paris" (01-09-2008).

"Online Etymology Dictionary: tour". Retrieved on 2008-03-01.

"Pak. Hockey Federation Secretary sacked", *Zee news*, United News of India (2008-06-16). Retrieved on 2008-08-05. "Sports Minister Najamuddin Khan said [..] "We have been watching with great distress the way hockey which is our national sport has been going downhill.""

"Paris Is The Most Visited City In The World" (01-09-2008).

"Paris: Most visited and most expensive city in the world" (01-09-2008).

"Paris—World's Most Visited City—Leisure and Statistics" (01-09-2008). This refers to 2002 .

"Puerto Rico Act 64 of 2000, S.B. 1856" (PDF). Office of Legislative Services of Puerto Rico (2000-04-11). Retrieved on 2008-07-14. "In 1966, the Public Parks and Recreation Administration and the Puerto Rico Olympic Committee awarded official recognition of the "paso fino" horse riding sport as the autochthonous sport of Puerto Rico."

"Scientists call for national flowers". *China Daily* (2005-08-09). Retrieved on 2008-07-21. "If you ask a Chinese person what the national wine is, you will no doubt be told it is Moutai. When asked what the national sport is, the answer will be table tennis."

"Some facts about the Dominican Republic". Embassy of the Dominican Republic, Washington. Retrieved on 2008-07-22. "Baseball is the Dominican Republic's national sport."

"Sport, Fitness and Leisure". *New Zealand Official Yearbook*. Statistics New Zealand (2000). etrieved on 2008-07-21. "Traditionally New Zealanders have excelled in rugby union, which is regarded as the national sport, and track and field athletics."

"The Flashpacker: A New Breed of Traveler", *Hotel Travel News* (2006-03-24). Retrieved on 2007-11-07.

"Tokelau FAQ's". Council for the ongoing government of Tokelau. Retrieved on 2008-07-21. "Many Tokelauan men and women regard cricket-island style (kilikiti) as their national sport, which can sometimes involve almost the entire village."

"UNWTO Tourism Highlights, Edition 2007". World Tourism Organization (2007). Retrieved on 2008-03-29.

"UNWTO World Tourism Barometer June 2008". World Tourism Barometer (June 2008). Retrieved on 2008-08-01. Vol. 6, No. 2

"Uruguay Law 17958 of 21 April 2006". Global Legal Information Network. Retrieved on 2008-07-14.

"Wales – a unique country, a unique culture". British Embassy, Warsaw.

Retrieved on 2008-07-21. "Wales is mainly associated with rugby. It is the national sport of Wales." Tourism in India.

"World Tourism Barometer (p. 8)". World Tourism Organization (2007). Retrieved on 2008-03-29.

Adamkus, Valdas (2005-07-28). "Address at Charles University, Prague". President of Lithuania official website. Retrieved on 2008-07-24. "Lithuania is a country that loves basketball. It is our national sport and we are proud to be reigning European Champions."

Aeberhard, Danny; Andrew Benson, Lucy Phillips, et al. (2001). *The Rough Guide to Argentina*, p. 198. ISBN 1858285690. "displays of traditional gaucho skills (*destrezas criollas*)"

Aidid, S. M. 'Penang (Malaysia) as a *Tourism Sport Centre*', (online), *Journal of Sport Tourism*, http://www.mcb.co.uk/journals/jst/archive/vol4no1/welcome.htm

Andueza, J. M. 'The Role of Sport in the Tourism Destinations Chosen by Tourists Visiting Spain', (online), *Journal of Sport Tourism*, http://www.mcb.co.uk/journals/jst/archive/vol4no3/jst15.htm

Anon. (1) 'Sport Tourism Consumer Motivation', (online), *Journal of Sport Tourism*, http://www.mcb.co.uk/journals/jst/archive/vol4no3/jst15.htm

Anon. (2) 'Sports Tourism—a Window of Opportunity', (online), *Journal of Sport Tourism*, http://www.mcb.co.uk/services/conferen/feb96/sports_tourism/backgrnd.htm

Anon. (3) 'Sports Tourism in the Barbados—the Development of Sports Facilities and Special Events', (online), *Journal of Sport Tourism*, http://www.mcb.co.uk/journals/jst/archive/vol4no1/welcome.htm

Australian Bureau of Statistics (1999) *More Australians are Going to Aussie Rules*, Australian Bureau of Statistics Media Release, 20 December 1999, 151/99

Australian Sports Commission (1990) *Hosting an International Sporting Event—A Guide for Australian Sporting Organisations*, Pirie Printers, Canberra

Australian Travel Research Workshop (1987) *The Impact and Marketing of Special Events*, Australian Standing Committee on Tourism

Barnard, C. L. P. (1988) *Sport Tourism...For You? a guide to develop a sport tourism strategy*, Recreation and Sport Branch, Ministry of Tourism, Recreation and Culture, British Columbia.

Basra, Sukhwant (2008-03-11). "No National status, except in NCERT textbooks". dnaindia. Retrieved on 2008-07-15. "The status of hockey as the national sport is not enshrined in any official proclamation by the Government of India. The NCERT textbook for Class XI does [..] state that India's national game is hockey and that, in a way, does make for an official take on the issue."

Batting For Grenada". *Grenada Life* p. 38. Grenada Board of Tourism (March 2007). Retrieved on 2008-07-21. "in the first Grenada Cricket Classics [, h]eroes such as Sir Viv Richards, Joel Garner and Curtley Ambrose came together to promote what is considered by many to be the national sport in Grenada."

Battisti, G. & Favretto, A. (1997) 'Sporting and Outdoor Activities in the Development.

Berglund, Nina (2006-02-20). "Few cheers for Norway", *Aftenposten*. Retrieved on 2008-07-21. "The scoreboard shows how the Norwegians placed, a performance considered much too poor in a country where cross-country skiing is a national sport."

Bramwell, B. (1997) 'A Sport Mega-event as a Sustainable Tourism Development Strategy', *Tourism Recreation Research*, Vol. 22(2), pp. 13-19.

Bull, C. & Weed, M. (1997) 'Influences on Sport-Tourism Relations in Britain: The Effects of Government Policy', *Tourism Recreation Research*, Vol. 22(2), pp. 5-12.

—— 'Integrating Sport & Tourism: A Review of Regional Policies in England', *Progress in Tourism and Hospitality Research*, Vol. 3, pp129-148.

Bull, C. & Weed, M. (1998) 'The Search for a Sport-Tourism Policy Network', *Leisure Management: Issues and Applications*, pp. 277-281

Bull, C. & Weed, M. (1999) 'Niche markets and small island tourism: the development of sports tourism in Malta', *Managing Leisure*, 4, pp. 142-155

Canada Tourism, 'The Canadian Sports Tourism Initiative', (online).

Caroline Bremner (2007-10-11). "Top 150 City Destinations: London Leads the Way". Euromonitor International. Retrieved on 2008-08-03. This article has the complete list of 150 cities.

Castro, Fidel (1999-). "Speech at a meeting with Pan American Games delegation members". cuba.cu. Retrieved on 2008-07-24. "the game that [..] is [..] our national sport [..] I am talking of baseball"

Chang-Shin, C. 'Benefiting from Mega Events: Olympics 2000, World Cup 2002 and 2005 World Exposition', (online), *Journal of Sport Tourism*, http://www.mcb.co.uk/journals/jst/archive/vol5no3/vol5no3.htm

Chernushenko, D. 'Sports Tourism Goes Sustainable—the Lillehammer Experience', The Delphi Group, Ottawa, Canada.

Cook L. (1999). The 1944 Education Act and outdoor education: from policy to practice. *History of Education, 28*(2), 157-172. ISBN 0-473-10583-7.

Craton, Michael; Gail Saunders (1998). *Islanders in the Stream: A History of the Bahamian People*. University of Georgia Press, p. 471. ISBN 0820322849.

De Knop, P. (1990) 'Sport for all and active tourism', *World Leisure and Recreation*, Vol. 32, No. 3, Fall 1990, pp. 30-36

Delpy, L. (1998) 'An overview of sport tourism: Building towards a dimensional framework', *Journal of Vacation Marketing*, Vol. 4, No. 1, January 1998, pp. 91-102

Delpy, L., Grabijas, M. & Stefanovich, A. (1998) 'Sport Tourism and corporate sponsorship: A winning combination', *Journal of Vacation Marketing*, Vol. 4, No. 1, January 1998, pp. 91-102

Department for Culture, Media and Sport (1999), 'Media Release—Government Acts to Boost Tourism', (online), 26 February 1999, London, http://195.44.11.137/coi/coipress.nsf

Department of Environment, Sport and Territories (1996) *Expanding Australia's sporting and recreational links with Asia*, Australian Government Publishing Service, Canberra

Douvis, J., Yusof, A. & Douvis, S. 'An Examination of Demographic and Psychographic Profiles of the Sport Tourist', (online), *The*

Cyber-Journal of Sport Marketing, http://www.cjsm.com/vol2/douvisyusof24.htm

Duquette, Jerold J. (1999). *Regulating the National Pastime: Baseball and Antitrust.* Greenwood, p. 104. ISBN 027596535X. Retrieved on 2008-07-21. "Baseball justified its privileged legal status by citing the special nature and cultural significance of America's national pastime."

Economic Potential of the Australian Sport and Recreation Industry, (unpublished report).

Embratur (2006). "Anúario Estatístico Volume 33 2006" (in Portuguese). Ministério do Turismo. Retrieved on 2008-06-27.

Encyclopedia of Marine Mammals, editors Perrin, Wursig and Thewissen, ISBN 0-12-551340-2. In particular the article *Whale watching* by Erich Hoyt.

Faulkner, B. & Tideswell, C. (1998)(1) *Leveraging Tourism Benefits from the Sydney 2000 Olympics* (unpublished paper)

Faulkner, B. (1993) *Evaluating the Tourism Impacts of Hallmark Events,* Occasional Paper No. 16, Bureau of Tourism Research, Canberra

Faulkner, B., Tideswell, C. & Weston, A. (1999) *Sydney Olympics and the Sports Tourism Nexus,* (unpublished paper) Griffith University Centre for Tourism and Hotel Management Research, and KPMG Management Consultants

Fernando, Leslie (2005-06-03). "Sponsors President's Gold Cup tourney: Dialog assures future of VB", *Daily News (Sri Lanka).* Retrieved on 2008-07-14. "Way back in 1991 volleyball was declared as the national sport of Sri Lanka but it was only name sake."

Forbes Traveller (2007-04-25). "Top 50 Most Visited Tourist Attractions". Retrieved on 2008-03-29.

Getz, D. (1997) 'Trends and Issues in Sport Event Tourism', *Tourism Recreation Research,* Vol. 22(2), pp. 61-62.

Gibson, H. J. (1998) 'Active Sport Tourism: Who Participates?', *Leisure Studies,* Vol. 17, No. 2, pp. 155-170.

Gibson, H. J. (1998)(2) 'Sport Tourism: A Critical Analysis of Research', *Sport Management Review,* 1, pp. 45-76.

Gibson, H. J. (1998)(3) 'The wide world of sport tourism', *P & R*, September 1998, pp. 108-114.

Gibson, H. J., Attle, S. P. & Yiannakis, A. (1998) 'Segmenting the active sport tourist market: A life-span perspective', *Journal of Vacation Marketing*, Vol. 4, No. 1, 1998, pp. 52-64.

Gonzalez Echevarria, Roberto (1999). "A Cuban *Belle Époque*", *The Pride of Havana: A History of Cuban Baseball*. Oxford University Press, p. 76. ISBN 0195146050. "Baseball is so ingrained in Cuba that it has thrived as the "national sport" through forty years of a bitterly anti-American revolution."

Grabowski, P. (1999) 'Tourism and sport: Parallel tracks for developing tourism in Brunei?', *Tourism Recreation Research*, Vol. 24(2), pp. 99-98.

Green, B. C. & Chalip, L. (1998) 'Sport Tourism as the Celebration of Subculture', *Annals of Tourism Research*, Vol. 25, No. 2, pp. 275-291.

Griffiths, M. (1999) *Positioning the Illawarra & Southern Highlands Region as a Sports Tourism Destination*, (unpublished thesis for Illawarra & Southern Highlands Tourism), University of Technology, Sydney.

Growing Lesbian and Gay Sports Tourism Industry', *Journal of Vacation Marketing*, Vol. 5, No. 1, pp. 31-50.

Hagan, J. & Patterson, E. (1991) *Oars Away—Assessing the Impact of the 1990 World Rowing Championships on Tasmania*, Department of Tourism, Sport and Recreation, Hobart.

Hall, C. M. (1997) 'Recent Progress of Sports Tourism in New Zealand', *Tourism Recreation Research*, Vol. 22(2), p. 63.

Harris, John (Summer 2006). "(Re)Presenting Wales: National Identity and Celebrity in the Postmodern Rugby World". *North American Journal of Welsh Studies* 6 (2). North American Association for the Study of Welsh Culture and History. Retrieved on 2008-07-14. "rugby used to be the undisputed national sport of Wales [..] Rugby Union's assumed position as "the national game" has often been questioned on the basis that it is predominantly a game played and followed in South Wales."

Hattie, J. A., Marsh, H. W., Neill, J. T. & Richards, G. E. (1997).

Adventure education and Outward Bound: Out-of-class experiences that have a lasting effect. *Review of Educational Research*, 67, 43-87.

Higham, J. (1999) 'Commentary—Sport as an Avenue of Tourism Development: An Analysis of the Positive and Negative Impacts of Sport Tourism', *Current Issues in Tourism*, Vol. 2, No. 1, pp. 82-90.

http://www.aboriginalbc.com/UserFiles/File/Haida%20Heritage%20Centre%20July%2027-07%20-%20Final.pdf

http://www.canadatourism.com/en/ctc/partner_centre/partnering/sports_initiative.htm

http://www.cornerbrook.com/business/pdf/2.Feb23.PR_SportTourism_N.pdf

http://www.cornerbrook.com/business/pdf/comprofilesm.pdf

http://www.mcb.co.uk/journals/jst/archive/vol4no1/welcome.htm

http://www.revelstokecf.com/newsletter/dev0101-1.htm

Industry Policy and Analysis Section (1996) *Sydney 2000 Olympics: Economic Benefits for the ACT Preliminary Estimates*, February 1999, Business and Regional Development Bureau—ACT.

International Association of Scientific Experts in Tourism. "The AIEST, its character and aims". Retrieved on 2008-03-29.

Irwin, R. L. & Sandler, M. A. (1998) 'An analysis of travel behaviour and event-induced.

Jackson, G. & Reeves, M. (1998) 'Evidencing the Sport-Tourism Interrelationship: a Case Study of Elite British Athletes', *Leisure Management: Issues and Applications*, pp. 263-275.

Kirby, David (September 27, 1998). "The Tourist Trap; With All Those Visitors Trampling the Welcome Mat, Can New York Be the Host With the Most for Everyone?" (Web). *News Article*. The New York Times. Retrieved on 2007-03-21.

Kurlantzick, Joshua (Sunday, January 9, 2005). "The True Meaning of the Tourist Trap" (Web). *News article*. The Washington Post. Retrieved on 2007-03-21.

Kurtzman, J. & Zauhar, J. (1995) 'Tourism Sport International Council', *Annals of Tourism Research*, Vol. 22, No. 3, pp. 707-708.

Kurtzman, J. & Zauhar, J. (1998) 'Sport Tourism: a business inherency or an innate compulsion?', *Visions in Leisure and Business*, Vol. 17(2), pp. 21-30.

Kurtzman, J. & Zauhar, J. 'A Wave in Time—The Sports Tourism Phenomena', (online), *Journal of Sport Tourism*, Vol. 3, No. 2, http://www.mcb.co.uk/journals/jst/archive/vol3no2/welcome.htm

Kurtzman, J. 'Sports Tourism Categories', (online), *Journal of Sport Tourism*, Vol. 3, No. 4, http://www.mcb.co.uk/journals/jst/archive/vol3no4/categories.htm

Lowell, John (1992). *Ring of Liberation: Deceptive Discourse in Brazilian Capoeira*. University of Chicago Press, p. 61. ISBN 0226476839.

Luke, Will (March 2007). "Cricket by association". The Wisden Cricketer. Retrieved on 2008-07-"Bermuda are one of the few sides who count cricket as a national sport."

Lynch, P. (?). *Camping in the Curriculum: A History of Outdoor Education in New Zealand Schools*. PML publications, Lincoln University, Canterbury, New Zealand.

Mckinley, James C., Jr (1999-03-26). "Baseball; Clash of Cultures, Pride and Passion", *The New York Times*. Retrieved on 2008-07-24. "Most Cubans, after all, consider baseball to be their national sport, a game entwined in history with their struggle for independence from Spain and the birth of their nation."

Mølster, Odd (1996). "Skiing and the Creation of a Norwegian Identity—part 2". *News of Norway, issue 2*. Norwegian Embassy, Washington. Retrieved on 2008-07-21. "the national sport could become a fine weapon in time of war. In 1943, Norway's resistance movement won an epochal victory — on skis, of course"

Moreira Recchione, Alberto (December 2007). "La Medialuna: un edificio para Chile" (in Spanish). *Revista de urbanismo* (No. 17). University of Chile. ISSN 0717-5051. Retrieved on 2008-07-14. "A reconocerse, en 1962, el rodeo como deporte nacional y oficial [10 de enero de 1962, oficio N°269 del Consejo Nacional de Deportes y Comité Olímpico de Chile]"

Mules, T., Burgan, B., Molloy, J., Redman, W. & Hudson, P. (1988) *Financial and Economic Modelling of Major Sporting Events in Australia*, Sport and Recreation Ministers' Council

Nash, D. (1999) Commentary on 'Sport Tourism as the Celebration of Subculture', *Annals of Tourism Research*, Vol. 26, No. 3, pp. 701-703.

Nicholls, Henry (Wednesday April 19, 2006). "The tourist trap (The Galapagos islands are the world's prime eco-tourism destination. Now the sheer number of visitors is endangering their future)" (Web). *News article*. Guardian. Retrieved on 2007-03-21.

Nogawa, H., Yamaguchi, Y. & Hagi, Y. (1996) 'An Empirical Research Study on Japanese Sport Tourism in Sport-for-All Events: Case Studies of a Single-Night Event and a Multiple-Night Event', *Journal of Travel Research*, Vol. XXXV, No. 2, pp. 46-54.

On the Trail of the Whale, Mark Carwardine, ISBN 1-899074-00-7.

Pigeassou, C. 'Sport and Tourism: The Emergence of Sport into the Offer of Tourism. Between Passion and Reason. An Overview of the French Situation and Perspectives', (online), *Journal of Sport Tourism*, Vol. 4, No. 2, http://www.mcb.co.uk/journals/jst/archive/vol4no2/welcome.htm

Pitts, B. G. (1999) 'Sports Tourism and Niche Markets: Identification and Analysis of the

Quintanar Hinojosa, Beatriz (August 2007). "[www.mexicodes conocido.com.mx Oaxaca: jubilo de los sentidos]". *Guía México Desconocido: Oaxaca* **137**: 8.

Sasi, V. K. 'Sports Tourism in India', (online), *Journal of Sport Tourism*,

Scarrott, M. (ed) (1999) *Exploring Sports Tourism: Proceedings of a SPRIG Seminar held at the University of Sheffield on 15 April 1999*, Sheffield Hallam University, Sheffield.

Schrag, Myles (2003). "Baseball as National Pastime Revisted: And a Little Town Shall Lead Them", in Peter Carino: *Baseball/literature/culture: Essays, 1995-2001*. McFarland, Chp. 13 p. 140. ISBN 0786416432. Retrieved on 2008-07-21. "Tradition — that quality so instrumental in elevating baseball to its century-old status as national pastime— has become less important".

Schwark, J. 'Forms of Supply and Individual Potential in Sport Tourism', (online), *Journal of Sport Tourism*, http://www.mcb.co.uk/journals/jst/archive/vol5no3/vol5no3.htm

Smith, C. & Jenner, P. (1998) 'The Impact of Festivals and Special Events on Tourism', *Travel & Tourism Intelligence*, No. 4, pp. 73-91

Sport Tourism, Vol. 3 No. 4, http://www.mcb.co.uk/journals/jst/vol3no4/bidding.htm

Stan Hagen—Tourism Minister of British Columbia.

Standeven, J. & De Knop, P. (1999) *Sport Tourism*, Human Kinetics, Champaign, Illinios.

Standeven, J. (1998) 'Sport Tourism: Joint marketing—A starting point for beneficial synergies' *Journal of Vacation Marketing*, Vol. 4, No. 1, pp. 39-51.

STIC Research Unit (1), 'Content Analysis of Tourism Schedules', (online), *Journal of Sport Tourism*, http://www.mcb.co.uk/journals/jst/archive/vol4no1/welcome.htm

STIC Research Unit (2), 'STIX (Sports Tourism Impact Index)', (online), *Journal of Sport Tourism*, http://www.mcb.co.uk/journals/jst/archive/vol4no1/welcome.htm

Swart, K. (1998) 'Visions for South African sport tourism', *Visions in Leisure and Business*, Vol. 17(2), pp. 4-12.

The Development of Social Network Analysis Vancouver: Empirical Press.

The Equity: "Esprit rafting to be featured in commercial", Wednesday, May 14th, 2008, print edition.

The Hopeful Traveler (2007-07-29). "Forbes Traveler 50 Most Visited Tourist Attractions". Retrieved on 2008-03-29. See the complete Top 50 list at this website.

The Whale Watcher's Guide: Whale-watching Trips in North America, Patricia Corrigan, ISBN 1-55971-683-5.

Theobald, William F. (1998). *Global Tourism*, p. 10. ISBN 0750640227.

Thomas, M. (1987) *Major Events—a descriptive and comparative analysis*, (unpublished thesis), University of New South Wales, Sydney

Tourism Canada (1993) *Spectator Sporting Activities in Canada—from a tourism perspective*, Department of Industry, Science and Technology.

Tourism Directorate (France) (2007). "Key facts on tourism 2007 Edition".

Tourism in Slovenia: The Case of the Triglav National Park', *Tourism Recreation Research*, Vol. 22(2), pp. 29-35.

Tourism Principles and Practice, C. Cooper, J. Fletcher, A. Fyall, D. Gilbert, S. Wanhill, Pearson Education, Third edition, Madrid 2005

Touristik report. January 2008 (German) .

Tow, S. (1997) 'Sports Tourism—the Benefits', (online), *Journal of Sport Tourism*, Vol. 3 No. 4, http://www.mcb.co.uk/journals/jst/vol3no4/benefits.htm.

Travel Industry Association of America (1), 'Sporting Events are a Draw for Many Travelers', (online), http://www.tia.org/press/093098sports.stm

Travel Industry Association of America (2), 'TIA Releases Landmark Report on Sports Travel', (online), http://www.tia.org/press/082599sports.stm

Travel Industry Association of America (3), 'Profile of Travelers Who Attend Sports Events', (online), http://www.tia.org/research/summsports.as

Travel Industry Association of America (4), 'Travelers Prefer Golf Over Tennis', (online), http://www.tia.org/press/051199poll.stm

Turco, D. & Eisenhart, H. (1998) 'Exploring the sport-tourism connection', *ICPER=SD*, Winter, pp. 24-27.

Turco, D. 'Are we there yet? Understanding the impacts of competitive vacations', (online), *The Cyber-Journal of Sport Marketing*, http://www.cjsm.com/vol1/turcov14.htm

Vienna University, 'Austrian Sport Tourism Profiles', (online), *Journal of Sport Tourism*, http://www.mcb.co.uk/journals/jst/archive/vol4no1/welcome.htm

Walsh, V., & Golins, G. L. (1976). *The exploration of the Outward Bound process*. Denver, CO: Colorado Outward Bound School.

Whale watching 2001: *Worldwide tourism numbers, expenditures and expanding socioeconomic benefits*, Erich Hoyt, ISBN 1-901002-09-8.

Whale watching, Discovery Travel Adventures Insight guide. ISBN 1-56331-836-9.

Whales and Whale Watching in Iceland, Mark Carwardine, ISBN 9979-51-129-X.

Where the Whales are!

Whitson, D. & Macintosh, D. (1996) 'The Global Circus: International Sport, Tourism and the Marketing of Cities', Journal of Sport & Social Issues, August 1996, pp. 278-295.

WWF-Philippines :: News and Facts.

Index